FEB 2008

D0204650

Bloom's Modern Critical Interpretations

Nathaniel Hawthorne's
The Scarlet Letter
Updated Edition

Edited and with an introduction by
Harold Bloom
Sterling Professor of the Humanities
Yale University

BLOOM'S
LITERARY CRITICISM
An imprint of Infobase Publishing

Bloom's Modern Critical Interpretations: The Scarlet Letter, Updated Edition

Copyright © 2007 by Infobase Publishing
Introduction © 2007 by Harold Bloom

Bloom's Literary Criticism
An imprint of Infobase Publishing
132 West 31st Street
New York NY 10001

ISBN-10: 0-7910-9424-3
ISBN-13: 978-0-7910-9424-2

Library of Congress Cataloging-in-Publication Data
Nathaniel Hawthorne's The scarlet letter / Harold Bloom, editor. -- Updated ed.
    p. cm. -- (Bloom's modern critical interpretations)
  Includes bibliographical references and index.
  ISBN 0-7910-9424-3 (hardcover)
 1. Hawthorne, Nathaniel, 1804-1864. Scarlet letter. 2. Mothers and daughters in literature. 3. Massachusetts--In literature. 4. Puritans in literature. 5. Adultery in literature. 6. Women in literature. I. Bloom, Harold. II. Title. III. Series.
 PS1868.N38 2007
 813'.3--dc22   2006036787

Contributing Editor: Pamela Loos

Cover designed by Ben Peterson

Cover photo The Granger Collection, New York

Printed in the United States of America

Bang EJB 10 9 8 7 6 5 4 3 2 1

This book is printed on acid-free paper.

Contents

Editor's Note

My Introduction ponders the creative (and defensive) misreading of Hawthorne-as-precursor by Henry James.

Joel Pfister concludes that Hawthorne implicitly identifies Hester Prynne's "transgression" with her full humanization, while Sacvan Bercovitch celebrates her "radicalism" as being in the American grain.

For Charles Swann, Hester ultimately represents a better future for American women, after which Emily Miller Budick intimates that Hawthorne is more of Emerson's "Party of Hope" than of his "Party of Memory."

Janice B. Daniel finds in Hawthorne's natural analogies a symbolic guide to his meanings, while Michael T. Gilmore offers a Marxist analysis of burgeoning class struggle in *The Scarlet Letter*.

In Hawthorne's sinuous, labyrinthine narrative, Leland S. Person uncovers similarities between Hester's motherhood and the same uneasy condition in slave narrative.

Richard Kopley believes that Hawthorne's romance form is transformed by a subtly subversive rhetoric, after which Margaret Reid concludes this volume by judging the mode of storytelling in *The Scarlett Letter* to be an ideal one for revealing cultural secrets.

Introduction

I

Henry James's *Hawthorne* was published in December 1879, in London, in the English Men of Letters series. Unique among the thirty-nine volumes of that group, this was a critical study of an American by an American. Only Hawthorne seemed worthy of being an English man of letters, and only James seemed capable of being an American critic. Perhaps this context inhibited James, whose *Hawthorne* tends to be absurdly overpraised, or perhaps Hawthorne caused James to feel an anxiety that even George Eliot could not bring the self-exiled American to experience. Whatever the reason, James wrote a study that requires to be read between the lines, as here in its final paragraph:

> He was a beautiful, natural, original genius, and his life had been singularly exempt from worldly preoccupations and vulgar efforts. It had been as pure, as simple, as unsophisticated, as his work. He had lived primarily in his domestic affections, which were of the tenderest kind; and then—without eagerness, without pretension, but with a great deal of quiet devotion—in his charming art. His work will remain; it is too original and exquisite to pass away; among the men of imagination he will always have his niche. No one has had just that vision of life, and no one has had a literary form that more successfully expressed his vision. He

was not a moralist, and he was not simply a poet. The moralists are weightier, denser, richer, in a sense; the poets are more purely inconclusive and irresponsible. He combined in a singular degree the spontaneity of the imagination with a haunting care for moral problems. Man's conscience was his theme, but he saw it in the light of a creative fancy which added, out of its own substance, an interest, and, I may almost say, an importance.

Is *The Scarlet Letter* pure, simple, and unsophisticated? Is *The Marble Faun* a work neither moral nor poetic? Can we accurately assert that man's conscience, however lit by creative fancy, is Hawthorne's characteristic concern? James's vision of his American precursor is manifestly distorted by a need to misread creatively what may hover too close, indeed may shadow the narrative space that James requires for his own enterprise. In that space, something beyond shadowing troubles James. Isabel Archer has her clear affinities with Dorothea Brooke, yet her relation to Hester Prynne is even more familial, just as Millie Theale will have the lineage of *The Marble Faun*'s Hilda ineluctably marked upon her. James's representations of women are Hawthornian in ways subtly evasive yet finally unmistakable. Yet even this influence and its consequent ambivalences do not seem to be the prime unease that weakens James's *Hawthorne*. Rather, the critical monograph is more embarrassed than it can know by James's guilt at having abandoned the American destiny. Elsewhere, James wrote to some purpose about Emerson (though not so well as his brother William did), but in *Hawthorne* the figure of Emerson is unrecognizable and the dialectics of New England Transcendentalism are weakly abused:

> A biographer of Hawthorne might well regret that his hero had not been more mixed up with the reforming and free-thinking class, so that he might find a pretext for writing a chapter upon the state of Boston society forty years ago. A needful warrant for such regret should be, properly, that the biographer's own personal reminiscences should stretch back to that period and to the persons who animated it. This would be a guarantee of fulness of knowledge and, presumably, of kindness of tone. It is difficult to see, indeed, how the generation of which Hawthorne has given us, in *Blithedale*, a few portraits, should not, at this time of day, be spoken of very tenderly and sympathetically. If irony enter into the allusion, it should be of the lightest and gentlest. Certainly, for a brief and imperfect chronicler of these things, a writer just touching them as he passes, and who has not the advantage of

having been a contemporary, there is only one possible tone. The compiler of these pages, though his recollections date only from a later period, has a memory of a certain number of persons who had been intimately connected, as Hawthorne was not, with the agitations of that interesting time. Something of its interest adhered to them still—something of its aroma clung to their garments; there was something about them which seemed to say that when they were young and enthusiastic, they had been initiated into moral mysteries, they had played at a wonderful game. Their usual mark (it is true I can think of exceptions) was that they seemed excellently good. They appeared unstained by the world, unfamiliar with worldly desires and standards, and with those various forms of human depravity which flourish in some high phases of civilisation; inclined to simple and democratic ways, destitute of pretensions and affectations, of jealousies, of cynicisms, of snobbishness. This little epoch of fermentation has three or four drawbacks for the critics—drawbacks, however, that may be overlooked by a person for whom it has an interest of association. It bore, intellectually, the stamp of provincialism; it was a beginning without a fruition, a dawn without a noon; and it produced, with a single exception, no great talents. It produced a great deal of writing, but (always putting Hawthorne aside, as a contemporary but not a sharer) only one writer in whom the world at large has interested itself. The situation was summed up and transfigured in the admirable and exquisite Emerson. He expressed all that it contained, and a good deal more, doubtless, besides; he was the man of genius of the moment; he was the Transcendentalist *par excellence*. Emerson expressed, before all things, as was extremely natural at the hour and in the place, the value and importance of the individual, the duty of making the most of one's self, of living by one's own personal light, and carrying out one's own disposition. He reflected with beautiful irony upon the exquisite impudence of those institutions which claim to have appropriated the truth and to dole it out, in proportionate morsels, in exchange for a subscription. He talked about the beauty and dignity of life, and about every one who is born into the world being born to the whole, having an interest and a stake in the whole. He said "all that is clearly due to-day is not to lie," and a great many other things which it would be still easier to present in a ridiculous light. He insisted upon sincerity and independence and spontaneity, upon acting in harmony with one's nature, and not conforming and compromising for the sake of being more comfortable. He urged that a man should await his call, his finding the thing to do which he should really believe in doing, and not be urged by the world's opinion to do simply the world's work. "If no call should come for years, for centuries, then I know that the want of the Universe is the attestation of faith by my abstinence.... If I cannot work, at least I need not lie." The doctrine of the supremacy of the individual to himself, of his originality, and, as regards his own character, *unique* quality, must have had a great charm for people living in a society in which introspection—thanks to the want of other entertainment—played almost the part of a social resource.

The "admirable and exquisite Emerson" was "as sweet as barbed wire," to quote President Giamatti of Yale. Any reader of that great, grim, and most American of books, *The Conduct of Life*, ought to have known this. James's Emerson, dismissed here by the novelist as a provincial of real charm, had provoked the senior Henry James to an outburst of more authentic critical value: "O you man without a handle!" Hawthorne too, in a very different way, was a man without a handle, not less conscious and subtle an artist than the younger Henry James himself. *The Scarlet Letter*, in James's *Hawthorne*, is rightly called the novelist's masterpiece, but then is accused of "a want of reality and an abuse of the fanciful element—of a certain superficial symbolism." James was too good a reader to have indicted Hawthorne for "a want of reality," were it not that Hawthornian representation had begun too well the process of causing a Jamesian aspect of reality to appear.

II

Of the four principal figures in *The Scarlet Letter*, Pearl is at once the most surprising, and the largest intimation of Hawthorne's farthest imaginings. There is no indication that Hawthorne shared his friend Melville's deep interest in ancient Gnosticism, though esoteric heresies were clearly part of Hawthorne's abiding concern with witchcraft. The Gnostic *Gospel of Thomas* contains a remarkable mythic narrative, "The Hymn of the Pearl," that juxtaposes illuminatingly with the uncanny daughter of Hester Prynne and the Reverend Mr. Dimmesdale. In Gnostic symbolism, the pearl is identical with the spark or *pneuma* that is the ontological self of the adept who shares in the Gnosis, in the true knowing that surmounts mere faith. The pearl particularly represents what is best and oldest in the adept, because creation is the work of a mere demiurge, while the best part of us, that which is capable of knowing, was never made, but is one with the original Abyss, the Foremother and Forefather who is the true or alien God. When Hawthorne's Pearl passionately insists she was not made by God, we hear again the most ancient and challenging of all Western heresies:

> The old minister seated himself in an arm-chair, and made an effort to draw Pearl betwixt his knees. But the child, unaccustomed to the touch or familiarity of any but her mother, escaped through the open window and stood on the upper step, looking like a wild, tropical bird, of rich plumage, ready to take flight into the upper air. Mr. Wilson, not a little astonished at this outbreak,—for he was a grandfatherly sort of personage, and usually a vast favorite with children,—essayed, however, to proceed with the examination.
>
> "Pearl," said he, with great solemnity, "thou must take heed to instruction, that so, in due season, thou mayest wear in thy bosom the pearl of great price. Canst thou tell me, my child, who made thee?"
>
> Now Pearl knew well enough who made her; for Hester Prynne, the daughter of a pious home, very soon after her talk with the child about her Heavenly Father, had begun to inform her of those truths which the human spirit, at whatever stage of immaturity, imbibes with such eager interest. Pearl, therefore, so large were the attainments of her three years' lifetime, could have borne a fair examination in the New England Primer, or the first column of the Westminster Catechism, although unacquainted with the outward form of either of those celebrated works. But that perversity, which all children have more or less of, and of which little Pearl had a tenfold portion, now, at the most inopportune moment, took thorough possession of her, and closed her lips, or impelled her to speak words amiss. After putting her finger in her mouth, with many ungracious refusals to answer good Mr. Wilson's question, the child finally announced that she had not been made at all, but had been plucked by her mother off the bush of wild roses, that grew by the prison-door.

That Pearl, elf-child, is the romance's prime knower no reader would doubt. The subtlest relation in Hawthorne's sinuously ambiguous romance is not that between Chillingworth and Dimmesdale, let alone the inadequate ghost of the love between Hester and Dimmesdale. It is the ambivalent and persuasive mother-daughter complex in which Hester is saved both from suicidal despair and from the potential of becoming the prophetess of a feminist religion only by the extraordinary return in her daughter of everything she herself has repressed. I will venture the speculation that both Hester and Pearl are intense representations of two very different aspects of Emersonianism, Hester being a prime instance of Emerson's American religion of self-reliance, while Pearl emerges from a deeper stratum of Emerson, from the Orphism and Gnosticism that mark the sage's first anarchic influx of power and knowledge, when he celebrated his own version of what he called, following the Swedenborgians, the terrible freedom or newness. Emerson, Hawthorne's Concord walking companion, is generally judged by scholars and critics to be antithetical to Hawthorne. I doubt that judgment, since manifestly Hawthorne does not prefer the pathetic Dimmesdale and the mock-satanic Chillingworth to the self-reliant Hester and the daemonic Pearl. Henry James, like T. S. Eliot, considered Emerson to be deficient in a sense of sin, a sense obsessive in Dimmesdale and Chillingworth, alien to Pearl, and highly dialectical in Hester.

In the Gnostic mode of Pearl, the young Emerson indeed affirmed: "My heart did never counsel me to sin. . . ./ I never taught it what it teaches me." This is the adept of Orphic mysteries who also wrote: "It is God in you that responds to God without, or affirms his own words trembling on the lips of another," words that "sound to you as old as yourself." The direct precursor to *The Scarlet Letter*'s Pearl is a famous moment in Emerson's "Self-Reliance," an essay surely known to Hawthorne:

I remember an answer which when quite young I was prompted to make to a valued adviser who was wont to importune me with the dear old doctrines of the church. On my saying, "What have I to do with the sacredness of traditions, if I live wholly from within?" my friend suggested,—"But these impulses may be from below, not from above." I replied, "They do not seem to me to be such; but if I am the Devil's child, I will live then from the Devil."

Call this Pearl's implicit credo, since her positive declaration is: "I have no Heavenly Father!" Even as Pearl embodies Emerson's most anarchic, antinomian strain, Hester incarnates the central impulse of "Self-Reliance." This is the emphasis of chapter 13 of the romance, "Another View of Hester," which eloquently tells us: "The scarlet letter had not done its office." In effect, Hawthorne presents her as Emerson's American precursor, and as the forerunner also of movements still working themselves through among us:

Much of the marble coldness of Hester's impression was to be attributed to the circumstance that her life had turned, in a great measure, from passion and feeling, to thought. Standing alone in the world,—alone, as to any dependence on society, and with little Pearl to be guided and protected,—alone, and hopeless of retrieving her position, even had she not scorned to consider it desirable,—she cast away the fragments of a broken chain. The world's law was no law for her mind. It was an age in which the human intellect, newly emancipated, had taken a more active and a wider range than for many centuries before. Men of the sword had overthrown nobles and kings. Men bolder than these had overthrown and rearranged—not actually, but within the sphere of theory, which was their most real abode—the whole system of ancient prejudice, wherewith was linked much of ancient prin-ciple. Hester Prynne imbibed this spirit. She assumed a freedom of speculation, then common enough on the other side of the Atlantic, but which our forefathers, had they known of it, would have held to be a deadlier crime than that stigmatized by the scarlet letter. In her lonesome cottage, by the sea-shore, thoughts visited her, such as dared to enter no other dwelling in New England; shadowy guests, that would have been as perilous as demons to their entertainer, could they have been seen so much as knocking at her door.

It is remarkable, that persons who speculate the most boldly often conform with the most perfect quietude to the external regulations of society. The thought suffices them, without investing itself in the flesh and blood of action. So it seemed to be with Hester. Yet, had little Pearl never come to her from the spiritual world, it might have been far otherwise. Then, she might have come down to us in history, hand in hand with Ann Hutchinson, as the foundress of a religious sect. She might, in one of her phases, have been a prophetess. She might, and not improbably would, have suffered death from the stern tribunals of the period, for attempting to undermine the foundations of the Puritan establishment. But, in the education of her child, the mother's enthusiasm of thought had something to wreak itself upon. Providence, in the person of this little girl, had assigned to Hester's charge the germ and blossom of womanhood, to be cherished and developed amid a host of difficulties. Every thing was against her. The world was hostile. The child's own nature had something wrong in it, which continually betokened that she had been born amiss,—the effluence of her mother's lawless passion,—and often impelled Hester to ask, in bitterness of heart, whether it were for ill or good that the poor little creature had been born at all.

Indeed, the same dark question often rose into her mind, with reference to the whole race of womanhood. Was existence worth accepting, even to the happiest among them? As concerned her own individual existence, she had long ago decided in the negative, and dismissed the point as settled. A tendency to speculation, though it may keep woman quiet, as it does man, yet makes her sad. She discerns, it may be, such a hopeless task before her. As a first step, the whole system of society is to be torn down, and built up anew. Then, the very nature of the opposite sex, or its long hereditary habit, which has become like nature, is to be essentially modified, before woman can be allowed to assume what seems a fair and suitable position. Finally, all other difficulties being obviated, woman cannot take advantage of these preliminary reforms, until she herself shall have undergone a still mightier change; in which, perhaps, the ethereal essence, wherein she has her truest life, will be found to have evaporated. A woman never overcomes these problems by any exercise of thought. They are not to be solved, or only in one way. If her heart chance to come uppermost, they vanish. Thus, Hester Prynne, whose heart had lost its regular and healthy throb, wandered without a clew in the dark labyrinth of mind; now turned aside by an insurmountable precipice; now starting back from a deep chasm. There was wild and ghastly scenery all around her, and a home and comfort nowhere. At times, a fearful doubt strove to possess her soul, whether it were not better to send Pearl at once to heaven, and go herself to such futurity as Eternal Justice should provide.

Only the emanation of Pearl from the spiritual world has saved Hester from the martyrdom of a prophetess, which is Hawthorne's most cunning irony, since without Pearl his romance would have been transformed into a tragedy. That may be our loss aesthetically, since every reader of *The Scarlet Letter* comes to feel a great regret at Hester's unfulfilled potential. Something in us wants her to be a greater heretic even than Ann Hutchinson. Certainly we sense an unwritten book in her, a story that Hawthorne did not choose to write. But what he has written marks the true beginning of American prose fiction, the absolute point of origin from which we can trace the sequence that goes from Melville and James to Faulkner and Pynchon and that domesticates great narrative art in America.

III

Hawthorne's highest achievement is not in *The Scarlet Letter* and *The Marble Faun*, distinguished as they are, but in the best of his tales and sketches. The last of these, the extraordinary "Feathertop," sub-titled "A Moralized Legend," is as uncanny a story as Kafka's "Country Doctor" or "Hunter Gracchus," and has about it the dark aura of Hawthorne's valediction, his farewell to his own art. In its extraordinary strength at representing an order of reality that intersects our own, neither identical with the mundane nor quite transcending the way things are, "Feathertop" may be without rivals in our language.

Mother Rigby, a formidable witch, sets out to create "as lifelike a scarecrow as ever was seen," and being weary of making hobgoblins, determines to give us "something fine, beautiful, and splendid." An authentic forerunner of Picasso as sculptor, the witch chooses her materials with bravura:

> The most important item of all, probably, although it made so little show, was a certain broomstick, on which Mother Rigby had taken many an airy gallop at midnight, and which now served the scarecrow by way of a spinal column, or, as the unlearned phrase it, a backbone. One of its arms was a disabled flail, which used to be wielded by Goodman Rigby, before his spouse worried him out of this troublesome world; the other, if I mistake not, was composed of the pudding-stick and a broken rung of a chair, tied loosely together at the elbow. As for its legs, the right was a hoe-handle, and the left, an undistinguished and miscellaneous stick from the wood-pile. Its lungs, stomach, and other affairs of that kind, were nothing better than a meal-bag stuffed with straw. Thus, we have made out the skeleton and entire corporosity of the scarecrow, with the exception of its head; and this was admirably supplied by a somewhat withered and shrivelled pumpkin in which Mother Rigby cut two holes for the eyes and a slit for the mouth, leaving a bluish-colored knob, in the middle, to pass for a nose. It was really quite a respectable face.

Gaudily attired, the scarecrow so charms its demiurgic creator ("The more Mother Rigby looked, the better she was pleased") that she emulates

Jehovah directly, and decides to breathe life into the new Adam by thrusting her own pipe into his mouth. Once vivified, Mother Rigby's creature is urged by her to emulate Milton's Adam: "Step forth! Thou hast the world before thee!" Hawthorne does not allow us to doubt the self-critique involved, as all romance is deliciously mocked:

> In obedience to Mother Rigby's word, and extending its arm as if to reach her outstretched hand, the figure made a step forward—a kind of hitch and jerk, however, rather than a step—then tottered, and almost lost its balance. What could the witch expect? It was nothing, after all, but a scarecrow, stuck upon two sticks. But the strong-willed old beldam scowled, and beckoned, and flung the energy of her purpose so forcibly at this poor combination of rotten wood, and musty straw, and ragged garments, that it was compelled to show itself a man, in spite of the reality of things. So it stept into the bar of sunshine. There it stood—poor devil of a contrivance that it was!—with only the thinnest vesture of human similitude about it, through which was evident the stiff, ricketty, incongruous, faded, tattered, good-for-nothing patchwork of its substance, ready to sink in a heap upon the floor, as conscious of its own unworthiness to be erect. Shall I confess the truth? At its present point of vivification, the scarecrow reminds me of some of the lukewarm and abortive characters, composed of heterogeneous materials, used for the thousandth time, and never worth using, with which romance-writers (and myself, no doubt, among the rest) have so over-peopled the world of fiction.

But the critique surpasses mere writers and attacks the greatest of romancers, Jehovah himself, as Mother Rigby deliberately frightens her pathetic creature into speech. Now fully humanized, he is named Feathertop by his creator, endowed with wealth, and sent forth into the world to woo the beautiful Polly, daughter of the worshipful Judge Gookin. There is only the one catch; poor Feathertop must keep puffing at his pipe, or he will dwindle again to the elements that compose him. All goes splendidly; Feathertop is a social triumph, and well along to seducing the delicious Polly, when he is betrayed by glances in a mirror:

> By and by, Feathertop paused, and throwing himself into an imposing attitude, seemed to summon the fair girl to survey his figure, and resist him longer, if she could. His star, his embroidery, his buckles, glowed, at that instant, with unutterable splendor;

the picturesque hues of his attire took a richer depth of coloring; there was a gleam and polish over his whole presence, betokening the perfect witchery of well-ordered manners. The maiden raised her eyes, and suffered them to linger upon her companion with a bashful and admiring gaze. Then, as if desirous of judging what value her own simple comeliness might have, side by side with so much brilliancy, she cast a glance towards the full-length look-ing-glass, in front of which they happened to be standing. It was one of the truest plates in the world, and incapable of flattery. No sooner did the images, therein reflected, meet Polly's eye, than she shrieked, shrank from the stranger's side, gazed at him, for a moment, in the wildest dismay, and sank insensible upon the floor. Feathertop, likewise, had looked towards the mirror, and there beheld, not the glittering mockery of his outside show, but a picture of the sordid patchwork of his real composition, stript of all witchcraft.

Fleeing back to his mother, Feathertop abandons existence in despair of his reality, and flings the pipe away in a kind of suicide. His epitaph is spoken by a curiously softened Mother Rigby, as though experience had rendered her a more maternal demiurge:

"Poor Feathertop!" she continued. "I could easily give him another chance, and send him forth again to-morrow. But, no! his feelings are too tender; his sensibilities too deep. He seems to have too much heart to bustle for his own advantage, in such an empty and heartless world. Well, well! I'll make a scarecrow of him, after all. 'Tis an innocent and a useful vocation, and will suit my darling well; and if each of his human brethren had as fit a one, 'twould be the better for mankind; and as for this pipe of tobacco, I need it more than he!"

Gentle and whimsical as this is, it may be Hawthorne's darkest irony. The witch is more merciful than the remorseless Jehovah, who always does send us forth again, into a world that cannot sustain us. Feathertop is closer to most of us than we are to Hester Prynne. That final dismissal of heroism is Hawthorne's ultimate legacy, glowing on still in the romances of Nathanael West and Thomas Pynchon.

JOEL PFISTER

Sowing Dragons' Teeth:
Personal Life and Revolution in
'The Scarlet Letter'

I proposed earlier that Medusa, the original "decapitated surveyor," be read as a symbol of revolutionary potential in Hawthorne's fiction, an unfeminine power that Hawthorne paradoxically identified with (himself a decapitated surveyor) and was petrified to look at. When young Perseus, in Hawthorne's "The Gorgon's Head" pulls Medusa's snaky severed head from his "wallet," he gives birth to a revolution: King Polydectes and his court are petrified. The fantasy is that the manipulation of a mythically dangerous female head makes revolution possible. This male fear of unfeminine power had historical coordinates; for there is also, as I noted, a similarity between the three gorgons ("terrible monsters") and Hollingsworth's depiction of women's rights advocates ("imaginary monster[s]," "petticoated monstrosities"). It is another aspect of this similitude that I now wish to elaborate.

These sister-monsters are also portrayed by Hawthorne's narrator as "a very frightful and mischievous species of dragon." Their wings were "exceedingly splendid ... pure, bright, glittering, burnished gold" and "when people happened to catch a glimpse of their glimmering brightness, aloft in the air, they seldom stopt to gaze, but ran and hid themselves as speedily as they could" (7: 13). Why this dread of winged "dragons"?

I suspect that here, as elsewhere, Hawthorne is expressing cultural anxieties about artistic or political women with a bite in corporeal terms and

From *The Production of Personal Life: Class, Gender, and the Psychological in Hawthorne's Fiction*, pp. 122–143. © 1991 by the board of trustees of the Leland Stanford Junior University.

that a dread of *dragonism*, like a fear of female monstrosity, should be situated in the context of anxieties about the "venomous" female "tongues" wagging in conventions and in print by the late 1840's. During the early part of my life", wrote Sarah Grimké, the outspoken women's rights advocate, "my lot was cast among the butterflies of the fashionable world; and of this class of women, I am constrained to say, both from experience and observation, that their education is miserably deficient; that they are taught to regard marriage as the one thing needful, the only avenue to distinction."[1] The winged, unwed dragon sisters, armed to the teeth and not easily crushed, are the antithesis of the shrinking "butterfly" or the paper-winged "angel" in the house.

I offer historical speculations on this undomesticated species of dragonism because the dragon theme resurfaces provocatively in Hawthorne's revision of the myths of Cadmus and Jason, published just two years after "The Gorgon's Head," in *Tanglewood Tales* (1853). In these myths, male warriors who originate from the mouth of a dragon threaten civilization itself. There may be a link in Hawthorne's mind between cultural anxieties surrounding dragon women with "terribly long tusks" (7: 13), and crazed warriors who sprout full-grown from the teeth of a dragon. The myths of Jason and Cadmus, as we shall see, suggest that Hawthorne saw the ideology of middle-class domesticity as potent enough to maintain a clearly mythic social order threatened by dragons' teeth. I shall propose, as my argument proceeds, that Hawthorne's determination to uphold this mythic *impression* of social order, over against those who would "sow" dragons' teeth, should be the key to our reading of *The Scarlet Letter*.

Our first task is to begin by unpacking the popular middle-class assumptions informing the "dragon" myths of Jason and Cadmus. In both myths our intrepid heroes must sow broadcast the "dragon's teeth," which yield a crop of spellbound soldiers poised for battle: "bright objects sprouted higher," before Jason's very eyes, "and proved to be the steel-heads of spears" (7: 359). Barely human incarnations of Ahab's "madness maddened," these warriors collectively had come into this beautiful world, and into the peaceful moonlight, full of rage and stormy passions, and ready to take the life of every human brother, in recompense of the boon of their existence (7: 360). So "fierce and feverish" was this army of armored monomaniacs that they turned on one another to a man, in response to a stone thrown by Jason, and reaped "the only enjoyment which they had tasted on this beautiful earth!" But why should they revel so in self-slaughter and "lopping of arms, head, and legs" (7: 361), something neither adult nor child should enjoy? Hawthorne offers a clue to his young readers: "They never had women for their mothers" (7: 360). And mother, mind you, should make all the difference.

Cadmus, like Jason, throws a stone at the charging soldiers, who then, in a blind rage, turn on one another "until the ground was strewn with helmeted heads" (7: 260). Five dragon's-teeth men remain standing, and Cadmus discovers that with a little domestic magic they can be put to good use. Cadmus is on a futile quest for his sister Europa ("everybody's queen"), who had been kidnapped long ago by Jupiter disguised as a white bull. In her place he is given as his wife Harmonia, "a daughter of the sky." At this juncture Hawthorne's retelling converts wholesale into a fantasy of middle-class domestic magic. Together King Cadmus and Queen Harmonia dwell in a "palace" where they find "comfort," "but would doubtless have found as much, if not more, in the humblest cottage by the wayside." In time Cadmus and Harmonia sprout some "rosy little children (but how they came thither, has always been a mystery to me)." The most dramatic transformation, however, is in the five surviving dragon's-teeth soldiers, who help build Cadmus a city and now delight in playing grandads to his "little urchins" (7: 264). Thus we learn that the profitable alembic of domesticity and maternal influence is capable of transmuting bloody competitors into cooperative workers and sentimental guardians.

The adult contemporary middle-class reader of Hawthorne's myths would have smiled at the popular assumptions and values of the "cult of domesticity" that informed these mid-century revisions. Both mid-century myths, for instance, pay holy tribute in ways obvious and subtle to the magical socializing powers of middle-class mothers. Without mother's magic little girls might grow up unruled, perhaps even tainted by dragonism. In "The Golden Fleece," for example, one of Jason's "oarsmen" is a woman, Atalanta, "who had been nursed among the mountains by a bear." Unlike Zenobia, she is unsinkable, and, like Christ, could walk on water "without wetting more than the sole of her sandal." There are, nevertheless, grave domestic deficiencies in this exceptional woman. Having been suckled outside a nursery, and not by a mother, she has imbibed a "very wild" disposition and thus talked much about the rights of women, and loved hunting and war far better than her needle (7: 345). Zenobia suffered similar deprivation. Her too fertile mind, Coverdale explains in *Blithedale*, sprouted "weeds" because "she lacked a mother's care" (3: 189). Mother is entrusted with weeding out combative dragonisms.

In *The Girl's Book*, first published during the Depression of 1837, Lydia Hunt Sigourney's authoritative maternal tone exemplifies Mother's role as agent of conformity and social order: "Shew respect to magistrates, and to all who are in places of authority. There would be fewer mutinies and revolutions; if children were trained up in obedience." Seeming to forget that Washington headed a Revolutionary army, and leaving aside his legendary naughty proclivity to hack down cherry trees, she writes: "It was said of Washington, by his mother, that 'his first lesson was to obey.'"[2]

The agenda of the mid-century Harmonia, however, was not simply to inculcate habits of obedience but to socialize girls and boys to be *middle class*. "Mother" was a bourgeois construction viewed as essential to the social reproduction of middle-class identity. Before the middle of the nineteenth century child rearing after infancy had been the responsibility of the patriarch, but, as historian Mary Ryan has observed, it gradually became the mother's job to impose "sweet control." She undertook to rule, not by corporal discipline, but by nurturing conscience so that the child "would become the emotional marionette of its parents, in a warm and morally salubrious environment devoid of all cause for rebellious expression." As Ryan describes it, mother's mission was to implant "petit bourgeois traits—honesty, industry, frugality, temperance, and, preeminently, self-control" in her wards. Harmonia's "emotional skills" were directed toward the social reproduction "of small families, conservative business policies, dogged work habits, and basic literary skills—that is, the attributes required of the owners of small shops and stores and an increasing number of white-collar workers."[3]

Ideally this ideological reproduction equipped boys for their eventual entry into the marketplace and girls for their adult role as emotional providers for the males who survived their labors in "the world." The capitalist marketplace was often portrayed in middle-class domestic tracts as a bloody battlefield where neither man nor woman, especially woman, would wish to go. Its portrayal was, in fact, often like the "dragon's teeth" clash witnessed by Jason and Cadmus. The Rev. E. H. Chapin sketched "the bitter world" of 1851 as a war zone in which man is "driven ... back on himself" and where "anger, scorn, or calumny" excite him to "madness."[4] In 1865 Ruskin described the public sphere outside of the "queen's" garden as "torn up by the agony of men, and beat level by the drift of their life-blood."[5] Dragon's-teeth soldiers personify the middle-class fear of "change and chaos" discussed by Carroll Smith-Rosenberg. This hysteria, notes Mary Ryan, commodified and intensified by the flourishing publishing industry of the 1840's and 1850's, "cast suspicion on the ties between the family and the community and discouraged involvement in social and political organizations, especially on the part of the fragile female."[6] The therapeutic "magic circle" became the ideological solution. Without the softening influences of mother, home, and family, men on the make might regress into the army of uncontrollable monomaniacs witnessed by Jason

and Cadmus, an army whose sole "enjoyment" resides in strewing the
ground with "helmeted heads."

The ameliorative cultural project of domestic alchemy, as exemplified
in Hawthorne's "The Old Manse," is that it promises to transform men in the
way that it seems to transmute the trees in the apple orchard: it "humanizes"
them. Dragon's-teeth warriors, once domesticized and mothered by the
Queen Harmonias of America, pay off. they build cities and homes, and play
with children. The socializing influences of domesticity and motherhood
help make middle-class capitalist culture possible.

Thus it is intriguing that in *The Scarlet Letter* Hawthorne brings to
life a "dragon's-teeth" child, Pearl, who, in accordance with the doctrine of
the transmission of impressions, has imbibed (like Atalanta from her bear)
the rebellious "turmoil" of her adulterous "mother's system." "She never
created a friend," writes Hawthorne, perhaps also reflecting on unpacified
tendencies in his own work, "but seemed always to be sowing broadcast the
dragon's teeth, whence sprung a harvest of armed enemies, against whom
she rushed to battle" (1: 95).[7] As Roger Chillingworth observes, with literary
allusiveness, the "child's composition" is based on no law, nor reverence
for authority, no regard for human ordinances or opinions, right or wrong
(1: 134). Like an author unable to get a handle on her composition, Pearl's
mother, Hester Prynne, "failed to win the master-word that should control
this new and incomprehensible intelligence" (1: 93). "I hardly comprehend
her"! (1: 203), Hester confesses to Dimmesdale. As a kind of creative
principle the illegitimate Pearl is, like the undomesticated "dragon's-teeth"
soldiers, combative, unfeminine, and unmotherly; indeed, she is singularly
"hostile" toward the imaginary "offspring of her own heart and mind"
(1: 95). In Pearl, then, Hawthorne incorporates aspects of the high-flying
dragon women as well as the dragon warriors.

Hawthorne seems to hint that the enigmatic Pearl can serve vigilantly
and even maliciously as a feminist conscience for Hester. Little Pearl proves
to be a strict mistress when her mother exhibits stereotypical signs of
feminine weakness or sentiment. When Hester, baffled by her "perverse"
daughter, would "burst into passionate tears," the "dragon's-teeth" child
would frown, and clench her little fist, and harden her small features into
a stern, unsympathizing look of discontent (1: 92–93). But often Pearl's
"perverse" behavior might be read as the quintessence of Hester's own
determination to resist puritan authority. Pearl refuses to let her mother
pacify herself by responding to her predicament in a conventionally feminine
manner. She outlaws in her mother what Mary Ryan terms the "tear-jerking"
responses cultivated by many mid-century sentimental novels.[8] Sometimes,

"but this more rarely happened," Pearl would respond differently to her mother's show of sentiment: "she would be convulsed with a rage of grief, and sob out her love for her mother in broken words, and seem intent on proving that she had a heart, by breaking it" (1: 93). Yet these hysterics also seem contrived to agitate rather than pacify Hester and to proscribe weeping as an emotional outlet for her mother.

Unlike the self-destructive dragon's-teeth soldiers, much of Pearl's hostility is recognizably political and retributive: her "incoherent exclamations" and witch's anathemas (1: 94) are directed toward the puritans and their children. It is possible at times to view Pearl as an angry, nascent, dragon revolutionary, pitting her "ever-creative spirit" (1: 95) against the patriarchal authority of the puritans. Pearl's furious imagination converted the pine trees of the forest into puritan fathers and the "ugliest weeds" into their offspring, whom Pearl smote down and uprooted, most unmercifully (1: 95). In "The Custom House", the autobiographical preface to the novel, Hawthorne admitted that as Salem's Surveyor of Customs he was no "exterminating angel" (1: 14) who could threaten the "patriarchal body" of indolent hangers-on with dismissal. Pearl would have had no such compunction, for she, in her insurrection against puritan children, "resembled, in her fierce pursuit of them, an infant pestilence,—the scarlet fever, or some such half-fledged angel of judgment,—whose mission was to punish the sins of the rising generation" (1: 102–3). It is as if Pearl, a lawless "composition" born of adulterous lovers, personifies a transgressive dimension of Hawthorne's own "creative force" which allows him to rebel against his "stern and black-browed" puritan fathers who, in his own mind, rebuke him as "a writer of story-books"! (1: 10).

Considered in the context of the history of mid-century childrearing, Pearl's temperament is significant because she bears no signs of having internalized the authority that marks the young middle-class conscience-under-construction. If the role of the mid-century Harmonia is to socialize her child to provide "the vital integrative tissue for an emerging middle-class," Hawthorne represents Hester as a flop. Rather than writing a good middle-class novel about "a kind of portable parent" lodged deep "within the child's personality," Hawthorne has reversed the process and, if anything, gives us a Pearl whose rebellious conscience is lodged deep within her mother.[9] As Richard Brodhead notes, the project of maternal socialization "supplied an emerging group with a plan of individual nature ... that it could believe in and use to justify its ways" and, furthermore, employ to promote its class specific norms as "American 'normality.'" Pearl rejects this middle-class "puritan" normality.[10]

Hawthorne, of course, did not have to wait for Max Weber to recognize that the "normality" prescribed by these puritans exemplified a protestant work ethic that nurtured the spirit of capitalism. Of the Election Day procession he writes, "Then, too, the people were countenanced, if not encouraged, in relaxing the severe and close application to their various modes of rugged industry, which, at all other times, seemed of the same piece and material with their religion" (1: 231). It is these nascent *middle-class* puritans who would, in Hawthorne's imagination, denounce him as an "idler" (i: 10).

But Hawthorne also identified with his stern puritan ancestors, whose administrative careers exemplified the "persecuting spirit." "And yet, let them scorn me as they will," he acknowledges, strong traits of their nature have intertwined themselves with mine (1: 10). "Neither cast ye your pearls before swine," we are advised in Matthew 6:6. It may be that Hawthorne, like the defiant and adulterous mother of Pearl, on one level identifies with his rebellious dragon's-teeth progeny. As Sarah Hale noted in *Flora's Interpreter*, the "hawthorne" bush bears "flowers scarlet." Nevertheless, an "angel of judgment,—whose mission was to punish the sins of the rising generation" is certainly not Sigourney's shrinking middle-class angel in the house. This probably made Hawthorne uneasy.[11] Insofar as Pearl can be read as the personification of a creative and rebellious tendency in his own "composition," a scarlet force that subverts middle-class socialization, perhaps Hawthorne himself tried to impose "a tender, but strict control" over his dragon child, but found, like Hester, that the task was beyond his skill. Yet Hawthorne does succeed in reprogramming her (and perhaps his own writing in the same way).

Hawthorne converts Pearl as he did the surviving dragon's-teeth warriors: he domesticates her in the most theatrical of circumstances. The scene" is the scaffold with the scarlet trio on stage: Rev. Dimmesdale, Hester, and Pearl. Dimmesdale, to the approbation of his daughter, appears to acknowledge his paternity in full view of his flock:

> Pearl kissed his lips. A spell was broken. The great scene of grief in which the wild infant bore a part, had developed all her sympathies; and as her tears fell upon her father's cheek, they were the pledge that she would grow up amid human joy and sorrow, nor forever do battle with the world, but be a woman in it. (1: 256)

The public gathering of her family as a family "humanizes" Pearl, like the grotesque apple trees in Hawthorne's orchard. Now she can be daddy's little girl, if only for a moment, for daddy—in what seems to be a parody of mid-nineteenth-century sentimental fatherhood—is about to perform a death scene.[12] We see that Pearl is "human" and can know "joy" again because, like a good girl, she weeps.

Harriet Beecher Stowe put Topsy, the "naughty" slave girl, through a similarly theatrical ideological conversion in *Uncle Tom's Cabin* (1852), which Stowe began publishing in serial form only one year after the appearance of *The Scarlet Letter*. Topsy, who inherits Pearl's naughtiness without her politics, creates domestic havoc and is in need of reformation. Since it "grieves" Eva, the white angel of the house, that Topsy is "so naughty," Stowe's little evaporating evangelist takes it upon herself, enacting the role of the middle-class mother, to subdue Topsy with sentiment and guilt ("I shan't live a great while ... be good, for my sake"). Stowe has Topsy respond to Eva's entreaty with a torrential downpour of tears. Stowe's language of redemption reveals its debt to an ethnocentric discourse of "dark continent" colonization: "Yes, in that moment, a ray of real belief, a ray of heavenly love, had penetrated the darkness of her heathen soul!"[13] Eva displays the redemptive power of middle-class femininity just as Hawthorne's reunited family on a scaffold manifests the transformative power of middle-class domesticity. Ostensibly both Pearl and Topsy are "humanized," but more particularly they are tamed through the act of crying.

Rebellious little Pearl, it can be argued, gets a bum rap from this "humanizing" sleight of hand. Pearl's tears, we are told, should be read as her "pledge that she would grow up amid human joy and sorrow" and, moreover, that she would not "forever do battle with the world, but be a woman in it." To qualify as a "woman" is to pledge to refrain from "battle with the world."

Hawthorne was not consistently disaffected with male revolutionaries who did "battle with the world." Perseus, wielding Medusa's head, carries out a revolution by petrifying the evil King Polydectes and his court and then trots home to mother. Jason, in pursuit of the golden fleece, is also seen in a glowing light as an avenging revolutionary who seeks "to punish the wicked Pelias for wronging his dear father, and to cast him down from the throne, and seat himself there instead" (7: 332). Nonetheless it is Medea whose powerful magic puts the dragon to sleep so that Jason can pull its teeth. Her power automatically makes her an object of suspicion: "These enchantresses, you must know, are never to be depended upon" (7: 364). Perseus and Jason (who would be stumped without the aid of Medusa and Medea respectively) are lionized as heroic social actors, while Pearl is sketched as an imaginative brat, a little girl "all in disorder" (1: 91).

Let us return to the scaffold and ask: does Pearl's tearful union with her family "humanize" her (no longer a dragon's-teeth child more predatory than human) or *feminize* her in the manner prescribed by so many writers on domesticity? I would argue for the latter, that Hawthorne's ideological pearl of wisdom for his middle-class female readers is that you cannot rebel and be feminine at the same time.[14] In this ideological equation, to lose your femininity is to surrender your humanity.[15]

Hester is subjected to the same politics of representation and sleight of hand as her Pearl. We know, for instance, that Hester's isolation has been a radicalizing process, enabling her to roam beyond the premises policed by the puritan fathers: "She assumed a freedom of speculation, then common enough on the other side of the Atlantic, but which our forefathers, had they known it, would have held it to be a deadlier crime than that stigmatized by the scarlet letter" (1: 164). Yet Hawthorne never divulges the "deadlier" contents of this scarlet "speculation."

Of course, Hester's manifestly radical accomplishment is the "fertility and gorgeous luxuriance of fancy" shown in the embroidery of her letter, which went "greatly beyond what was allowed by the sumptuary regulations of the colony" (1: 53). One of the merciless "female spectators" of Hester on the scaffold is correct to recognize in her embroidery a refusal to obey to the letter. Hester is aware that her ideological function is to serve as a living stereotype not simply of sinfulness or adultery but of "woman's frailty and sinful passion" (1: 79). By taking liberties with her letter, by showing skill, intelligence, creativity, and pride rather than shame, she is engaged in a semiotic battle with a puritan patriarchy that seeks to regulate biological and ideological reproduction.[16]

This ideological reproduction is at one point symbolized as a mirror. In Governor Bellingham's mansion Hester views herself in the breastplate of standing armor, a "convex mirror" which exaggerates the size of her letter so as to render it "the most prominent feature of her appearance" and to obscure her behind it (1: 106). The "mirror" is reminiscent of Aylmer's daguerreotype of Georgiana, which, like the alchemist's fixating imagination, reproduces only the "hand" where her cheek should have been (10: 45). Bellingham's mirror can be read as a symbol of the way the puritan fathers would like Hester to view herself and her transgression. Hester's "voluptuous" art, if anything, functions to parody this "convex" puritan vision. It is significant that it is the dragon's-teeth child who directs Hester to gaze into the mirror. Hawthorne represents this as another sign of Pearl's impishness and naughtiness; yet Pearl's action signals to her mother exactly how the puritan fathers will try to contort her vision of herself in the interview which is to follow.

Hester does well as a cultural critic, given the fact that her author, that ambivalent descendant of puritan administrators, granted her merely one letter of the alphabet to work with. Only one letter makes it difficult for Hester to lead what Margaret Fuller aspired to and achieved, a "life of letters."[17] She remains a seamstress rather than a lecturess or an authoress.[18] Hawthorne has this woman of one letter earn her living, not without irony, by adorning the puritan patriarchy. Her embroidery distinguishes those "dignified by rank or wealth" from the plebian (1: 82) and thus helps legitimize the authority of the "new government" (1: 82) that censured her.[19]

However empowering Hester's revolutionary thoughts may be for her, Hawthorne makes her pay for them: as she gains in vision, she loses her "looks." When we first see the scarlet woman she is like a Lady of Shalott or a magnificent Medusa before being transformed into a gorgon: "She had dark and abundant hair, so glossy that it threw off the sunshine with a gleam" (1: 53). On the scaffold this woman of vision exhibited "a burning blush, and yet a haughty smile, and a glance that would not be abashed" (1: 52–53). Hester confines her "rich and luxuriant hair" (1: 163) in a cap and increasingly entertains radical thoughts.[20] Hawthorne has this intellectual activity wither her looks, all within seven years. It is difficult not to think of the way Hawthorne may have perceived his recently deceased friend, Margaret Fuller, when he writes of Hester: "All the light and graceful foliage of her character had been withered up by this red-hot brand, and had long ago fallen away, leaving a bare and harsh outline, which might have been repulsive, had she possessed friends and companions to be repelled by it" (1: 163).[21] Hester, like a queen, is now "majestic and statue-like"; but she is no longer, Lord help her, someone Hawthorne deems fit to cuddle: her "bosom" offers no "pillow of Affection" (1: 163).

Hawthorne explains that her "marble coldness ... was to be attributed to the circumstance that her life had turned, in a great measure, from passion and feeling, to thought" (1: 164). Then we learn of her egregious "freedom of speculation." All that sexy hair stuffed under her cap makes Hester not only think too much, but lose her femininity (her humanity): "She who has once been a woman, and ceased to be so, might at any moment become a woman again if there were only the magic touch to effect the transfiguration" (1: 164). If Hester, when free to "speculate," has perforce "ceased" to be a "woman," then what is she? Hawthorne's sleight of hand (his own crafty "magic touch") is here installing ideological criteria for what qualifies a female to be a "woman." Hester deviates from Hawthorne's discursive construction of "woman."

Hawthorne constructs "motherhood" as Hester's redemption. This conventional middle-class faith in the saving grace of Motherhood can also be seen in Horace Greeley's quip about Margaret Fuller (who had been one of his most successful columnists): "A good husband and two or three bouncing babies would have emancipated her from a great deal of cant and nonsense."[22] Hawthorne may have felt that one "bouncing" baby should be enough to drive the dragonism ("cant and nonsense") out of a radical woman. If not for Pearl, he assures us, the scarlet mother "might have come down to us in history, hand in hand with Anne Hutchinson, as the foundress of a religious sect. She might, in one of her phases, have been a prophetess" (1: 165). Just as sewing clothing may well have diverted Hester from unambiguously sowing broadcast the "dragon's teeth" in other forms, so does child rearing, which gave the mother's enthusiasm of thought ... something to wreak itself upon (1: 165).

Yet it seems as if Pearl, from birth, has fired up her mother's radical "enthusiasm of thought." Her "fierce" reactions to the "little Puritans" who scorn them "had a kind of value, and even comfort, for her mother; because there was at least an intelligible earnestness in the mood, instead of the fitful caprice that so often thwarted her in the child's manifestations" (1: 94). Pearl's "fitful caprice," by contrast, often operates to "thwart" her mother's "enthusiasm of thought." This would seem to present us with an enigma. If Pearl's only "discoverable principle of being" is, as Hester tells Dimmesdale, the freedom of a broken law (1: 134), and if she takes the lead in repelling "little Puritans" who torment the wearer of the scarlet letter, why then does Pearl demand that her mother refasten the scarlet badge of puritan authority to her bosom in the forest, and kiss it when Hester gives in? I shall suggest later that this "perverse" tormenting of her mother and this expression of allegiance to a symbol of puritan authority be read as the Dimmesdale side of Pearl.

Hawthorne, despite what appears to be conflicting evidence about the effect of Pearl on Hester, wants his readers to regard sewing and motherhood as fulfilling the cultural function later attributed by Oliver Wendell Holmes to the piano. In *Elsie Venner* Holmes profiles women as naturally secretive, resentful, and dangerous—ready to combust. They possess, for some unprobed reason, a "stormy inner life" that demands "free utterance" in "words or song." He gratefully concludes: "What would our civilization be without the piano?"[23] Hawthorne, by invoking the mid-century construction of middle-class motherhood, frames the question somewhat differently: what would our civilization be without the safety valve of "motherhood"?

Hawthorne's more fundamental question underlying this one is: what would our middle-class civilization be without feminized women? By "our civilization" both Holmes and Hawthorne mean a "civilization" based on the unquestionable primacy of patriarchal authority ("our"). Defeminized behavior, more than sexual transgression per se, is what Hawthorne sees as the "deadlier" (1: 164) threat to the puritan patriarchs as well as to the middle-class "civilization" of his own day. Although Hawthorne chooses not to disclose the details of Hester's scarlet "speculation," his allusion to the comprehensiveness of her vision of the revolutionary task before her is telling:

> As a first step, the whole system of society is to be torn down, and built up anew. Then, the very nature of the opposite sex in its long hereditary habit, which has become like nature, is to be essentially modified, before women can be allowed to assume what seems a fair and suitable position.... woman cannot take fair advantage of these preliminary reforms, until she shall have undergone a still mightier change; in which, perhaps, the ethereal essence, wherein she has her truest life, will be found to have evaporated. (1: 165–66)

In his Hutchinson piece of 1830 Hawthorne maintained that a "false liberality ... mistakes the strong division-lines of Nature for arbitrary distinctions."[24] But here, twenty years later, Hawthorne acknowledges that women and men inhabit "opposite" gender roles, which, though they become "like nature," are not quite "nature" ("hereditary habit") and can be changed. The phrasing does not specify what authority will at long last "allow" women to take up what "*seems* a fair and suitable position" (emphasis mine); nor does it spell out this new "position." Nevertheless, the radicalism here is in Hawthorne's suggestion that there is a vital *connection* between sex roles and specific forms of society. If sex roles change, everything changes, for these roles legitimize, enforce, and symbolize the larger "system," however unfree and contradictory this "system of society" may be. Hawthorne's perception of a link between gender reform and social change is, as we have seen, also overt in Coverdale's paranoid representation of Zenobia's catastrophic feminism ("oversetting all human institutions"). Defeminization leads not only to unlearning assumptions about gender but to dismantling assumptions undergirding patriarchal bourgeois constructs of "civilization" and "humanity." In this respect Hawthorne may well have made a connection between the "dragon's" mouth and a powerful force issuing from it that did indeed menace "civilization" as he knew it and wanted it to be.[25]

Hawthorne, then, may not have just been ambivalent about female sexuality or procreativity, or simply ambivalent about poetical and political "monsters" who deviate from prescribed roles; he may have felt distinctly uneasy about his own apocalyptic vision that "the whole system of society" as he knew it *had* to be "torn down" to set things right. Here Hawthorne is thinking expansively about why "our civilization," which implies a particular power structure, relies on the binary classification of "opposite" sexes. His theorizing resembles that of historian Joan W. Scott on the ways in which sexual difference becomes "one of the recurrent references by which political power has been conceived, legitimated, and criticized." What is at issue in Hawthorne's novel and his culture is not solely the control of women's bodies, behavior, and thinking, but in a more encompassing sense the "consolidation" of middle-class power and identity: in Scott's words, "The binary opposition and the social process of gender relationships both become part of the meaning of power itself; to question or alter any aspect threatens the entire system."[26] Paulina Wright Davis, the pioneer women's rights advocate who edited *The Una* in the early 1850's, also recognized this when, in 1870, she averred that the women's rights movement was "intended from its inception to change the structure, the central organization of Society."[27]

The fundamental inquiry for both Hawthorne and Scott is the ideological use of "the feminine in the political order." Once sexual difference seems "sure and fixed, outside of human construction," it can be used ideologically to naturalize and therefore legitimize other social relations, such as class divisions and the unequal distribution of wealth and power. This is what Melville was thinking about five years later in "The Tartarus of Maids", when he hinted that nature and feminized women workers were being transformed into signs intended to advertise the presence of the factory as a wholesome American institution. On the cutting edge of Hawthorne's middle-class consciousness was some awareness that, as Scott maintains, "the concept of class in the nineteenth century relied on gender for its articulation."[28]

Of course, Hawthorne's sketch of Hester's revolutionary vision ("the whole system of society is to be torn down, and built up anew") could have been a good deal more specific. For it may have been a theoretical *abstraction* of criticisms launched by the members of female reform and benevolent associations. Hester is herself a one-woman benevolent association in Salem, aiding the poor, ministering to the sick, and counseling abused and confused women. Concomitantly she is, all wrapped into one, exactly the kind of woman whom mid-century benevolent associations sought to assist: a seamstress, a fallen woman, and, at the outset, a prisoner.

Barbara Berg has advanced the thesis that in these associations, which flourished between 1830 and the 1850's, one can locate important origins of American feminism. The women who volunteered for these associations were middle-class and upper-class, and one lesson they learned (perhaps like Hester) as they moved out of their conventional "spheres" was that middle-class "motherhood" had indeed privatized them. "Many a woman is lost to society" once she becomes a mother, concluded one reformer in 1852."[29]

Coming face to face with exploited seamstresses, starving widows, and prostitutes, these reformers began not only to develop a sense of sisterhood with such women but to criticize *specific* structural contradictions that accounted for their plight.

In 1839, the year Hawthorne began work as a weigher and gauger of coal and salt at the Boston Custom House, one woman, a member of the Boston Seaman's Aid Society, wrote about the socioeconomic predicament of seamstresses. Her vision of the relationship between gender and exploitation is more focused than the revolutionary vision that Hawthorne attributes to Hester. "The irresistible influence of the Government, by its agents, is brought to operate directly to beat down the price of wages on the only kind of labor which a considerable class of females in every large city can perform." The year before, another member of the society observed in their publication: "The only means of earning money for those who cannot go out to labor in families, nor take in washing, is by needlework." They blamed not only government, and employers, but men for allowing this to happen: it is, charged another member, "a shame and disgrace for any one, who writes himself a man, to make a fortune out of the handy-work of poor females!"[30]

Hawthorne was not oblivious to this and may have been cognizant of criticisms leveled by these associations. Two years after he left his Boston Custom House post and one month after he published "The Birthmark", he published "The Procession of Life" (1843). In this sketch he describes a "crowd of pale-cheeked, slender girls, who disturb the ear with their multiplicity of short dry coughs" (10: 209). They are seamstresses who suffer under the rule of "master-tailors and close-fisted contractors" (10: 210). But what these reformers grasped, perhaps more firmly than Hawthorne, was that the feminization that had prevented them in their middle-class homes from being aware of such laboring-class realities was also the feminization that, by prohibiting women from being trained in and taking up a range of employments, created an ever-present female underclass, a well-stocked labor pool of easily exploited and, due to socialization, often docile wage slaves. A New York reformer, well aware of the *economic* reasons why some women often became prostitutes, wrote in the *Advocate of Moral Reform* (1846): "Women are thus limited to a few employments, hence these are overstocked with laborers." Another woman, writing for the same periodical in 1836, acknowledged that men speak "in extravagant terms on the excellence of women," but for her this now evoked the economic ramifications of such pedestal elevation and incited her to rock the belle-tower by demanding: "How is her labor requited?"[31]

In their criticisms there is a developing awareness that gender is a social construct. "Does the delicate mother fear that I would make her daughters masculine?" inquired one moral reform member in 1846. "Does she mean by masculine—thoughtful, judicious, wise, learned, independent, self, respecting—I plead guilty."[32] By the 1840's some reformers recognized that "masculine," as a construct, encompassed a congeries of activities and experiences that all human beings were entitled to share in.

These women of letters were discovering not that they could, in spite of censure from the clergy and elsewhere, retain their "humanity" even if they engaged in public reform, but that this process was enabling them to *redefine* humanity and to appropriate it for themselves and for the women they aided, perhaps for the first time. For some reformers this meant that their notion of "humanizing" would have to clash with the bourgeois notion of "humanizing" that had been part of their socialization as middle-class feminine women. Like Hester, many of these women had learned these lessons by helping "deviant" women and recognizing their sisterhood with them. But unlike Hawthorne, many of these women reformers were able to give their readers detailed reports of how gender socialization helps to produce and legitimize certain economic conditions inimical to laboring women and why, therefore, certain ideological and economic systems in a class stratified society should indeed in Hawthorne's words "be torn down, and built up anew."

Hawthorne's resistance to Hester's rather abstract vision of structural social change is not only political but emotional: the delicate femininity ("truest life") he reveres must evaporate in the change. The process of feminine evolution that produces Priscilla and other "true" women would be reversed, perhaps leaving us with the likes of the "man-like" Queen Elizabeth and Anne Hutchinson.

Hence Hawthorne proposes another solution. If woman embraces her role as Heart, he advises, these complex problems will "vanish." Hester's defeminized heart "had lost its regular and healthy throb, [she] wandered without a clew in the dark labyrinth of mind" (1: 166). A fastidious heaven will not award the sacred role of "prophetess" to a woman stained with sin, bowed down with shame, or even burdened with a life-long sorrow (1: 263). Instead heaven, in its "own time," will send an angel to the house. This "apostle" will bring revelation rather than revolution; not an "angel of judgment" or an "exterminating angel," but an angel of domesticity: The angel and apostle of the coming revelation must be a woman, indeed, but lofty, pure, and beautiful; and wise, moreover, not through dusky grief, but the ethereal medium of joy (1: 263).

Anne Hutchinson, Margaret Fuller, Hester, and Zenobia, all grounded by their politics and passion, were no angels. If Hester possesses wings, they are bedaubed wings of scarlet. Through a sleight of hand presented as Hester's "revelation," the scarlet woman is made to read herself as did Hawthorne, the nineteenth-century, middle-class son of the puritans, and to acknowledge that, stained "with a life-long sorrow," her domestic wings have forever been clipped.

Hawthorne managed to yank Hester's dragon's teeth with a sleight of hand even more subtle than that which had her bow to the cultural supremacy of the angel in the house. In "The Custom House" Hawthorne's statement of objective seems innocent enough: in "dressing up" Surveyor Pue's brief history, he has issued himself an artistic license to imagine "the motives and modes of passion that influenced the characters who figure in it" (1: 33). In doing so, I suggest, he contributes to the construction of a middle-class psychological "self" and that it is this we must continue to problematize as we did in Chapter 1.[33] This notion becomes essential to the way his reader is encouraged to imagine not only the "self," but power and social authority. *The Scarlet Letter* is one of a number of "puritan" texts in which Hawthorne psychologizes the wielding of cultural power. Hawthorne's insight that gender roles, though they are represented to seem "like nature," are not natural, becomes the theoretical road not taken. I shall argue that Hawthorne's critical consciousness of the discursive production of the gendered self is made subordinate to the idea that desire is the defining factor of the "self," that desire is at the root of the drive to possess cultural power.
From the first we are exposed to a number of mild double entendres that analogize writing with desire. In the intellectually sterile Custom House "lettered intercourse" (1: 27) is rare. The collection of official documents disappoints Hawthorne as "worthless scratchings of the pen" (1: 28). Hawthorne's "dressing up" of Dimmesdale's "motives and modes of passion," however, may well have gratified his own "scratchings" by way of compensation. For the writing and desire analogy is conspicuous in Hawthorne's description of Dimmesdale's triumphant all-nighter spent composing his Election sermon: daylight found him "with the pen still between his fingers" (1: 225). This presumably more fluid version of the sermon was inked with "an impulsive flow of thought and emotion," and in spite of the good minister's doubt that "Heaven should see fit to transmit the grand and solemn music of its oracles through so foul an *organ-pipe* as he" (1: 225) (emphasis mine).[34]
Religion is consistently represented as a substitutive form of sexual expression for Dimmesdale and even some of his flock. Dimmesdale's "popularity" as preacher of the Word reflected his great "intellectual gifts, his moral perceptions, his power of experiencing and communicating emotion";

but all of these qualities were kept in a state of preternatural activity by the prick. and anguish of his daily life (1: 141). His guilt, appropriately termed "prick and anguish," and his sexuality, sublimated through the Word, make him an impassioned preacher. He ignites the faith of his flock with a *Tongue of Flame* (1: 142). Hot stuff, we learn, for the pubescent "virgins of the church grew pale around him, victims of a passion so imbued with religious sentiment that they imagined it to be all religion, and brought it openly, in their white bosoms, as their most acceptable sacrifice before the altar" (1: 142). They get turned on, and Dimmesdale himself gets turned on, by his confessions that "he was altogether vile, a viler companion of the vilest." "They heard it all"—but not quite all—and did but reverence him the more (1: 144). Dimmesdale's confessions, like Hawthorne's rendition of Hester's revolutionary vision, stay abstract. D. H. Lawrence knew this game; the itchy minister gets the same substitutive pleasure out of flagellating himself by preaching in public as he does by mortifying his flesh in private: "It's a form of masturbation."[35]

Dimmesdale seems like a lubricious lad liberated from the pages of antimasturbation tracts of the 1830's and 1840's penned by Sylvester Graham, John Todd, and the Fowler brothers. As we have seen in Chapter I, phrenological and antimasturbation authors advised readers on how to decode signs of a libidinal interiority that their own texts constructed and implanted as natural. Hawthorne has done what these writers did in their "manuals": he has locked up desire inside the self, privileged it as the essence of the self, and designated it as the explanatory key to the allegory of behavior. Note the language of interiority used to describe Dimmesdale, whose "Tongue of Flame" has been relighted in the forest by Hester:

> Before Mr. Dimmesdale reached home, his inner man gave him other evidence of a revolution in the sphere of thought and feeling. In truth, nothing short of a total change of dynasty and moral code, in that interior kingdom, was adequate to account for the impulses now communicated to the unfortunate and startled minister. At every step he was incited to do some strange, wild, wicked thing or other, with a sense that it would be at once involuntary and intentional, in spite of himself, yet growing out of a profounder self than that which opposed the impulse. (1: 217)

Dimmesdale surrenders to an "inner" man, an "interior kingdom," a "profounder self." This model of sexual interiority governs how he and we as readers imagine character and conceive of liberation. His "revolution," by the by, seems less ambitious than Hester's. The scarlet woman's speculative freedom pushes her toward questioning why the architects of a power structure would want to create and enforce sexual difference as a strategy to legitimize their authority. Dimmesdale's "revolution in the sphere of thought and feeling," on the other hand, arouses him to be naughty in public and private whenever he can get away with it.

Hawthorne's construction of the naughty psychological self also provides the theoretical basis for a cultural theory. Not only is Dimmesdale naughty and repressed, so are the governing puritans in several of Hawthorne's puritan tales. In "The Maypole of Merrymount" (1836), "Endicott and the Red Cross" (1838), and "Main-Street" (1849), desire underlies the puritans' motives for enforcing cultural power. Hawthorne's cultural theory resembles Freud's in "'Civilized' Sexual Morality and Modern Nervousness" (1908), in which the father of psychoanalysis encodes "civilization" as a form of necessary sexual repression, but advises that this repression be made less severe. "Our civilization is, generally speaking, founded on the suppression of instincts."[36] Puritan semiotic control is represented by Hawthorne as symbiotic with sexual control.

In "The Maypole of Merrymount", for instance, the puritan whipping post gratifies unacknowledged libidinal satisfactions not all that different from the sexual desires that the merrymounters are being whipped for celebrating around the maypole. Cultural conflict is thus translated into a sexual power struggle. William Bradford *Of Plymouth Plantation* and Thomas Morton *New English Canaan*, as seventeenth-century accounts of the puritan suppression of the merrymounters, stress economic and religious causes. Hawthorne, writing within the bourgeois "deployment of sexuality" described by Foucault, psychologizes their motives.

In "Main-Street" Hawthorne implicates his own ancestor as he depicts Ann Coleman being dragged and whipped through the streets "naked from the waist upward": A strong-armed fellow is that constable; and each time that he flourishes his lash in the air, you see a frown wrinkling and twisting his brow, and, at the same instant, a smile upon his lips. He loves his business, faithful officer that he is, and puts his soul into every stroke, zealous to fulfil the injunction of Major Hathorne's warrant, in the spirit and to the letter (11: 70). One can almost imagine Hawthorne smiling when writing *The Scarlet Letter* and musing self-critically whether he was putting "his soul into every stroke, zealous to fulfil the injunction of Major Hathorne, in the spirit and to the letter." Hawthorne gives us puritan authorities, seemingly bound to the logic of Freud's "projection," who get turned on by punishing in others impulses they would publicly deny in themselves.[37]

Of course, this twist was one way for Hawthorne to handle his own ambivalence about those iron-faced practical ancestors who in his imagination scoffed at him as a writer of mere "story-books." Hawthorne's "Freudian" joke is on them and their collective unconscious. The repression model gives him a means of controlling how interiority is imagined by his readers and authorizes him to assign his puritan fathers subterranean (sexual) "motives."

Hawthorne's assumptions about interiority in *The Scarlet Letter* often seem closer to Freud's than to Foucault's or Joan Scott's. This privatized model of the self and of culture competes with and perhaps towers over Hester's more politicized understanding of gender identity as a construction and culture as the site of political struggle. Hawthorne seems to marginalize, if not quite dismiss, the insights of Hester into social construction theory as the misleading lessons of a scarlet letter that "had not done its office" (1: 166).

The final scaffold scene allows Hawthorne to return us to what I take to be his principal ideological scheme. The Pearl who throws stones and utters "witch's anathemas" at her little puritan persecutors is expressing the antagonistic fertility and political rebelliousness of her mother. Of course, her "sowing" is at last domesticated. But Pearl has also inherited the naughtiness of her father. One day Hester gazed into the little imp's eyes and "fancied that she beheld ... a face, fiend-like, full of smiling malice, yet bearing the semblance of features that she had known full well, though seldom with a smile, and never with malice in them" (1: 97). The Pearl who delights in tormenting her mother with guilt is, in part, daddy's little girl. Once Pearl is domesticated on the scaffold, she is something other than socially rebellious or perversely naughty. Hawthorne's real "pearl" of wisdom is that domesticity "humanizes" both the maternal political self and the paternal psychological self in Pearl.

Perhaps the domestic theme is also what Hawthorne deploys to "humanize" these two theoretical tendencies in his art. When domesticity "humanizes" the self, for example, an extended criticism of gender and social structure in one's writing is rendered superfluous. At the same time, this process of domestic "humanizing" presumably diminishes one's susceptibility to the psychological creatures lurking in the darker regions that one has figured within one's text.

To conclude, the fundamental ideological project of *The Scarlet Letter* seems contradictory but self-consciously so: Hawthorne reinforces *and* problematizes the middle-class ideology that domesticity "humanizes." One can argue persuasively that the former tendency prevails over the latter in the climactic "humanizing" of a teary-eyed and heart-inflated Pearl on the scaffold and in Hester's own ironclad acknowledgment that she is disqualified to be a ministering "angel" of celestial "revelation." Yet the text also allows us to question the authority of its narration by wondering whether Hester would have been at all interested in sentimental "revelation" anyway. If *The Scarlet Letter* sets out to affirm motherhood as that which saves Hester from becoming Anne Hutchinson, the scarlet mother remains, nevertheless, an unorthodox mother. To make matters more complex, the scarlet family winds up not on a pedestal but on a scaffold. The image, despite the middle-class domestic message we might draw from it, is way off balance.[38]

Hawthorne states in his preface that by leaving the Salem Custom House for Home and Hearth he was able to transform his "snow-images into men and women" (1: 36). Yet he seems to have converted his snow-images into what Mrs. Oliphant and other contemporary reviewers saw as an almost unrecognizable group of misfits. Because Hester shattered the feminine stereotype, she was seen by some reviewers to be as shocking as any other character in the novel. Indeed, in 1852 Charles Hale profiled Hawthorne's unsentimental heroines in terms that conjure Hawthorne's three "dragon" women in The Gorgon's Head: "They are all weird, and as much a creation of his fancy as the three sisters in MacBeth are Shakespeare's.... We never fell in love with such. In truth, they are not lovable; they are incomprehensible, and full of mystery."[39]

Hawthorne's "romance" did not sit right as a reassuringly domestic novel because it was not intended to. One half-expects Hester, given the odd tilt of the book, to contest the official "humanizing" (feminizing) ideology of the narrative with a counterargument. This argument could easily be what Hawthorne certainly recognized while penning his sometimes kinky "romance": that transgression, given the puritan or mid-nineteenth-century middle-class context, is what potentially makes a woman fully "human" (begrimed with "dusky grief").

NOTES

1. Grimké, *Letters*, pp. 46–47. On "butterflies" see Berg (*The Remembered Gate*, pp. 98–99), who quotes from "Young Ladies at Home," *Golden Keepsake* (1851): the author criticizes "female characters who spend their time and talents in as useless a manner as possible and with the same superficial appearance as the painted butterfly." In addition note Fanny Fern's "The Women of 1867," reprinted in Ruth Hall: "A woman—but not necessarily a butterfly—not necessarily a machine, which, once wound up by the marriage ceremony, is expected to click with undeviating monotony till Death stops the hands" (p. 344). In Hawthorne's *The Artist of the Beautiful* (1844), Owen Warland mechanical butterfly can be read as a miniature technological substitute for a shrunken "angel" in the house.

2. Sigourney, *The Girl's Book*, p. 47.

3. M. P. Ryan, *Cradle*, p. 232; *Empire of the Mother*, p. 52; *Cradle*, p. 161; *Empire of the Mother*, p. 57; *Cradle*, p. 238.

4. Chapin, *Duties*, p. 15.

5. Ruskin, *Queens' Gardens*, p. 115.

6. M. P. Ryan, *Empire of the Mother*, p. 39.

7. See Larry J. Reynolds's *Revolutions Abroad* (pp. 46–47, 59–60); Reynolds suggests that Hawthorne may have read Margaret Fuller's dispatches to the *New York Tribune* in 1849 about the Italian Revolution and borrowed the image from her: "Every struggle made by the old tyrannies ... only sows more dragon's teeth," she wrote.

8. M. P. Ryan, *Cradle*, p. 17.

9. M. P. Ryan, *Empire of the Mother*, pp. 18, 51.

10. Brodhead, *Sparing the Rod*, p. 77.

11. For the story of how Hawthorne's daughter's occasionally unfeminine autonomy made him uneasy, see Herbert, "Nathaniel Hawthorne, Una Hawthorne," especially pp. 292–95. Una may have been the model for Pearl, and her father refused to allow her to read *The Scarlet Letter*.

12. Dimmesdale, who does not fit the pedagogical mold of the seventeenth-century father, seems to parody mid-nineteenth-century sentimental fatherhood on stage. See Demos, *The Changing Faces of Fatherhood*, pp. 41–67 in *Past, Present, and Personal*.

13. Stowe, *Uncle Tom's Cabin*, p. 410.

14. David Leverenz develops the gender politics of Pearl's pacification: the kiss "pacifies her.... Now Pearl gains her narrator's praise for returning to femininity" (*Manhood*, p. 269). For Larry J. Reynolds, Pearl's pacification is also paid off with upward mobility: "In what seems to be a reward for her docility she marries into European nobility (thereby accomplishing a restoration of the ties with aristocracy her maternal relatives once enjoyed)" (*Revolutions Abroad*," p. 65).

15. For a clever reading of Pearl's "humanizing" worked out within the terms of Hawthorne's discourse, see Ragussis, *Family Discourse*," especially p. 885.

16. Amy Schrager Lang points out that Hester's letter "ties the liberation of the creative, the generative, impulse to lawlessness" (An American Jezebel: Hawthorne and The Scarlet Letter, in *Prophetic Woman*, p. 167.)

17. Blanchard, *Margaret Fuller*, p. 46.

18. See Sarah J. Hale's *The Lecturess*: "Mother ... I try to make other women do something more than sew" (p. 17). Also see Ware's *Zenobia*, in which Zenobia, on the verge of being defeated, asks herself rhetorically: "Should I have done better to have sat over my embroidery, in the midst of my slaves, all my days, than to have spent them in building up a kingdom?" (2: 142). Fanny Fern points to the significance of the needle as a symbol of domesticized woman when parodying the patriarchal ideology which predicted that Stowe's Uncle Tom's Cabin would be a flop: "You see you had no 'call,' Mrs. Tom Cabin, to drop your babies and darning-needle to immortalize your name.... Women should have their ambition bounded by a gridiron, and a darning needle" (*Mrs. Stowe's Uncle Tom*," in *Ruth Hall*, p. 256).

19. See Pease, *Visionary Compacts*, pp. 89, 91. Yet her embroidery, as Pease notes, might also be read not "as a form of repentance but [as] public restatements of her private relationship with Arthur" (p. 91).

20. As Judith Fetterley points out, "the containment of Hester constitutes a primary action of the text. Although flashes of Hester's power occur and reoccur, they serve essentially to rationalize the systematic reduction of her power: her sexuality is imprisoned

beneath her drab clothing and severe cap; her artistry is diverted from rebellious self-expression into the works of charity; her maternal force is converted into the ineffectual fumblings of a mother with a 'bad' child whom she cannot control" (*Provisions*, p. 26). Yet by containing her hair in a cap, Hester seems able to break away from the way the townspeople see her and the way she has been taught to see herself.

21. Francis E. Kearns makes parallels between Hester and Fuller's advocacy of female prisons, her "conversations" with women, and her cultural role as a "prophetess" (Margaret Fuller as a Model for Hester Prynne). As I noted earlier, Larry J. Reynolds also notes the correspondence of their revolutionary thoughts in *Revolutions Abroad*," p. 66.

22. Greeley quoted in A. Douglas, *Feminization of American Culture*, p. 339.

23. Holmes, *Elsie Venner*, p. 341.

24. Hawthorne, *Mrs. Hutchinson*," *Works: Riverside Edition* 4: 168.

25. On Hawthorne's "liberal" representation of Hester's radicalism ("fear of process run amok," p. 649) see Bercovitch, "A-Politics". David Stineback offers a useful discussion of the radicalism underlying Hawthorne concerns with gender in "Gender, Hawthorne, and Literary Criticism".

26. Scott, "Gender: A Useful Category," pp. 1072–73.

27. Davis quoted in M. P. Ryan, *Cradle*, pp. 228–29.

28. Scott, "Gender: A Useful Category," p. 1073.

29. Berg, *The Remembered Gate*, p. 248.

30. Ibid., pp. 168, 171.

31. Ibid., pp. 206, 204–5.

32. Ibid., p. 207.

33. For a discussion of how the novel both reflects and participates in one aspect of this construction, see Brodhead, "Sparing the Rod". Brodhead's analysis of shifts in modes of disciplinary punishment in the middle-class leads him to suggest that "Hawthorne's whole project in *The Scarlet Letter* could be thought of as an attempt to weigh the methods and powers of a newer against an older disciplinary order, by juxtaposing a world of corporal correction (embodied by the Puritans' punishment of Hester) and a world of correction-by-interiority (embodied in Chillingworth and Dimmesdale)" (p. 78). The Foucauldian outcome seems to be something like the institutionalization of a peculiarly middle-class superego.

34. On sexual imagery in *The Scarlet Letter*, see Michael Davitt Bell, "Arts of Deception," p. 49; Bell notes Hawthorne's irony in making Dimmesdale oblivious to the sexual pun on "organ-pipe."

35. Lawrence, *Studies*, p. 90.

36. S. Freud, "'Civilized' Sexual Morality and Modern Nervousness," in *Sexuality*, p. 25.

37. Freud observes that socially prescribed "punishment will not infrequently give those who carry it out an opportunity of committing the same outrage under colour of expiation. This is indeed one of the foundations of the human penal system and it is based, no doubt correctly, on the assumption that the prohibited impulses are present alike in the criminal and in the avenging community" (*Totem and Taboo*, p. 72).

38. For David Leverenz, Hawthorne "seems fully aware that his readers will accept Hester only while she suffers for her sin.... Yet though he silences Hester with values he and his audience hold dear, he makes his readers uncomfortable with those values.... His narrative continuously invokes and undermines prevailing conventions of womanhood and manhood" (*Manhood*, p. 277).

39. C. Hale, "Nathaniel Hawthorne," p. 179.

SACVAN BERCOVITCH

The A-Politics of Ambiguity

The drama of Hester Prynne's return has gone unappreciated, no doubt because it is absent from the novel. At a certain missing point in the narrative, through an unrecorded process of introspection, Hester abandons the high, sustained self-reliance by which we have come to identify her, from her opening gesture of defiance, when she repels the beadle and walks proudly "into the open air" (162), to the forest scene seven years later, when she casts off her A and urges Dimmesdale to a new life—choosing for no clear reason to abandon her heroic independence and acquiescing to the A after all. Voluntarily she returns to the colony that had tried to make her (she once believed) a "life-long bond-slave," although Hawthorne pointedly records the rumors that Pearl "would most joyfully have entertained [her] ... mother at her fireside" (313–14, 344). And voluntarily Hester resumes the letter as a "woman stained with sin, bowed down with shame," although, he adds, "not the sternest magistrate of that iron period would have imposed it" (344). As in a camera obscura, isolation and schism are inverted into vehicles of moral, political; and historical continuity:

> Women, more especially ... came to Hester's cottage, demanding
> why they were so wretched, and what the remedy! Hester com-
> forted and counseled them, as best she might. She assured them,

From *The Office of* The Scarlet Letter, pp. 1–31. © 1991 by The Johns Hopkins University Press.

too, of her firm belief, that, at some brighter period, when the
world should have grown ripe for it, in Heaven's own time, a new
truth would be revealed, in order to establish the whole relation
between man and woman on a surer ground of mutual happiness. Earlier in life, Hester had vainly imagined that she herself
might be the destined prophetess, but had long since recognized
the impossibility that any mission of divine and mysterious truth
should be confided to a woman stained with sin, bowed down
with shame, or even burdened with a life-long sorrow. The angel
and apostle of the coming revelation must be a woman, indeed,
but lofty, pure, and beautiful; and wise, moreover, not through
dusky grief, but the ethereal medium of joy; and showing how
sacred love should make us happy, by the truest test of a life successful to such an end! (344–45)

The entire novel tends toward this moment of reconciliation, but the
basis for reconciliation, the source of Hester's revision, remains entirely
unexplained. The issue is not that Hester returns, which Hawthorne does
account for, in his way: "There was a more real life for Hester Prynne,
here, in New England" (344). Nor is it that she resumes the A: we might
anticipate that return to beginnings, by the principles of narrative closure.
What remains problematic, what Hawthorne compels us to explain for
ourselves (as well as on Hester's behalf), is her dramatic change of purpose
and belief. Throughout her "seven years of outlaw and ignominy," Hester
had considered her A a "scorching stigma" and herself "the people's victim"
(331, 291, 313–14). Only some "galling" combination of fatalism and love,
Hawthorne tells us early in the novel, had kept her from leaving the colony
at once, after her condemnation (188). She had been "free to return" to
England; she had also had

the passes of the dark, inscrutable forest open to her, where the
wildness of her nature might assimilate itself with a people whose
customs and life were alien from the law that had condemned
her.... But [Hester was possessed by] ... a fatality, a feeling so
irresistible and inevitable that it ha[d] the force of doom.... Her
sin, her ignominy, were the roots which she had struck into the
soil. It was as if a new birth, with stronger assimilations than the
first, had converted the forest-land ... into Hester Prynne's wild
and dreary, but life-long home.... The chain that bound her here
was of iron links, and galling to her inmost soul.... What she
compelled herself to believe,—what, finally, she reasoned upon,

as her motive for continuing a resident of New England,—was half a truth, and half a self-delusion. Here, she said to herself, had been the scene of her guilt, and here should be the scene of her daily punishment; and so, perchance, the torture of her daily shame would at length purge her soul, and work out another purity than that which she had lost; more saint-like, because the result of martyrdom. (186–87)

Something of that force of necessity attends Hester's return, together with that earlier self-denying, self-aggrandizing quest for martyrdom. But it now conveys a far less "wild and dreary" prospect. Hester chooses to make herself not only an object of the law, "saint-like" by her resignation to "daily punishment," but more largely an agent of the law, the sainted guide toward "another purity," "some brighter period" of "sacred love" foreshadowed by her agon (344–45). What had been half-truth, half-delusion is rendered whole as a vision of progress through due process. And the bond she thus forges anew with the community lends another moral interpretation to her "new birth" as American. It recasts her adopted "forest-land" into the site of prophecy, home to be of the "angel or apostle of the coming revelation"; it reconstitutes Hester herself, *as a marginal dissenter*, into an exemplum of historical continuity (344–45).

We accept all this as inevitable, as readers did from the start, because Hawthorne has prepared us for it. His strategies of ambiguity and irony *require* Hester's conversion to the letter. And since the magistrates themselves do not impose the A; since the community has long since come to regard Hester as an "angel or apostle" in her own right; since, moreover, we never learn the process of her conversion to the A (while her development through the novel tends in exactly the opposite direction); since, in short, neither author nor characters help us—we must meet the requirement ourselves.

"The scarlet letter had not done its office," and, when it has, its office depends on our interpretation—or, more precisely, on our capacities to respond to Hawthorne's directives for interpretation. The burden this imposes can be specified by contrast with Dimmesdale's metamorphosis, earlier in the story, from secret rebel into prophet of New Israel. Hawthorne details the state of despair in which the minister agrees to leave, elaborates the disordered fantasies that follow, and yet leaves it to us to explain Dimmesdale's recantation. In this case, however, the explanation emerges directly from character and plot. "The minister," Hawthorne writes, "had never gone through an experience calculated to lead him beyond the scope of generally received laws; although, in a single instance, he had so fearfully transgressed one of the most sacred of them. But this had been a sin of passion, not of principle, nor even purpose" (290). When, accordingly, Dimmesdale decides to leave with Hester, he does so only because he believes he is "irrevocably doomed" (291), and we infer upon his return that he has regained his faith after all—that he has made peace at last with the Puritan ambiguities of mercy and justice, good and evil, head and heart, which he had abandoned momentarily in the forest.

The reasons for Hester's reversal are far more complex. It takes the whole story to work them through. To begin with, there is the problem of form, since in her case (unlike Dimmesdale's) the reversal so, conspicuously defies tradition. I refer to the genre of tragic love to which *The Scarlet Letter* belongs. Had Hester returned for love alone (the A for Arthur) or under the cloud of disaster abroad (the A for adversity), we could follow her reasoning readily enough. But Hawthorne asks us to consider the disparity between these familiar tragic endings and Hester's choice. The familiar endings, from *Antigone* and *Medea* through *Antony and Cleopatra* and *Tristan and Isolde*, are variations on the theme of love against the world. Hester's return merges love *and* the world. In this aspect (as in others) it offers a dramatic contrast with European novels of adultery, which narrative theorists have classified in terms either of subversion or of containment, as implying "a fatal break in the rigid system of bourgeois realism," or as "working to subvert what [the novel] aims to celebrate," or else (because of the "nearly universal failure of the adulterous affair") as serving "closurally to reinstate social norms."[1] *Madame Bovary* and *Anna Karenina* can be said to fit any of these descriptions. *The Scarlet Letter* fits none. Hester neither reaffirms her adulterous affair nor disavows it; her actions neither undermine the social order nor celebrate it; and at the end she neither reinstates the old norms nor breaks with them. Instead, she projects her dream of love onto some "surer ground" in the future, when "the whole relation between man and woman" can be reestablished. In other words, her return deliberately breaks with tradition by its emphasis on the political implications of process as closure.

The political emphasis is appropriate for the same reason that it is problematic: Hawthorne's portrait of Hester is a study of the lover as social rebel. Not as antinomian or witch, as he explicitly tells us, and certainly not as adulteress—if anything Hester errs at the opposite extreme, by her utter repression of eros. This emphasis on the non- or even antierotic is also to highlight sexual transgression, of course, but wholly by contrast; and it is to reinforce the contrast that Hawthorne insinuates by his often-remarked parallels between Hester and "unnatural" Anne Hutchinson, mother of "monstrous misconceptions"[2] as well as imperious, "bitter-tempered" Mistress Hibbins (217). Hawthorne remarks, with a note of disgust, that

Hester had lost her "womanly" qualities, had become almost manlike in her harshness of manner and feature:

> Even the attractiveness of her person had undergone a ... sad transformation ... [so that] there seemed to be no longer any thing in Hester's face for Love to dwell upon; nothing in Hester's form, though majestic and statue-like, that Passion could ever dream of clasping in its embrace; nothing in Hester's bosom, to make it ever again the pillow of Affection. Some attribute had departed from her, the permanence of which had been essential to keep her a woman. (258–59)

Hester errs, then, not in her sexual transgression but in her "stern development" as an individualist of increasingly revolutionary commitment (259). At the novel's center is a subtle and devastating critique of radicalism that might be titled "The 'Martyrdom' of Hester Prynne." It leads from her bitter sense of herself as victim to her self-conscious manipulation of the townspeople, and it reveals an ego nourished by antagonism; self-protected from guilt by a refusal to look inward; using penance as a refuge from penitence; feeding on shame, self-pity, and hatred; and motivated by the conviction that society is the enemy of the self.

Let me recall the scene I began with, in the chapter midway through the novel. Seven years have passed and the townspeople have come to regard Hester with affection, admiration, even reverence. On her part, Hester has masked her pride as humility, has repeatedly reminded them, by gesture and look, of her "saint-*like*" suffering, and in general has played upon their guilt and generosity until "society was inclined to show its *former* victim a more benign countenance than she cared to be favored with, or, perchance, than she deserved" (187, 257; my emphasis). And like other hypocrites in Hawthorne's work, Hester pays a heavy price for success. "All the light and graceful foliage of her character had been withered up," he tells us, "leaving a bare and harsh outline, which might have been repulsive, had she possessed friends or companions to be repelled by it" (258). She has none because she wants none. The "links that united her to the rest of human kind had all been broken," save for "the iron link of mutual crime" (255). She considers Pearl, whom she loves, an instrument of "retribution" (273): Concerning those to whom she ministers—not only "her enemies" but also those for whom "the scarlet letter had the effect of a cross on a nun's bosom"—Hawthorne points out that Hester "forebore to pray for [them], lest, in spite of her forgiving aspirations, the words of the blessing should stubbornly twist themselves into a curse" (258, 191).

It is worth stressing the severity of Hawthorne's critique. After seven
years Hester has become an avenging angel, a figure of penance unrepentant,
a so-called Sister of Mercy who not only scorns those who call her so
but who has developed contempt for all "human institutions," "whatever
priests or legislators had established" (257, 290). Despairing, therefore, of
any improvement short of tearing down "the whole system of society" and
doubtful even of that "remedy," she turns her energies first against "the
world's law" and then against her daughter and herself (260, 259). Her heart,
Hawthorne tells us,

> had lost its regular and healthy throb, [and she] wandered with-
> out a clew in the dark labyrinth of mind; now turned aside by an
> insurmountable precipice; now starting back from a deep chasm.
> There was wild and ghastly scenery all around her, and a home
> and comfort nowhere. At times, a fearful doubt strove to pos-
> sess her soul, whether it were not better to send Pearl at once to
> heaven, and go herself to such futurity as Eternal justice should
> provide. (261)

Here is the allegorical landscape of misguided rebellion: a wild, self-vaunting
independence leading by a ghastly logic of its own to the brink of murder and
suicide. No wonder Hawthorne remarks at this point that "the scarlet letter
had not done its office."

I do not mean by this to deny the obvious. Hester is a romantic heroine.
She is endowed with all the attributes this term implies of natural dignity,
generosity of instinct, and what Hawthorne calls "a woman's strength" (257).
Although she persistently abuses or represses these qualities, nonetheless they
remain potential in her—dormant but felt in her every thought and action—
and Hawthorne clearly means them to move us all the more forcefully for the
contrast. As he remarks after detailing her "sad transformation," "She who
has once been a woman, and ceased to be so, might at any moment become a
woman again, if there were only the magic touch to effect the transfiguration.
We shall see whether Hester Prynne were ever afterwards so touched, and so
transfigured" (260). While we wait to see, Hester persistently invites our pity
and praise, and by and large she succeeds, as she did with the Puritans. But
to take her point of view is to prevent the scarlet letter from doing its office.
It leads us, as it did Hester, into conflict—compels us to choose between the
reasons of the heart and the claims of institutions—and conflict is precisely
what the letter is designed to eliminate.

Again, a distinction is called for. Conflict is also a form of process, of
course, but one that assumes inherent antagonism; it derives from a partiality

that inspires partisanship. Conflict forces us to take positions and thus issues in active oppositions: one certainty against another, one generation against the next, one class or gender against another. Process (for Hawthorne) is a form of partiality that accepts limitation, acknowledges its own incompleteness, and so tends toward tolerance, accommodation, pluralism, acquiescence, inaction.

The contrary tendency toward conflict is the dark side of Hawthorne's chiaroscuro portrait of Hester. Her black eyes and hair—always a danger signal in Hawthorne's (culture's) symbolic system—are complemented, so to speak, by his relentless critical commentary on her every misstep into independence. We feel it the moment she crosses the prison threshold to his gently mocking "as if by her own *free-will*" (162; my emphasis). We see it detailed in her radical speculations, when her mind wanders

> without rule or guidance, in a moral wilderness as vast, as intri-
> cate and shadowy, as the untamed forest.... Her intellect and heart
> had their home, as it were, in desert places, where she roamed as
> *freely* as the wild Indian in his woods.... Shame, Despair, Solitude!
> These had been her teachers,—stern and wild ones,—and they
> had made her strong, but taught her much amiss. (290; my
> emphasis)

This running gloss on the ways that the letter has not done its office reaches its nadir in her forest meeting with Dimmesdale. Amidst the fallen autumn leaves, Hester discards the A in a gesture of defiance for which (Hawthorne reminds us) her entire seven years had been the preparation. "The past is gone!" she exclaims. "With this symbol, I undo it all, and make it as it had never been!" (292). And the narrator adds, with characteristic irony (characteristic, among other things, in that the irony borders on moralism):

> O exquisite relief! She had not known the weight, until she felt
> the *freedom!* ... All at once, as *with* a sudden smile of heaven, burst
> forth the sunshine.
>
>   Such was the sympathy of Nature—that wild, heathen Nature
> of the forest never subjugated by human law, nor illumined by
> higher truth—with the bliss of these two spirits! (292–93; my
> emphasis)

The narrator's ironies are not Hawthorne's precisely, and the difference, as we shall see, allows for a significant leeway in interpretation. But even within this larger perspective the contrast in forms of process is unmistakable.

The radicalization of Hester Prynne builds on the politics of either/or. Hawthorne's symbolic method requires the politics of both/and. To that end, in the forest scene, Pearl keeps Hester from disavowing the office of the A, as earlier she had kept her from becoming another antinomian Anne or Witch Hibbins. Indeed, it is worth digressing for a moment to point out how closely for these purposes Pearl is bound to the A—with what painstaking care this *almost* anarchic figure is molded into a force for integration. Hawthorne presents in Pearl a profound challenge to the boundaries of socialization,[3] but he also details her restraining role with a consistency that verges on the didactic. He sustains this technique through virtually all her dialogues, with their conspicuously emblematic messages. And he reinforces it with his every definition of Pearl: as "imp" of the "perverse" *and* "pearl of great price," as "demon offspring," "Red Rose," "elf-child," and "mother's child" (Hester's "blessing" and "retribution" all in one); as the image simultaneously of "untamed nature" and the "angel of judgment," and, at the climactic election-day ritual, as (successively) "sin-born child," "witch-baby," the quintessential outsider who engages with and so weaves together all sections of the diverse holiday crowd—"even as a bird of bright plumage illuminates a whole tree of dusky foliage"—and, finally, as the fully "human" daughter who breaks once and for all the "spell" of mutual isolation (208, 211, 210, 215, 202–3, 205, 329, 330, 336, 339). Throughout this *development*—in effect, our developing sense of Pearl as "the scarlet letter endowed with life"—Pearl serves increasingly to underscore what is wrong with Hester's radicalism, what remains "womanly" about Hester despite her manlike "freedom of speculation," and what sort of politics Hester must adopt if she is to help effect the changes that history calls for (200, 210, 259).

No other character in the novel, not even the shadowy Roger Chillingworth, is more carefully orchestrated into the narrative design or more single-mindedly rendered a means of orchestration. Midway through the story, at the midnight scaffold, Hawthorne pointedly presents us with a *figura* of things to come: "There stood the minister, with his hand over his heart; and Hester Prynne, with the embroidered letter glimmering on her bosom; and little Pearl, herself a symbol, and the connecting link between these two" (251). At the last scaffold scene Pearl kisses the minister, now openly her father at last, and Hawthorne remarks: "Towards her mother, too, Pearl's errand as a messenger of anguish was all fulfilled" (339). And with that office accomplished—by the one character, it will bear repeating, who might be imagined to offer an alternative vision in the novel—Hester can choose in due time to become the agent of her own domestication.

There is a certain irony here, to be sure, but it functions to support Hester's choice by reminding us of the burden of free will, when freedom is properly willed, for, although the burden is a tragic one, it alone carries the prospect of progressive (because incremental, nonconflictual) change. I discuss this use of irony in chapter 3. Let me say for the moment that it pertains above all to historical process and that it is perhaps especially prominent in Hawthorne's tales of the Puritans. The obvious contrast to Hester's return in this respect is the fate of Young Goodman Brown. Unlike Hester, Brown insists on alternatives when he rejoins the settlement—innocence or guilt, the truths of the town or those of the forest—and so finds himself in a hermeneutical impasse, a paralysis of thought and action whose issue is unambiguous "gloom." The no less obvious parallel (in view of Hester's propensities for the unillumined "sympathy of Nature") is the lovers' choice that ends "The May-Pole of Merry Mount." Strictly speaking, it is John Endicott, "the Puritan of Puritans," who forces the former "Lord and Lady of the May" into history. But in fact, Hawthorne emphasizes, they had started on that harsh, necessary road to progress long before, of their own free will: "From the moment they truly loved, they had subjected themselves to earth's doom of care, and sorrow, and troubled joy, and had no more a home at Merry Mount."[4]

Much the same might be said of Hester and Dimmesdale, although they must learn the lesson for themselves, separately, and offstage as it were—Dimmesdale, in the privacy of his study (following a "maze" of Goodman Brown-like temptations); Hester across the ocean, in the "merry old England" that the Puritans had rejected together with the Maypole (303, 211). Like Dimmesdale, she comes back home as a mixed figure of "pathos" and promise (333)—"angel of judgment" and mercy, "messenger of anguish" and hope. Hawthorne writes of the fully humanized Pearl, the former "wild child" who has at last "developed all her sympathies," that she would no longer need to "do battle with the world, but [could] be a woman in it" (339). It might be said of Hester upon her return that she can leave Pearl behind because she has taught herself to play Pearl to her own former Hester. She no longer needs restrictions because, after her long battle with the world, she has learned how to restrict herself—how to obviate the conflict between self and society, between the certainty of love and certain prospects of social change, between prophetic hope and politics as usual. As a woman in the world, she has learned to deflect, defuse, or at least defer that inherently explosive conflict and at best to transmute it, freely, into a faith that identifies continuity with progress.

This political level of meaning is closely connected to the moral. What I just called Hawthorne's politics of both/and is directly based upon his concept of truth. Critics often remark on the moral he draws from Dimmesdale's experience: "Be true! Be true! Be true!" (341). But, as usual with Hawthorne, it is hinged to the narrative by ambiguities. He tells us that he has culled the moral ("among many" others) from "a manuscript of old date," which he has "*chiefly* followed" (341; my italics). And he prefaces the moral with a dazzling variety of reports about the scarlet letter (or the absence of it) on the minister's breast. For Hawthorne, partiality is to process what multiplicity is to truth—a series of limited perspectives whose effectiveness depends on their being partial without becoming exclusive and partisan in such a way as gradually, by complementarity rather than conflict, to represent the whole. His political meaning here points us toward the premises of liberal society. His moral meaning is grounded in the premises of Puritan thought. The connection between the two is that between the Hobbist and the Calvinist meanings of the Fall. *The Scarlet Letter* is a story of concealment and revelation, where the point of revelation is not to know the truth but to embrace many truths and where concealment is not a crime, but a sin.

Not crime, but sin: Hawthorne adopts this fine theological distinction for his own liberal purposes. A crime pertains to externals, and, as a rule, it involves others, as in the case of murder or adultery. A sin pertains to the spiritual and internal, to an act of will. It may or may not involve crime, just as a crime (murder, for example, or adultery) *may* not involve sin. It depends on the inner cause, the motive. The issue, that is, is guilt, not shame: not the deceiving of others, but the skewing of one's own point of view. The political office of the A is to make partisanship an agent of reciprocity. Its moral office is to lead from the willful self-binding of a truth—paradigmatically, a truth of one's own—to the redemptive vision of many possible truths.

In the next-to-last chapter, that office is rendered (as the chapter title tells us) through "The Revelation of the Scarlet Letter" (332). The action centers on the scaffold, as it does twice previously. The first time is at Hester's midday "public exposure" (172), where the A denotes various kinds of division (within the community, within Dimmesdale, and, most dramatically, between Hester and the community). The second scaffold scene comes midway through the novel, in the midnight meeting that draws the main characters together, and by implication, the townspeople as well, for the A that flashes across the night sky lights up the entire town "with the distinctness of mid-day ... [lending] another moral interpretation to the things of this world than they had ever borne before ... as if [this] ... were the light that is to reveal all secrets, and the daybreak that shall unite all who belong to one another" (251).

In short, the novel tends increasingly toward reconciliation through a series of ambiguous unveilings, each of which might be titled "The Revelation of the Scarlet Letter." In that penultimate chapter Dimmesdale reconciles himself with his guilt, with Pearl, with Hester, with Chillingworth, and, in "words of flame," with the destiny of New Israel (332). Now it only remains for Hester to join the telos in process. When she does so, in the conclusion, her moral interpretation of things past and future may be seen to reverse her first misstep across the prison threshold. Indeed, the scene deliberately echoes that initiation into concealment so as emphatically to invert it. When Hester returns, she pauses "on the threshold" of her old home—as many years before she had paused "on the threshold of the prison door"—long enough to display to the onlookers a scarlet letter on her breast (162, 343). It is a nice instance of liminality serving its proper conservative function at last. Then, at the start of her trials, Hester had repelled the beadle, representative of "the Puritanic code of law" (162), in order to assert "her own free-will." Now she returns as representative of the need for law and the limits of free will. Having abandoned the hope of erasing the past, Hester internalizes the past in all its shame and sorrow. Franz Kafka's penal colony requires a fatal mechanism of authority in order to make the prisoner accept his guilt; Hester preempts the mechanism by authorizing her own punishment and inscribing her guilt upon herself. In a gesture that both declares her independence *and* honors her superiors, she re-forms herself, voluntarily, as the vehicle of social order.

This moral design parallels the political process I outlined, but with an important difference. Hester's radicalism sets her apart and sustains her marginality to the end. The sin she commits (her double act of concealment, first of her lover, then of her husband) links her to everyone else. She is unique as a rebel but typical as a liar. Indeed, telling lies is the donnée of the novel as for the Puritans the prison is the donnée of their venture in utopia. It establishes the terms of human possibility in an adulterated world. Directly or indirectly—as deception, concealment, or hypocrisy, through silence (in Hester's case), cunning (in Chillingworth's), eloquence (in Dimmesdale's), or perversity (in Pearl's)—lies constitute the very texture of community in *The Scarlet Letter*. But the texture itself is not simply evil. All of Hawthorne's main characters are good people trapped by circumstance, all are helping others in spite of themselves, and all are doing harm for what might justifiably be considered the best of reasons: Hester for love, Dimmesdale for duty, and the Puritan magistrates for moral order. Even Chillingworth, that least ambiguous of villains, is essentially a good man who has been wronged, who lies in order to find the truth, who prods his victim to confess (partly, perhaps, through love), and who, in leaving his wealth to Pearl (gratuitously), provides the basis for whatever there is of a happy ending to the story.

Hawthorne owes this *complex* view of evil—good and evil entwined, the visible "power of blackness" symbiotically augmented by the pervasive if sometimes oblique power of light—to Puritan theology. As the New England primer put it, Adam's fall did much more than fell us all. It also brought the promise of grace through Christ, the Second Adam. Justice *and* mercy, law *and* love: from these twin perspectives, the Puritans built the scaffold and imposed the A. Restrictions were necessary because the Fall had sundered the affections from the intellect; it had set the truths of the heart at odds with the truths of the mind. Now only faith could reconcile the two kinds of truth. They who bound themselves to a single view, *either* justice *or* mercy, were entering into a Devil's pact. They were committing themselves to a lie by concealing a part of reality from themselves, including the reality of the self in all its ambiguity, both human and divine—hence, the degeneration of Chillingworth, "demon of the intellect" (321), and Dimmesdale, until he manages to harmonize the minister's gospel of love with the lover's self-punishment. Hence, too, Pearl's fragmented identity: she is a shifting collage of retribution and love, seeking integration; and, hence, the reciprocal movement of Hester and the community, from opposition to mutuality. As she acts the Sister of Mercy toward those who merely judged her, and so judged too harshly, Hester increasingly touches the people's "great and warm heart" (226). At the end, after she has passed judgment on herself, Hester gains a fuller, more generous vision of reality than she dreamed possible in the forest. Then it was love with a consecration of its own. Now her love has the consecration of justice, morality, and community.

I rehearse this familiar pattern in order to point out that nothing in it is random or arbitrary. Not a single aspect of this apparent multiplicity (reversals, revisions, and diverse points of view) permits free choice. Hawthorne's celebrated evasiveness comes with a stern imperative. Penitence, he would urge us, has more substance than the absolutism of either/or. Drab though it seems, the morality of both/and heightens personal vision by grounding it in the facts of experience. It takes more courage to compromise. It is a greater act of self-assertion to recognize our limits—to "be true" to what we most deeply are while admitting the fragmentary quality of our truth—to keep faith in our boldest convictions while acknowledging the incompleteness of those convictions, and so to discipline ourselves, of our "own free-will," to the pluralist forms of progress.

It amounts to a code of liberal heroics. Hawthorne's focus is first and last upon the individual; his emphasis on perspective assumes faith in ambiguity; and his ambiguities compel resolution through the higher laws of both/and. Through those higher laws we learn how to sustain certain ideals *and* deny the immediate claims of their certainty upon us; how to possess the self by being self-possessed (which is to say, to hold the self intact by holding it in check); and, from both of these perspectives, how voluntarily to embrace gradualism and consensus in the expectation that, gradually, "when the world should have grown ripe for it," consensus will yield proximate justice for the community and, for the individual, the prospect of unadulterated love.

The prospect leads from the moral to the aesthetic level of the novel. Again, Hawthorne himself provides the link—in this case through the parallel he assumes between moral bivalence and symbolic ambiguity. Consider the title he gives to that chapter midway through the novel. "Another View of Hester" means an inside view of her secret radicalism; it also means a public view of Hester through her acts of charity, which in turn involves a distinction between the view of the many, who consider her "angelic," and the view of the few, "the wise and learned men" who were reluctant to give up earlier "prejudices" (257). "Another view" means a true sight of Hester, as she really is (rather than as she appears), *and* it means a glimpse of Hester in medias res, in the process of development. Above all, it means another view in the sense of differences of interpretation: interpretation in the form of rumor and legend (the A that magically protects Hester "amid all peril"); interpretation as a mode of sacralization (the A as a nun's cross); interpretation as agent of social change; and interpretation as vehicle of manipulation (Hester "never raised her head to receive their greeting. If they were resolute to accost her, she laid her finger on the scarlet letter, and passed on. This might be pride, but was so like humility that it produced all the softening effects of the latter quality on the public mind"); and, of course, interpretation as the avenue to multiple meanings—the A as sign of infamy, pillow for the sick, shield against Indian arrows, "glittering" and "fantastic" work of art (257–58, 255).

All this and more. No critical term is more firmly associated with *The Scarlet Letter* than ambiguity. What has not been adequately remarked, and questioned, is the persistent, almost pedantic pointedness of Hawthorne's technique. F. O. Matthiessen defined Hawthorne's ambiguity as "the device of multiple-choice"[5]—and so it is, if we recognize it as a device for enclosure and control. That strategy can be traced on every page of the novel, from start to finish, in Hawthorne's innumerable directives for interpretation: from the wild rose he presents to his readers in chapter 1—in a virtuoso performance of multiple choice that is meant to preclude choice (for it instructs us *not* to choose between the local flower, the figural passion flower, and the legacy of the ambiguously "sainted Anne Hutchinson")—to the heraldic device with which the novel ends: the "engraved escutcheon" whose endlessly interpretable design (one "ever-glowing point of light gloomier than the shadow" but a source of relief nonetheless) "*might* serve for a motto or brief description of our now concluded tale" (345; my emphasis). Concluded *then*, but, by authorial direction, it is *now* in process, a prod to our continuing speculations. The "curious investigator may still discern [it]," Hawthorne remarks, "and perplex himself with the purport" (345), and the interplay between our perplexity and its purport, like that between process and telos in the description of the rose ("It *may* serve, let us hope, to symbolize *some* sweet moral blossom, that *may* be found along the track, or relieve the darkening close tale of human frailty and suffering"), tells us that meaning, while indefinite, is neither random nor arbitrary; rather, it is gradual, cumulative, and increasingly comprehensive (159; my emphasis).

The Scarlet Letter is an interpreter's guide into perplexity. As critics have long pointed out, virtually every scene in the novel is symbolic, virtually every symbol demands interpretation, and virtually every interpretation takes the form of a question that opens out into a variety of possible answers, none of them entirely wrong, and none in itself satisfactory. But the result (to repeat) is neither random nor arbitrary. It is a strategy of pluralism—issuing, on the reader's part, in a mystifying sense of multiplicity—through which each set of questions and answers is turned toward the same solution: all meanings are partly true, hence, interpreters must choose as many parts as possible of the truth and/or as many truths as they can possibly find in the symbol.

Let me illustrate my point through the single most straightforward instance of choice in the novel. Describing Hester's "sad transformation" (midway through the story), Hawthorne remarks that her "rich and luxuriant hair had either been cut off, or was ... completely hidden by the cap" (259). For once, it seems, we have a plain truth to discover. Something has been hidden, a question about it has been raised, and we await the moment of disclosure; that moment reveals, of course, in "a flood of sunshine" (292), that Hester had *not* cut off her hair. But of course, too, Hawthorne means for us to recognize that in some sense she *had*—had cut off her "essential womanhood," had cut herself off from community, and had cut away her natural luxuriance of character by willfully hiding it beneath an Odysseus' cloak of conformity. These are metaphors, not facts. But in Hawthorne's ambiguous world a main function of choice is to blur the commonsense lines between metaphor and fact, and nowhere is that blurring process better demonstrated than at the moment of revelation, during her forest meeting with Dimmesdale, when Hester discards the A:

> By another impulse, she took off the formal cap that confined her hair; and down it fell upon her shoulders, dark and rich, with at once a shadow and a light in its abundance, and imparting the charm of softness to her features. There played around her mouth, and beamed out of her eyes, a radiant and tender smile, that *seemed* gushing from the very heart of womanhood.... Her

sex, her youth, and the whole richness of her beauty, came back
from *what men call* the irrevocable past. (292–93; my emphasis)

Shadow and light, seemed and was, irrevocable and renewed,
womanhood cut off/hidden/lost/restored: *The Scarlet Letter* is a novel of
endless points of view that together conspire to deprive us of choice. We are
enticed by questions so that we can be allowed to see the polarity between
seeking *the* answer, any answer, and undertaking an interpretation. The
option is never one thing or another; it is all or nothing. We are offered
an alternative, not between different meanings, but between meaning
or meaninglessness, and it is meaning in that processual, pluralistic, and
therefore (we are asked to believe) progressivist sense that Hester opts for
when she returns to New England.

In that option lies the moral-aesthetic significance of Hawthorne's
representation of crime as sin. Crime involves social transgression, as in
the tradition of the detective story, which centers on the discovery of the
criminal. Or, more equivocally, it might involve a conflict of rights that must
be decided one way or another, as in the tradition of the novel of adultery,
which opposes the claims of the heart to those of civic order. Hawthorne
makes use of both kinds of plot, only to absorb them—climactically, through
Hester's return—into a story about the trials and triumphs of ambiguity.
Through the office of the scarlet letter, all particulars of the criminal act,
together with the conflicts they entail, dissolve into a widening series of
reciprocities. We come to see that the issue is not a breach of commandment,
but (as Hawthorne signals by the conspicuous absence from the novel of
the word "adultery") an incremental process of interpretation by which we
discern the purport of the broken law for ourselves, and we do so by turning
speculation against the tendency either to take sides or to view conflicting
sides as irreconcilable.

To represent crime as sin is first of all to universalize the legal problem.
It forces us to read a particular transgression in terms of innate human defects
and the recurrent conflict of good and evil. But more comprehensively it
makes the universal itself a curious object of interpretation—not in order
to demystify it, not even to analyze it (in any cognitive sense), but, on
the contrary, to invest it with richer significance and a more compelling
universality. The ambiguities of *The Scarlet Letter* lead us systematically
forward, from the political to the moral or religious to the aesthetic levels,
toward what we are meant to understand is a series of broader and ampler
meanings. Always ampler, and therefore at any given point indefinite: a
spiral of ambiguities whose tendency to expand in scope and depth is all the
more decisive for the fact that the process occurs in unexpected ways. The

result is a liberal hierarchy of meaning, a series of unfoldings from simple to complex, "superficial" to "profound," which is as schematic, comprehensive, and coercive as the medieval fourfold system. Hawthorne's representation of crime as sin requires us to remain vague about all issues of good versus evil (except the evils of partiality and partisanship) in order to teach us that the Puritans' final, relatively nonconflictual view of Hester is deeper than the single-minded judgment reflected in the governor's iron breastplate, just as her final, relatively nonconflictual position toward their bigotry opens the way for both personal and historical development.

I have been using the term "option" in connection with Hester's return in order to stress the overriding distinction in Hawthorne's "device of multiple-choice" between making choices and having choice. His point is not that Hester finally makes a choice against adultery. It is that she has no choice but to resume the A. To make choices involves alternatives; it requires us to reject or exclude on the ground that certain meanings are wrong or incompatible or mutually contradictory. To have choice (in Hawthorne's fiction) is to keep open the prospects for interpretation on the grounds that reality never means either one thing or another but, rather, is Meaning fragmented by plural points of view, for, although the fragmentation is a source of many a "tale of frailty and sorrow," such as *The Scarlet Letter*, it is also, as *The Scarlet Letter* demonstrates, the source of an enriched sense of unity, provided we attend to the principles of liberal exegesis. And by these principles, to opt for meaning in all its multifariousness—to have your adulterous love and do the work of society too—is to obviate not only the conflicts embodied in opposing views but also the contradictions implicit in the very act of personal interpretation between the fact of multiple meaning and the imperative of self-assertion.

In other words, to interpret is willfully, in the interests of some larger truth, *not to choose*. Ambiguity is a function of prescriptiveness. To entertain plural possibilities is to eliminate possible divisions. We are forced to find meaning in the letter, but we cannot choose one meaning out of many: Chillingworth's fate cautions us against that self-destructive act of exclusion. Nor can we choose to interpret any of the novel's uncertainties as contradictions: the antagonism between Hester and the townspeople (or between Chillingworth and Dimmesdale, or between the minister and his conscience) cautions us repeatedly against that abuse of free will. What remains, then, is the alternative that symbols are lies, multiple choice is a mask for absence of meaning, and the letter is an arbitrary sign of transient social structures. And Hester's incipient nihilism cautions us at every turn against that flight from responsibility: in the first scene, by her instinctive attempt to conceal the letter; then, three years later, by concealing its meaning from Pearl (to Hawthorne's suggestion that "some new evil had crept into [her heart], or some old one had never been expelled"); later, in the forest scene, by flinging the letter "into infinite space" and drawing an (infinitely illusory) "hour's free breath"; and, finally, at the election day ritual, by gloating secretly at the prospect of its annihilation, a prospect that Hawthorne opens to her imagination so that, by absorbing it into what the entire novel makes us think *must* be some larger, truer interpretation, we can effectually exclude it as an alternative from our own (162, 274, 300).

If we refuse to exclude it—if we are tempted like Hester in the forest to reject meaning, if we make Chillingworth's choice at the scaffold against mercy or Dimmesdale's in his "secret closet" for contradiction (242)—then interpretation has not done its office. And lest, like these characters, we find ourselves wandering in a maze, Hawthorne points us toward the true path, midway in our journey through the novel. In "Another View of Hester" he impresses upon us: the need for personal interpretation; the inevitably partial nature of such interpretation; the richly varied experiential bases of interpretation; the tendency of these partial and shifting interpretations to polarize into symbolic oppositions, such as rumor and event, metaphor and fact, natural and supernatural, good and evil, head and heart, concealment and revelation, fusion and fragmentation; the need to recognize that these polarities, because symbolic, are never an inherent source of conflict, but instead they are always entwined in symbiotic antagonism and therefore mutually sustaining; and, as the key to it all, the *clavis symbolistica*, the need for faith both in the value of experience (shifting, private, and partial though it is) and in some ultimate hermeneutical complementarity, as in an ideal prospect that impels us toward an ever-larger truth.

That faith involves a *certain* activity on the reader's part. We need to make sense of the entire process for ourselves so that the process can in turn make sense of our partial contributions. The text elicits personal response in order to allow each of us to contribute to the expanding continuum of liberal reciprocity. It is a hermeneutics designed to make subjectivity the primary agency of change while keeping the subject under control, and it accomplishes this double function by representing interpretation as multiplicity flowing naturally into consensus. For, as oppositions interchange and fuse in the text, they yield a synthesis that is itself a symbol in process, an office not yet done. It is a richer symbol now than it was before, a higher office, but still veiled in the winding *perhapses*, *ors*, and *mights* that simultaneously open new vistas of meaning and dictate the terms of closure.

It may be helpful to distinguish this strategy from others to which it has been compared. Hawthorne does not deconstruct the A; he does not anticipate the principle of indeterminacy; and he offers neither an aesthetics of relativism nor a dialectics of conflict. We might say that in some sense he is doing all of these things, but only in the sense that to do so is to dissipate the integral force of each. His purpose is to rechannel indeterminacy into pluralism, conflict into correspondence, and relativism into consensus. Insofar as terms such as "instability" and "self-reflexiveness" apply to *The Scarlet Letter*, they are agencies of a certain kind of interpretation, much as private enterprise and self-interest were said to be agencies of the general good in antebellum America. Frank Kermode's claim for Hawthorne's modernity—"his texts ... are meant as invitations to co-production on the part of the reader"—is accurate in a sense quite different from that which he intended. Kermode speaks of "a virtually infinite set of questions." *The Scarlet Letter* holds out that mystifying prospect, much as Jacksonian liberals held out the prospect of infinite possibility, in order to implicate us as coproducers of meaning in a single, coherent moral-political-aesthetic design.[6]

    This contrast pertains even more pointedly to Mikhail Bakhtin's concept of the dialogic imagination, which it has recently become fashionable to apply to American novels, and *The Scarlet Letter* in particular. Dialogics is the process by which a singular authorial vision unfolds as a "polyphony" of distinct voices. It entails a sustained open-ended tension between fundamentally conflicting outlooks. They are said to be conflicting insofar as they are not partial reflections (such as good or evil) of a more complex truth but each of them, rather, the expression of a separate and distinct way of understanding, a substantially different conception or configuration of good and evil. And they are said to be open-ended because the tension this involves is sustained not through the incremental layers of meaning but through the dynamics of diversity itself, which is, by definition, subversive of any culturally prescribed set of designs, including those of group pluralism. Bakhtin's dialogics denies telos through a "modernist" recognition of difference. Hawthornes ambiguities imply telos through the evasion of conflict. They are modernist in the sense of modern middle-class culture— which is to say, in their use of difference (including marginality, complexity, and displacement) for purposes of social cohesion. Recent theorists such as Paul Ricoeur and Hans Blumenberg tell us that the novel (the genre par excellence of the dialogic) "legitimates the aesthetic qualities of novitas, ... removes the dubiousness from what is new, and so terra incognita, or the *munda novus*, becomes possible."[7] Hawthorne seeks precisely to rein in what becomes possible. Aesthetically, it is the letter's office, as *novitas*, to enclose "the new world," whether as alternative order or as Bakhtinian carnival, within culture, *as* culture.

We might term this strategy the "monologics of liberal ambiguity." It serves to mystify hierarchy as multiplicity and diversity as harmony in process. Dialogics unsettles the link between process and closure. Hawthorne details the manifold discrepancies between process and closure in order to make discrepancy itself—incompleteness, concealment, the distance between penance and penitence—a vehicle of acculturation. To that end he guides his readers (as he does his errant heroine) to a *certain* belief in the unity of the symbol. He shows us that, precisely by insisting on difference, we can fuse an apparently (but not really) fragmented reality. Augustine's answer to Manichaean dualism was to redefine evil as the absence of good. Hawthorne's answer to the threat of multiplicity is to redefine conflict as the absence of ambiguity, and ambiguity, therefore, as the absence of conflict.

Ambiguity is the absence of conflict: Hawthorne's logic is as simple in theory as it is complicated in application. Historical facts tend toward fragmentation, but ambiguity brings this tendency under control, gives it purpose and direction, by ordering the facts into general polarities. Fragmentation itself thus becomes a function of consensus. For once the fragments have been ordered into polarities, the polarities can be multiplied ad infinitum, since each polarity entails or engenders other parallel, contrasting, or subsidiary sets of polarities. The process is one of endless variation upon a theme. And vice versa: it is a process of variation endlessly restricted to a single theme, because (in Hawthorne's fiction) all polarity is by definition ambiguous, all ambiguity is symbolic, and all symbols tend toward reconciliation—hence, the distinctly narrowing effect of Hawthorne's technique, in spite of his persistent allusions and deliberate elusiveness. He himself wrote of *The Scarlet Letter* to his publisher, James T. Fields, on November 3, 1850, that since the novel was "all in one tone" it could have gone on "interminably."[8] We might reverse this to say that what makes the novel hermeneutically interminable also makes it formally and thematically hermetic. In that sustained counterpoint between endlessness and monotone lies the dynamic behind Hawthorne's model of pluralist containment. Process for him is a means of converting the *threat* of multiplicity (fragmentation, irreconcilability, discontinuity) into the pleasures of multiple choice, where the implied answer, "all of the above," guarantees consensus.

The process of conversion follows the symbolic logic of the scarlet letter. It is the office of the A to demonstrate that naturally, organically, pluralism tends to absorb differences into polar opposites, and that bipolarity, properly interpreted, tends of its own accord toward integration. So conceived, the monologics of ambiguity in *The Scarlet Letter* extend to structures of gender, religion, history, psychology, aesthetics, morality, and epistemology. One instance, a minor one but suggestive of Hawthorne's range, is the

imaginary "Papist" at the first scaffold scene (166), who sees Hester as the
Virgin Mother and who seems to offer an option—an oppositional view,
in Raymond Williams's sense, or, more accurately (in light of Hawthorne's
emphasis on the relative newness in 1642 of the Reformation), a residual
view—that goes deeper than personal and partial differences of perspective.[9]
But here, as elsewhere, Hawthorne's point is to intrigue us with notions
of conflict in order to disperse them. He can be said to have invented the
Papist (that Puritan symbol of irreconcilable antagonism) on our behalf as
an early step in our education in ambiguity, and the education proceeds
through our recognition, in due time, that the putative contrast is really just
one pole in the reciprocity between justice and love. Thus, Catholic and
Protestant outlooks merge, midway through the novel, in the townspeople
who interpret the A sympathetically as "a cross on a nun's bosom" and, more
powerfully, at the final scaffold scene, in the apparent pietà, where Hester (in
an image that prepares us for her final role as prophet) plays Sacred Mother
to Dimmesdale's Christ (258, 339).

It makes for a rich fusion of polarities, with multiple implications for
Hawthorne's symbolic method. For example, the papist perspective (if I may
call it so) clearly parallels the compassionate view of Hester expressed by
the young mother at the prison door, and clearly, Hawthorne presents *her*
view mainly for purposes of contrast, as he does the Papist's, to highlight
the harshness of Puritan judgment, whether from magistrates or from
"matrons" (161). In each case the contrast turns out to be a form of symbolic
doubling. The "young wife, holding a child by the hand," in some sense
mirrors Hester; the embittered matrons in some sense preview Hester's
later "injustice"—her impenitent, sometimes brutal judgments (variously
motivated by "scorn," "hatred," and "asperity") of her perceived "enemies,"
her husband, and even her daughter (161, 269, 274). The result is a spiral of
symbolic reciprocities, reinforced by principles of psychology (head–heart)
and morality (good–evil), which grow increasingly comprehensive in their
image of womanhood—increasingly comprehensive and, proportionately,
increasingly positive. They find their high point in Hester the prophet: the
rehumanized (because refeminized) heroine whose fall, though it warrants
"strict and severe" censure (274), augments the promise she represents of
future good things. The revelation is still to come, but Hester at last has
reached the proper womanly vantage point for perceiving something of
its import; she has earned the privilege of paying homage, if not directly
to Hawthorne's "little Dove, Sophia," as several critics have argued, then
to the dream of "sacred love," which Sophia shared with Nathaniel and
which largely derived from the mid-nineteenth-century cult of domesticity
(344).[10]

A similar strategy of incorporation applies to the parallel between the Papists and the other non-Puritan culture represented at the first scaffold scene. I refer to the local Indians, who judge from Hester's "brilliantly embroidered badge" that she "must needs be a personage of high dignity among her people" (330). Hawthorne invests the story's Indians with much the same processual-symbolic effect as lie does the Catholic. He juxtaposes the outsider's perspective, in both cases, to that of the Puritans in order to absorb historical difference into what we are meant to think of as broader, universal categories. To that end he deploys the keywords of savagism: "stone-headed" implements, "snake-like" features, "savage finery," "painted barbarians," and, most frequently, "wild"—"wild Indian," "wild men ... of the land," the "wildness" of their "native garb" (318, 329, 315, 330, 169).

It makes for an all-too-familiar Romantic Jacksonian configuration: the primitive as an early stage of social growth, which the civilized state not only supersedes but (in the process) ingests, so that at its best society combines the "natural" state with the "higher" advantages of culture. Hence, the Indian aspect of Pearl, the "wild child" (329), and, above all, the Indian wildness of Hester's radicalization:

> Her intellect and heart had their home, as it were, in desert places, where she roamed as freely as the wild Indian in his woods ... criticizing all with hardly more reverence than the Indian would feel for the clerical band, the judicial robe, the pillory, the gallows, the fireside, or the church. (290)

An entire culture is represented in these cunningly compressed polarities. Hawthorne appreciates the natural freedom of the "red men" (287), just as he deplores the civilized excesses of the Puritan pillory—and vice versa; he recognizes the dangers of "desert places" just as he acknowledges the need for fireside and church. It is an ambiguity that effectually deprives the Indians of both nature and civilization, a high literary variation on an imperial rhetoric that ranges from Francis Parkman's elegies for a "noble," "primitive," "dying" race to what Herman Melville satirized as "the metaphysics of Indian-hating."[11] Here it serves to empty the "savages" of their own history so as to universalize them as metaphors for Hester's development.

As all of these examples suggest, the basic symbolic opposition in *The Scarlet Letter* is that between self and society. I said earlier that Hawthorne portrays Hester as an individualist of increasingly radical commitment. I might as well have said a radical of increasingly individualist commitment, for Hawthorne's aim is to counter the dangerously diverse social possibilities to which she has access, in fantasy or fact—Indian society, witch covens,

Elizabethan hierarchy, Leveler and Ranter utopia (289, 313–30)—to bring all such unruly alternatives under control, rhetorically and hence morally and politically, by implicating them all under the symbol of the unrestrained self.

No symbol was better calculated to rechannel dissent into the gradualism of process. And no symbol was more deeply rooted in the culture. As *The Scarlet Letter* reminds us, it served as a major Puritan strategy of socialization, through a process of inversion that typifies all such strategies. Society in this polar opposition became the symbol of unity, and the unsocialized self was designated the symbol of chaos unleashed—"sin, in all its branches," as the Reverend John Wilson details them in the first scaffold scene for "the poor culprit's" sake (176). Or, mutatis mutandis, the unsocialized self was a morass of "monstrous misconceptions," as John Winthrop labeled Anne Hutchinson, and society stood not just for legal order (as against antinomianism), but for Order at large—"the laws of nature and the laws of grace" (to quote Winthrop again) through which "we are bound together as one man."[12]

In either case, the polarity of self and society remained central through the successive discourses of libertarianism, federalism, republicanism, and Jacksonian individualism. Its negative pressures, implicit in Hawthorne's reference to "the sainted Anne Hutchinson" (and explicit in his essay on "Mrs. Hutchinson")—as well as in recurrent charges of antinomianism against those who were said to have "sprung up under her footsteps" (159), from Edwards through Emerson—are memorably conveyed in Alexis de Tocqueville's contrast between "traditional" and "modern" modes of control: "The ruler no longer says: 'You must think as I do or die.' He says: 'You are free to think differently, and to retain your life, your property, and all that you possess; but from this day on you are a stranger among us.'" Its positive form can be inferred from Edwin Chapin's Massachusetts election day sermon of 1844, *The Relation of the Individual to the Republic*. The self, Chapin argues, denotes "matters of *principle*" and society entails "matters of *compromise*," but in the American way of "self-government" (as nowhere else) it is "compromise not *of* principle but *for* principle."[13]

The Scarlet Letter is the story of a stranger who rejoins the community by compromising for principle, and her resolution has far-reaching implications about the symbolic structures of the American ideology. First, the only plausible modes of American dissent are those that center on the self: as stranger or prophet, rebel or revolutionary, lawbreaker or Truth seeker, or any other adversarial or oppositional form of individualism. Second, whatever good we imagine must emerge—and, properly understood, has emerged and is continuing to emerge—from things as they are, insofar as these are conducive to independence, progress, and other norms of group pluralism. And third, radicalism has a place in society, after all, as the example of Hester demonstrates—radicalism, that is, in the American grain, defined through the ambiguities of both/and, consecrated by the tropes of theology ("heaven's time," "justice and mercy," "divine providence"), and interpreted through the polar unities at the heart of American liberalism: fusion and fragmentation, diversity as consensus, process through closure.

NOTES

1. Joseph Allen Boone, *Tradition Counter Tradition: Love and the Form of Fiction* (Chicago: University of Chicago Press, 1987), 48; Tony Tanner, *Adultery in the Novel: Contract and Transgression* (Baltimore: Johns Hopkins University Press, 1979), 13.

2. Amy S. Lang, *Prophetic Woman: Anne Hutchinson and the Problem of Dissent in the Literature of New England* (Berkeley: University of California Press, 1987), 58, 67.

3. I take up this issue in the last chapter, but it may be noted here, as intrinsic to Hawthorne's mode of ambiguity, that Pearl, who forces Hester to restore the A, is among other things an incarnation of Emersonian whim (not to say Poesque perversity)—a figure of "infinite variety," "mutability," and "caprice," with "wild, desperate, defiant" proclivities; the very spirit of negation, toward her inwardly rebellious mother no less than toward the apparent consensus of Puritan Boston (269–74)—and that all these traits, including the most "freakish" ("fiend-like," "demon offspring"), give symbolic substance to the "imperious gesture" with which Pearl asserts her "authority" in the forest scene (298–99):

> Pearl still pointed with her forefinger; and a frown gathered on her brow; the more impressive from the childish ... aspect of the features that conveyed it....
>
> "Hasten Pearl; or I shall be angry with thee!" cried Hester Prynne....
>
> But Pearl, not a whit startled at her mother's threats, any more than mollified by her entreaties, now suddenly burst into a fit of passion, gesticulating violently, and throwing her small figure into the most extravagant contortions.... Seen in the brook, once more, was the shadowy wrath of Pearl's image, crowned and girdled with flowers, but stamping its foot, wildly gesticulating, and, in the midst of it all, still pointing its small forefinger at Hester's bosom! ....
>
> "Come thou and take it up!" (298–300)

Pearl's reflection in the brook is a memorable representation of the reciprocities of process and telos. It stands for nature (and the natural) as an office of repression. Equally and *simultaneously*, it stands for the demands of social conformity, indifferent to threat and entreaty, and conveyed through an impassioned willfulness. It is the letter of the law conceived in the spirit of resistant individuality, and vice versa.

4. Hawthorne, "The May-Pole of Merry Mount," in *Tales and Sketches*, ed. Roy Harvey Pearce (New York: Library of America, 1982), 370, 367, 363.

5. F. O. Matthiessen, *American Renaissance: Art and Expression in the Age of Emerson and Whitman* (New York: Oxford University Press, 1941), 276.

6. Frank Kermode, *The Classic: Literary Images of Permanence and Change* (New York: Knopf, 1975), 43.

7. Mikhail Bakhtin, *Problems in Dostoevsky's Poetics*, ed. and trans. Caryl Emerson (Minneapolis: University of Minnesota Press, 1984), passim; Hans Blumenberg, "The Concept of Reality and the Possibility of the Novel," in *New Perspectives in German Literary Criticism*, ed. Richard Amacher and Victor Lange (Princeton: Princeton University Press, 1979), 32.

8. Hawthorne, *Letters, 1843–1853* ed. Thomas Woodson, L. Neal Smith, and Norman Holmes Pearson, in Works, Centenary Edition (Columbus: Ohio State University Press, 1985), 16: 371.

9. Raymond Williams, *Marxism and Literature* (Oxford: Oxford University Press, 1977), 121–27.

10. T. Walter Herbert, Jr., "Nathaniel Hawthorne, Una Hawthorne, and *The Scarlet Letter*: Interactive Selfhoods and the Cultural Construction of Gender," *PMLA* 103 (1988): 285–97.

11. Francis Parkman, *The Jesuits in North America in the Seventeenth Century* (1867), in *France and England in North America*, ed. David Levin (New York: Library of America, 1983), 1: 343, 461, 466; Herman Melville, *The Confidence-Man: His Masquerade*, 994.

12. John Winthrop, *The History of New England*, ed. James Savage (Boston: Phelps and Farnham, 1825), 1:166; and "A Model of Christian Charity" (1630), in *Winthrop Papers*, ed. Stewart Mitchell (Boston: Massachusetts Historical Society, 1931), 2:124.

13. Alexis de Tocqueville, *Democracy in America*, ed. J. T. Mayer, trans. George Lawrence (Garden City, N.Y.: Doubleday, 1969), 72; Edwin Chapin, *The Relation of the Individual to the Republic* (Boston: Dutton and Wentworth, 1844), 27, 31.

CHARLES SWANN

The Scarlet Letter *and the Language of History: Past Imperfect, Present Imperfect, Future Perfect?*

I

But the object that most drew my attention, in the mysterious
package, was a certain affair of fine red cloth, much worn and
faded ... It had been intended, there could be no doubt, as an
ornamental article of dress; but how it was to be worn, or what
rank, honor, and dignity, in by-past times, were signified by it,
was a riddle which (so evanescent are the fashions of the world in
these particulars) I saw little hope of solving. And yet it strangely
interested me. My eyes fastened themselves upon the old scarlet
letter, and would not be turned aside. Certainly, there was some
deep meaning in it, most worthy of interpretation, and which, as
it were, streamed forth from the mystic symbol, subtly communicating itself to my sensibilities, but evading the analysis of my
mind. (145–6)

The first appearance of the scarlet letter is particularly striking in that
everything about the artefact is remarkably obscure—except for its ambiguous
historicity: "time, and wear, and a sacrilegious moth, had reduced it to little
other than a rag." Initially it is not even recognizable—merely "a certain affair
of fine red cloth," an object stripped of its glamour, its "glitter." Its history is

From *Nathaniel Hawthorne: Tradition and Revolution*, pp. 75–95. © 1991 by Cambridge
University Press.

Its history is doubly one of loss for not only is it "defaced" but, even in its decayed state, it "gives evidence of a now forgotten art." Its very form has to be recovered: only careful examination allows it to assume "the shape of a letter" (145). However, although its shape may have been established, form does not confer meaning, but only the strong possibility that the letter has significance: "there was *some* deep meaning in it, most worthy of interpretation." For that interpretation to be possible, story is needed—Mr. Surveyor Pue's narrative which reveals the meaning (which is to say the social function) of the letter. Hawthorne makes it clear that his central symbol belongs to, is the product of history and therefore can only be understood in terms provided by narrative, by a (fictional) historiography. And, as "The Custom-House" further indicates, history is not only a crucial subject of the fiction as a whole, but the very existence of *The Scarlet Letter* is the product of history—as Hawthorne's personal history intersects with a wider public history.

If the Democrats had won the Presidential election of 1848 and if we are to believe Hawthorne, *The Scarlet Letter* would most likely not have been written. It is then as Hawthorne tells us, the product of contemporary political history, of "the period of hardly accomplished revolution, and still seething turmoil, in which the story shaped itself" (156). The period between Hawthorne losing his job in the Salem custom-house in June, 1849 and his departure for England in July, 1853 (when he had acquired, largely thanks to his campaign biography of Pierce, the best paid job of his life as consul in Liverpool) is the most remarkable in his life for sustained and successful literary production—productions all strikingly marked by a concern with history, politics, and the problematic nature of the contemporary. Most important, of course, are the three full-length fictions. *The Scarlet Letter* (1850) starts from an autobiographical meditation on the present before turning back to the seventeenth century, to end with Hester's prophecy of an utopian future of sexual equality—a prophecy which has conspicuously not been fulfilled in the America of 1850 (nor in that of 1990). *The House of the Seven Gables* (1851) begins from an act of expropriation in the 1690s and goes right up to the autumn of 1848, ending with an apparent (but only apparent) reconciliation of class tensions in New England history. *The Blithedale Romance* (1852), though set some ten years in the past, takes as its subject an attempt radically to transform the present state of things in the name of a desired Utopian future, an attempt which belongs crucially to American history in that it is overtly analogous both to the Puritan project of the Pilgrim Fathers and to 1776.

Though these were the major works of those remarkably productive years, the other literary enterprises also bear on the history/politics/

modernity nexus. Thus, the campaign biography—Hawthorne's most rewarding work in the financial sense and probably the most widely read in his life-time—is, however modestly, an attempt to make history through writing. Even the two volumes of Greek myths retold for children—*A Wonder-Book for Girls and Boys* (1851) and *Tanglewood Tales* (1853)—are offered as ways of making modern ("Gothic or romantic") those pre-historic stories: "an attempt to render the fables of classical antiquity into the idiom of modern fancy and feeling" (T&S, 1,163, 1,235). Here with *A Wonder-Book* we have at last a version of that dream of the 1830s, *The Story Teller*—a framed set of stories, as the story-teller (the college student, Eustace Bright) with his audience of children provide a context in which the myths are told and set—and Hawthorne insists that the reader should be conscious of the fictitiousness of that context with a sophistication surely aimed at adults rather than children:

> "Hush, Primrose, hush!" exclaimed Eustace ...
> "Our neighbor [Hawthorne] in the red house is a harmless sort of person enough, for aught I know, as concerns the rest of the world; but something whispers me that he has a terrible power over ourselves, extending to nothing short of annihilation."
> (T&S, 1,301)

Hawthorne ends *A Wonder-Book* with a jokey reminder that what we are reading is a fiction, that whatever the origin of these myths, their interpreter has the power not only to create or transmit, but to destroy.

It is no longer necessary to argue that "The Custom-House" is to be considered as an intrinsic part of *The Scarlet Letter*—that, in other words, it is a variant on the strategy of *The Story Teller*. It is in "The Custom-House" that Hawthorne offers a semi-fictive genetic account of the origin of his fiction of the scarlet letter, beginning from a reminder of the previous production of his pen ("The Old Manse") before foregrounding the question of the writer/reader relationship. Hawthorne repudiates the romantic ambition "to find out the divided segment of the writer's own nature and complete his circle of existence" but insists that "thoughts are frozen and utterance benumbed, unless the speaker stand in some true relation with his audience" (121). Readers quickly understand the running pun on "custom"—once they realize they have entered the Interpreter's House through which they must pass before encountering the main structure of the story of the letter. The story proper is carefully situated in its social, historical and psychological contexts—for the work of art is not allowed to appear to float free, but is rooted in the concrete historical situation of its genesis and production. It is in "The Custom-House" that Hawthorne launches an investigation of the relationships of fiction to the real world and indicates a subtle and complex interrelationship between the two worlds. By describing his surroundings in the custom-house he goes a long way towards justifying his historical fiction by suggesting the inadequacies of that way of life. To be a custom-house officer is to be excluded from the ethical world of men in a way which ironically parallels Hester's situation: "the very nature of his business ... is of such a sort that he does not share in the united effort of mankind" (151). Punning on "custom," Hawthorne argues that the experience which is dependent on habit destroys the historical imagination on which a true recognition of reality must be based. The elderly members of the Custom-House are condemned for their inability to have made anything useful or valuable from their pasts. And—given that the stars and stripes flies over the Custom-House, given the explicit references to the patriarchs of the Custom-House—Hawthorne surely intends to suggest a wider placing: is this what the seventeenth century patriarchy even with its admitted faults and inadequacies has come to, with its "fortitude ... self-reliance" and "natural authority" (323)?

Seeing Salem as a dust-heap of history, Hawthorne creates the impression that his tale has an authentic base, and obliquely suggests its nature and the nature of his fictional developments, as he famously describes the conditions where his imagination works best: "the floor of our familiar room has become a neutral territory, somewhere between the real world and fairy-land, where the Actual and the Imaginary may meet, and each imbue itself with the nature of the other" (149). But the historical imagination is necessary to perceive the reality of anything but the world of pure objects, as Hawthorne makes clear when discussing the old General. He can be described as he appears, but this is to miss the true, the important realities. The General has a public, an historic identity, but, if that is to be recovered, Hawthorne has to become, so to speak, an archaeologist:

> To observe and define his character, however ... was as difficult a task as to trace out and build up anew, in imagination, an old fortress, like Ticonderoga, from a view of its gray and broken ruins. Here and there, perchance, the walls may remain almost complete; but elsewhere may be only a shapeless mound, cumbrous with its very strength, and overgrown, through long years of peace and neglect, with grass and alien weeds. (136)

The General's identity can be recreated, as Hawthorne shows when he looks at him "affectionately." And he suggests that the true reality for the General himself lies within his own consciousness as he recreates and inhabits his past. As the scarlet letter initiates Hawthorne's desire to retell Hester's story and come to terms with old New England, so it is one item from the General's past that makes it possible for Hawthorne to understand him:

> There was one thing that much aided me in *renewing and recreating* the stalwart soldier of the Niagara frontier,—the man of true and simple energy. It was the recollection of those memorable words of his,—"I'll try, sir!"—... breathing the soul and spirit of New England hardihood, comprehending all perils, and encountering all. (138–9, my emphasis)

It is the (historical) imagination that makes it possible for Hawthorne to comprehend what the General was—which is at least as important as what he is.

One purpose of "The Custom-House" is, then, to demonstrate that the past can be reconstructed through the sympathetic and informed imagination—an imagination whose other name should be the historical sense. Hawthorne stresses that he has a double past, and with that emphasis he prepares us for his concern with the different but ideally united realms of the public and private sides of human identity which is so crucial in the main story. One of Hawthorne's pasts is his immediate personal past when he defined himself as a writer (but, of course, that is not totally private in that he is also publicly known as a writer—that, after all, is largely why he got the Custom-House job). He emphasizes that the "discovery" of the letter re-awoke his literary feelings and made him realize that neither his own past as writer nor the public, historical past was dead. That fictive fragment from history is presented as having a wider function than re-awakening his old artistic impulses for it also brings into focus a concern with a wider history, with Hawthorne's evocation of the past of Salem and his seriocomic account of his relationship with his ancestors. And, as I began by implying, it is with the way that Hawthorne introduces the letter and the question of its original meaning that it can be seen that, while Hawthorne is profoundly concerned with the functions and powers of symbols, his fiction is really a criticism of symbolic modes of perception and definition—a criticism made in the name of historical, of narrative modes of knowing the world. The fact that the discovery of the only too clearly symbolic A is so obviously at the centre of "The Custom-House" might seem to contradict this. But, as I have tried to suggest, while the reader is told that the letter is an artefact containing considerable power, as long as its meaning remains unknown, which is to say as long as its historical context is unknown, as long as it lacks a placing narrative, it can only communicate itself to Hawthorne's "sensibilities" while "evading the analysis of" his "mind." However "worthy of interpretation" the sign in isolation may be, it cannot be decoded until the accompanying text is read, when it can take its meaning from its place in a story. Until then, what it "signified" is an insoluble "riddle" because of the way in which meanings can be lost from history, "so evanescent are the fashions of the world" (145–6).

Not that Pue's narrative is unproblematic: the discovery of the letter and the text is, of course, a fictional origin for Hawthorne's fiction—an origin that, however, does not significantly contradict the known facts and thus claims the authority of history—or demands, at the least, a willing suspension of disbelief on the part of his audience: "the reader may smile, but must not doubt my word" (146). Yet, however much Hawthorne may claim Pue's story as an authentic authorization for his tale, he almost immediately undercuts that authority in a way that has understandably bothered many readers: "I have allowed ... myself nearly or altogether as much license as if the fact had been entirely of my own invention." Something of a solution to this difficulty lies in the fact that the wearing of an A was a New England punishment for adultery—and in Hawthorne's next paragraph, where he seems to have done his homework in taking an appropriate metaphor from needlework: "There seemed to be here the groundwork of a tale" (147). "Ground-work" is nicely chosen given an OED definition: "The body or foundation on which parts are overlaid, as in embroidery work, painting and the like." The dictionary gives a seventeenth-century (1655) illustration: "In needlework, the sad groundwork is laid before the beautiful colours." The production of the text of *The Scarlet Letter* is, then, presented as analogous to Hester's elaboration of the letter. Hawthorne transforms the sad groundwork of a simple fact about a way that seventeenth-century New England punished adultery into a complex narrative meditation on signs and meanings in history: Hester transfigures a simple sign of society's condemnation of her transgression of its rules into a work of art. And that subversion of the sign of society's intention to define (to limit) the transgressor, to reduce Hester's very self to a sign reading "Thou shalt not ..." problematizes the symbolic definition to which that society is committed and by which the society had intended to limit the transgressor. Society's intention—or, rather, the intention of those in power who claim to represent the society—had been to contain Hester in, so to speak, an eternal present so that her life would largely be constituted by a sense of history as repetition and she would be stripped of the social relationships that make so much of our identity:

To-morrow would bring its own trial with it; so would the next day, and so would the next; each its own trial, and *yet the very same* that was now so unutterably grievous to be borne ... Throughout them all, *giving up her individuality*, she would become *the general symbol* at which the preacher and moralist might point ... Thus the young and pure would be taught to look at her ... as the figure, the body, the reality of sin. (185–6, my emphases)

But that intention to reduce Hester to a government moral health warning would involve the impossible—the elimination of process—whether that process takes the form of the history of a community, of a self, or the interactions between the two.

If the main narrative argues that history will vanquish symbolism's attempt to freeze time and meaning, "The Custom-House" suggests that the present is in any case both a fragile and a problematic concept. There Hawthorne makes a confession of failure yet the very fact of making the confession invites us to consider whether the question of (social) reality in the present is not always dependent on history. His fiction of contemporary life, *The House of the Seven Gables*, is overtly built on history, connecting as the Preface tells us "a by-gone time with the very present that is flitting away from us"—and it is that historical narrative which enables Hawthorne to offer a picture of the modern world (351). One crucial problem in producing or, rather, reproducing the realistic text that Hawthorne might have written instead of *The Scarlet Letter* is the way in which contemporary reality is always vanishing—not so much into history as into limbo because Hawthorne lacks the proper perspective to deal with the experience even though contemporary reality appears to him as an already written text:

A better book than I shall ever write was there; leaf after leaf presenting itself to me, just as it was written out by the reality of the flitting hour, and vanishing as fast as written, only because my brain wanted the insight and my hand the cunning to transcribe it. (151)

Hawthorne fails to write his full-length book about contemporary life partially at least because he could not stop time, because memory is not enough on its own—yet, and surely it is a deliberate irony, one point about "The Custom-House" is that he has shown ways that such a work might be constructed with its necessary roots in private and public history. Another related point is that the difference between Hawthorne's historical romance and a realistic fiction of contemporary life is one of degree, not kind. The rupture with the Custom-House means that the immediate past is in danger

of being lost to history even if it is history as autobiography—were it not for
"The Custom-House":

> The life of the Custom-House lies like a dream behind me. The
> old Inspector ... and all those other venerable personages who sat
> with him at the receipt of custom, are but shadows in my view;
> white-headed and wrinkled images, which my fancy used to sport
> with, and has now flung aside for ever. The merchants ... —these
> men of traffic, who seemed to occupy so important a position
> in the world,—how little time has it required to disconnect me
> from them all, not merely in act, but recollection! It is with an
> effort that I recall the figures and appellations of these few. Soon,
> likewise, my old native town will loom upon me through the haze
> of memory, a mist brooding over and around it; as if it were no
> portion of the real earth, but an overgrown village in cloud-land,
> with only imaginary inhabitants to people its wooden houses ...
> Henceforth, it ceases to be a reality of my life. (157)

Dream, shadows, images, fancy, haze of memory, mist cloud-land, imaginary:
these are the words that Hawthorne uses to describe his sense of his very
recent past. This is analogous to the equally radical break with the past
evidenced by Hester's reflections in the first scaffold scene where her
memories of her European past take the shape of "phantasmagoric forms"
under the pressures of the "weight and hardness of the reality" (167). After
those phantasmagoric memories have flashed across the screen of Hester's
mind, Hawthorne returns to that key term which resonates throughout the
novel: reality. The letter, "the infant and the shame were real. Yes!—these
were her realities,—all else had vanished!" (168) Hester, having lost her
past through her sin and society's punishment of it, has to construct a new
history, a new identity for herself which will go beyond the limitations of
symbolic definition until, by the end of the novel, there is "a more real life"
for her in New England (344). For Hawthorne, all fiction should necessarily
be historical fiction—and the worlds both of nineteenth-century Salem and
seventeenth-century Boston are not so much to be read as inventions or
creations but as re-creations.

II

> One thing that quickned [sic] his Resolution to do what might be
> in this Matter expected from him, was a Passage which he heard
> from a Minister Preaching on the Title of the *Fifty-first* Psalm:
> *To make a publick and an open Profession of Repentance, is a thing not*

mis-becoming the greatest Man alive.

Every disease is the penalty for what the Salteaux call "bad conduct." ...

The illness can be combated in only one way—by confession. But it is a different idea of confession from what we are used to. We assume that any confession made to a priest, psychoanalyst, friend, or lawyer will be held in strictest confidence; it is a private matter. But among the Salteaux, the whole point of confession is that it must be public; the transgressor must suffer all the shame of self-exposure. By confessing his guilt and telling the members of the band exactly what he did wrong, the sinner deters others from making the same mistake in the future.[1]

Here, both Mather the minister and Farb the anthropologist discuss social contexts in which public confession is valued, and their very different perspectives help to illuminate Hawthorne's concern with what he sees as the necessary relationship between the public and private sides of man's being—necessary for full humanity. The minister speaks from the structure of feeling of the society that Hawthorne is re-creating—and (up to a point—the point perhaps where symbolic definition of a person negates social relationships) respecting if only for the seriousness with which it responds to experience, its refusal to trivialize as (and this is surely Hawthorne's implication) is the tendency of the modern world:

The scene was not without a mixture of awe, such as must always invest the spectacle of guilt and shame in a fellow-creature, before society shall have grown corrupt enough to smile, instead of shuddering, at it. The witnesses of Hester Prynne's disgrace ... were stern enough to look upon her death, had that been the sentence, without a murmur at its severity, but had none of the heartlessness of another social state, which would find only a theme for jest in an exhibition like the present. (166)

The anthropologist contrasts the world view of the primitive Indian to that of modern liberalism—a world view which not so much accepts as endorses a split between the public and private sides of man's being and which, I would argue, does not necessarily see adultery as wrong because an anti-social act as Hawthorne most certainly does. Hawthorne's emphasis that meaning must be socially negotiated to be valid, that morality is above all social morality, means that, however palliated, Hester's and Dimmesdale's adultery must be seen as wrong. Adultery destroys the possibility of the fulfilment of private relationships and of wider public relationships. For Hawthorne it is only when the two are brought together that there is the possibility of sustained authentic life. It is to take the diseased Dimmesdale seven years to learn the lesson that public confession is necessary to heal the split not only between the way he sees himself and the way he is seen but also to heal the relationship between father and daughter, and, indeed, to enable Pearl to escape from the solitary confinement of symbolic definition imposed by her mother.

It is crucially important to realize the value that Hawthorne places in living in right relationship in society, in living a life of open and spontaneous reciprocity, because it is only by remembering this that we can adequately recognize the way symbolism is presented and judged in the fiction. It cannot be emphasized too strongly that Hawthorne is writing a fiction critical of symbolic definition rather than a symbolist work. Thus, Pearl is forced to exercise the function of a symbol not by the reader but by Hester as she replicates what the authorities had done to her. Pearl's whole appearance

> was the scarlet letter in another form; the scarlet letter endowed with life! The mother herself—as if the red ignominy were so deeply scorched into her brain, that all her conceptions assumed its form—had carefully wrought out the similitude; lavishing many hours of morbid ingenuity, to create an analogy between the object of her affection, and the emblem of her guilt and torture. But in truth, Pearl was the one, as well as the other; and only in consequence of that identity had Hester contrived so perfectly to represent the scarlet letter in her appearance. (204–5)

Hester makes Pearl into "the living hieroglyphic ... the symbol" of her sin, a sign that she can redeem herself, and by doing so she depersonalizes, dehumanizes Pearl. It is only with Dimmesdale's public confession that Pearl can become fully human and escape from the narrowness and distortion inherent in symbolic identity (296). If Pearl is Hester's victim, so is Chillingworth (*né* Prynne)—only his symbolic self-definition is self-imposed. He takes up a symbolic function, defining and limiting himself by the new name he has chosen, until he becomes fully "unhumanized" (342). By his allegorical/symbolical way of viewing the world, he abnegates human responsibility for actions. He tells Hester

> "It is not granted me to pardon ... By thy first step awry, thou didst plant the germ of evil; but, since that moment, it has all

been a dark necessity. Ye that have wronged me are not sinful, save in a kind of typical illusion; neither am I fiend-like, who have snatched a fiend's office from his hands. It is our fate. Let the black flower blossom as it may!" (268)

Since Hawthorne tells us elsewhere explicitly that Chillingworth is to be seen as a self-made fiend, we know how to place this abnegation of responsibility. But in this way of seeing experience symbolically, as "a kind of typical illusion," it can be seen that he shares the way of seeing of the "highly respectable" but mistaken Calvinist witnesses who wish to deny the particular historical meaning of Dimmesdale's confession on the scaffold: "After exhausting life in his efforts for mankind's spiritual good, he had made the manner of his death a parable, in order to impress on his admirers the mighty and mournful lesson, that, in the view of Infinite Purity, we are sinners all alike" (341).

Those witnesses have failed to comprehend the change in Dimmesdale's scaffold confession from his earlier pulpit rhetoric where his confession of his specific sin is interpreted as sublime humility, as he predicted, "subtle, but remorseless hypocrite" that he is (242). But despite the self-hatred that his double-dealing induces, paradoxically his very consciousness of his sinfulness moves him towards comprehension of his congregation. "this very burden it was that gave him sympathies so intimate with the sinful brotherhood of mankind" (240). One effect of the sin on Hester has been to make her doubt the virtues of others. One effect on Dimmesdale has been to make him doubt the very nature of reality itself. Hester has the advantage of being a confessed and known sinner—and it is a very real advantage for Hawthorne. But Dimmesdale cannot dare to communicate in any sincerity with his fellow-men:

> It is the unspeakable misery of a life so false as his, that it steals the pith and substance out of whatever realities there are around us, and which were meant by Heaven to be the spirit's joy and nutriment. To the untrue man, the whole universe is false, it is impalpable,—it shrinks to nothing with his grasp. And he himself, in so far as he shows himself in a false light, becomes a shadow, or, indeed, ceases to exist. (243)

Reality is a social construct: it comes from sharing experience and emotion. To live privately is to live immorally and to destroy one's identity. For Hawthorne, social being is at the core of all identity and of all virtue. The only "truth" that gave Dimmesdale "a real existence" was the strength in his inmost soul, and *the undissembled expression of it in his aspect*. Had he once found power to smile and wear a face of gayety, *there would have been no such man!*" (243–4, my emphases).

Dimmesdale, in his search for "a moment's peace" ascends the scaffold at night but as carefully dressed "as if it had been for public worship" as if in unconscious rehearsal of his final confession (244). When Hester and Pearl join him on their return from Governor Winthrop's death-bed, there is a temporary escape from isolation in this social contact. As the minister takes Pearl's hand:

> there came what seemed like a tumultuous rush of new life, other life than his own, pouring like a torrent into his heart, and hurrying through all his veins, as if the mother and the child were communicating their vital warmth to his half torpid system. The three formed an electric chain. (250)

But the minister still lacks the courage to stand with them in the public light of noontide, as Pearl asks him to do, and says that he will stand with them only on one other day—the judgement day (which tells the reader how to place the community and the occasion when Dimmesdale does make his open confession). At this point, however, only a symbolic and therefore inadequate harmony can be achieved. The position is unreal because it is private. Dimmesdale can only gain subjective meaning from it rather as he imposes meaning on the meteor. And here Hawthorne seems to distinguish between the communal interpretation of a natural phenomenon as they read the meteor as a sign welcoming Winthrop to Heaven, which he respects if he does not endorse, over against Dimmesdale's private reading which he unequivocally condemns, imputing it "solely to the disease in his own eye and heart," his "egotism" (252).

If the significance of the first meeting lies in the stress on the inadequacy of symbolic definition and the impossibility for the guilty sinner to escape from this straitjacket, the meeting in the forest deals with the impossibility of escape from one's personal history and the inadequacy of the appeal to nature. Seven years have passed since the birth of Pearl. Hester and Dimmesdale have acquired new histories since the break caused by the discovery of their sin, though these new histories have pushed them in different ways. (Pearl has not changed: her symbolic status prevents significant human development.) Hester no longer measures her idea of right and wrong by any standard external to herself. "The scarlet letter had not done its office" (261). The symbol has had the effect of creating a split between her public appearance and her private thoughts. Dimmesdale similarly suffers from the division between private and public identity: "No man, for any considerable period, can wear one face to himself, and another to the multitude, without finally getting bewildered as to which may be the true" (304). In the forest, Hester can make a bid for life in her appeal to Dimmesdale to escape into the wilderness or to the old world. In spite of the fact that the minister, with his fixed place in the social system, "was only the more trammelled by its regulations, its principles, and even its prejudices," he feels the attraction of Hester's plea: "there appeared a glimpse of human affection and sympathy, a new life, and a true one" (290, 291). Hester explicitly attempts to deny the past any validity: "Let us not look back ... The past is gone! See! With this symbol, I undo it all, and make it as it had never been!" (292). "Make it new" with a vengeance! But her attempt to escape from her past by identifying herself with a Nature "never subjugated by human law" is doomed (and rightly doomed) to failure, for Hawthorne sees a romantic assertion of the value of passion based on the appeal to nature as immoral and unworkable. Ironically, at the very moment that Hester attempts to repudiate the authority of the past, her abandonment of the symbol shows how the past can erupt into the present: "Her sex, her youth, and the whole richness of her beauty, came back from what men call the irrevocable past" (293). Pearl, at once their past and their future, shows that they cannot escape from time or society by her insistence that Hester must wear the letter.

Dimmesdale returns from the forest full of an amoral energy produced by his dislocation from his previous history and by the feeling that he can now have hopes for the future. When he returns to his house, this vitality needs to be channelled, and, as Male puts it, "nourished by a communion with the tomb-fed faith and the tome-fed wisdom of the past":[2]

> Here he had studied and written; here, gone through fast and vigil, and come forth half alive; here, striven to pray; here, borne a hundred thousand agonies! There was the Bible, in its rich old Hebrew, with Moses and the prophets speaking to him, and God's voice through all! (310)

Here the private and the public selves can begin to be reintegrated. The minister is greatly relieved that the ship in which he and Hester intend to escape to Europe will not be sailing until after the day appointed for the Election Sermon which is to prove his salvation. Hawthorne apparently criticizes him for this, describing his desire to "leave no public duty unperformed, nor ill performed!" as "pitiably weak," as evidence of "a subtle disease" (304). But it is the public duty of the Election Sermon which is to prove his salvation. It is because he has to preach that he returns to his study. It is because of his awareness of his public duty that he can bring himself to

confess: it is the sermon and its effects which enables him to decide which
is his real self. The sermon does not have an effect on Dimmesdale alone.
It enables him to open a reciprocal intercourse with the world (and here we
look back to Hawthorne's suggestion that "thoughts are frozen and utterance
benumbed, unless the speaker stand in some true relation to his audience"
[121]). The sermon inspires both audience and speaker, and by inspiring his
audience the minister can no longer evade his responsibility to them and
to Hester and Pearl. He has been *both* "so etherealized by spirit" *and* "so
apotheosized by worshipping admirers" (334). The sermon, given before
the whole known community, has two levels of meaning: first, the prophecy
about the political future of New England, expressed by conventional
language; and second, the private cry, expressed by his tone of voice—the
universal language of the heart. It is "The complaint of a human heart,
sorrow-laden, perchance guilty, telling its secret, whether of guilt or sorrow,
to the great heart of mankind; beseeching its sympathy or forgiveness, ... and
never in vain" (328).

For such a short fiction, *The Scarlet Letter* covers a remarkable length
of time—and a period which has a considerable historical resonance:
seven years—1642–49. Whatever the reason for choosing the period
of England's Civil War for the main action of the novel, a substantial
length of time is necessary for Hester to build a new identity after her
old European self had been destroyed by her sin and its punishment on
the scaffold: "It was as if a new birth, with stronger assimilations than the
first, had converted the forest-land ... into Hester Prynne's ... life-long
home" (186). And not only Hester's construction of a new self but also
the related matter of the mutual relationships between herself and the
community have to be given time to develop so that a long revolution in
the community's interpretation of the letter and Hester can take place.
That relationship is not only long but complex—and not without its
ironies. One irony is that her subversion by decoration of the letter not
only enables Hester to find a place in the community's economy but also
that art of needlework, that labour of the outsider, in large part reinforces
the power structure of the society—even though her own thoughts
radically question that structure:

> Public ceremonies, such as ordinations, the installation of magis-
> trates, and all that could give majesty to the forms in which a new
> government manifested itself to the people, were, as a matter of
> policy, marked by a stately and well-conducted ceremonial, and
> a sombre but yet a studied magnificence. Deep ruffs, painfully
> wrought bands, and gorgeously embroidered gloves, were all

deemed necessary to the official state of men assuming the reins of power; and were readily allowed to individuals dignified by rank or wealth, even while sumptuary laws forbade these and similar extravagances to the plebeian order. (188)

There is much that could be said about this passage—but one obvious point is that Hawthorne is drawing attention to the class structure of the infant democracy. In so far as her identity is constituted by the letter signifying one meaning along with her labour for the establishment, the patriarchy could hardly ask for a more useful "citizen" than Hester—at once a strong warning against hiding the father who has broken the rules and a figure who enables the patriarchy (both fathers in Christ and fathers in the law) symbolically to declare their command over "painfully wrought" labour—a labour which in its products signifies their power, their difference from "the plebeian order." But the simplicity of symbolic labelling cannot, over time, survive the necessary multiplicity of Hester's relationships with the society as a whole. For example, not all Hester's labour (if all her paid work) goes towards making the symbols of power: she uses the profit ("all her superfluous means") to make "coarse garments for the poor" (189). Though that activity certainly reflects and by reflecting may endorse class difference within the society, it is also a response to need—and in that response a beginning to her social work as well as private penance (remorse for past sins, in its technical meaning—but not, significantly, yet penitence—technically the resolve to sin no more).

The original interpretation of the letter can survive over a limited period of time especially when it is confined to the class that imposed the definition. Pearl is three when she and Hester go to the Governor's Hall and Hester, notoriously, sees an image of herself in the breast-plate of his armour. As Hawthorne forcibly suggests, authority's definition has to be seen as a distortion: "owing to the peculiar effect of this convex mirror, the scarlet letter was represented in exaggerated and gigantic proportions, so as to be greatly the most prominent feature of [Hester's] appearance" (208). But one point to make about that representation is that the breast-plate may embody as well as reflect a truth—that the sign on Hester's breast may not only distort other's perceptions of her but may also be a protective device behind which her (possibly irresponsible) subversive ideas can shelter, grow, and flourish. More obviously, that breast-plate definition of Hester is not stable: under the pressure of historical experience, the sign's meaning has shifted. Hester's new social role, after seven long years, is not so much a production intended by either Hester or the society as something that the history of the interaction between the two parties has rendered up:

> She was self-ordained a Sister of Mercy; or so we may rather say,
> the world's heavy hand had so ordained her, when neither the
> world nor she looked forward to this result. The letter was the
> symbol of her calling. Such helpfulness was found in her,—so
> much power to do, and power to sympathize,—that many people
> refused to interpret this scarlet A by its original signification.
> They said it meant Able; so strong was Hester with a woman's
> strength. (257)

Authority had once, we have to infer, defined Hester as Adulteress: now
the people define her not by the static reductiveness of a noun, but by an
adjective—an attribute, not an identity. Notably, it is "the men of rank,"
conscious of their role as guardians "of the public morals" who are slow to
accept any redefinition of the sign, while it is "the people" and those "in
private life" (significant terms) who, having redefined the sign, incorporate
Hester, a person not a symbol, into the community: "our Hester,—the town's
own Hester" (258). Of course, their Hester may not be Hester's Hester—and
Hester may not accept, may not deserve this incorporation—as Hawthorne
subtly indicates. And, following from her secret resistance to incorporation
into the town's ideology, society's redefinition of the sign is not enough to
heal the split between the way society sees Hester and the way she sees not
only this society but, it would appear, all societies in which men dominate
women—a view of the world about which at this stage Hawthorne seems
profoundly ambivalent. If this split is to be healed—and, from Hester's point
of view, it may matter little whether she is labelled as Adulteress or Able—
then the story has to go beyond the moment of Dimmesdale's confession and
death which, though convenient for him, Pearl and, no doubt, the author,
leaves Hester still at the centre of the stage. For her, neither death, nor
escape are real options.

I have already argued that one consequence of Dimmesdale's public
acknowledgement of his connection with Pearl and Hester is that Pearl can
escape from her limiting status as symbol and become fully human, a woman
in the world. It is this that explains her movement to Europe. Pearl is not
a Jamesian heroine who has somehow strayed into the wrong book, as is
occasionally suggested. She can go to Europe because she has no historical
ties with New England. Her only identity there has been as symbol, used by
others but without independent existence: when that is destroyed, she is free.
Hester must return, because it is New England and her sin that has given
some sort of organizing principle to her life. After her first appearance on the
scaffold, "Her sin, her ignominy, were the roots which she had struck into
the soil ... The chain that bound her here was of iron links ... but never could

be broken" (186). During Dimmesdale's sermon, Hester stands at the foot of the scaffold "whence she dated the first hour of her life of ignominy ... There was a sense within her.... that her whole orb of life, both before and after, was connected with this spot, as with the one point that gave it unity" (328). To be true, as Hawthorne admonishes us, is freely to declare ourselves to the world, to recognize that we cannot reject or deny the personal history that defines us. We must choose reality over symbol, as Hester chooses to return to New England to live the ethical life: "But there was a more real life for Hester Prynne, here, in New England, than in that unknown region where Pearl had found a home. Here had been her sin; here her sorrow; and here was yet to be her penitence" (344). That last sentence is a more economical version with authorial approval of a feeling that Hester had experienced at the beginning of her life of isolation:

> Here, she said to herself, had been the scene of her guilt, and here should be the scene of her earthly punishment; and so, perchance, the torture of her daily shame would at length purge her soul, and work out another purity than that which she had lost; more saint-like, because the result of martyrdom. (187)

III

> "Frailty, thy name is WOMAN."
> "The Earth waits for her Queen."
> The connection between these quotations may not be obvious, but it is strict.

The connection may not be obvious, but I want to argue that this, the opening of Margaret Fuller's *Woman in the Nineteenth Century* provides the right perspective in which to see the following crucial passage from *The Scarlet Letter*—crucial, that is, for the sexual politics of the novel—right, in that Fuller's epigraphs link a present definition (if not condition) with a desired Utopian future, very much as the narrative of Hester does:

> Women ... —in the continually recurring trials of wounded, wasted, wronged, misplaced, or erring and sinful passion,—or with the dreary burden of a heart unyielded, because unvalued and unsought,—came to Hester's cottage demanding why they were so wretched, and what the remedy! ... She assured them ... of her firm belief, that, at some brighter period, when the world should have grown ripe for it, in Heaven's own time, a new truth would

be revealed, in order to establish the whole relation between man and woman on a surer ground of mutual happiness. Earlier in life, Hester had vainly imagined that she herself might be the destined prophetess, but had long since recognized the impossibility that any mission of divine and mysterious truth should be confided to a woman stained with sin, bowed down with shame, or even burdened with a life-long sorrow. The angel and apostle of the coming revelation must be a woman, indeed, but lofty, pure, and beautiful; and wise, moreover, not through dusky grief, but the ethereal medium of joy; and showing how sacred love should make us happy, by the truest test of a life successful to such an end! (344–5)

With this passage as evidence, I want to argue that Hester finishes as rather more than a social worker specializing in female clients whom "she counselled as best she might," more than just an early representative of the caring professions—and doing more than running a seventeenth-century counselling group. She is genuinely subversive in that she desires and prophesies a radical subversion of the patriarchal structures of the society and, most significantly, of the religion that legitimates that patriarchy. Such a view, however, seems to run counter to the comparatively few recent critics who have found the passage worthy of notice.

Michael Colacurcio in an important and learned article has argued convincingly for the relevance of Ann Hutchinson's moral and intellectual structure of feeling for the world inhabited by Hester Prynne and Dimmesdale. But he does not go further when describing Hester's final position than to say that it is "in Hawthorne's mental universe, just about half way between Ann Hutchinson and Margaret Fuller." This could mean almost anything, but Colacurcio has made it clear that he does not want to see Hester as making a radical critique: "What Hester's experience came to finally—in an epilogue, and after a painful and complicated development forced upon her by others—is some insight about the double standard, or perhaps about the new morality."[3] Is that all? It hardly seems an adequate commentary on a statement asking for a total restructuring of the relations between man and woman—one which rewords and makes public Hester's private feelings about male female relations in chapter XIII. However, he does realize that the passage matters. One of the few other critics to have paid serious attention to these words of Hester's is Austin Warren in an excellent piece, though I cannot go along with his gloss on the passage ("falsetto" strikes me as a peculiarly unfortunate and tasteless epithet):

Whether applied to Hester specifically or to the mysterious revelation to come—reminiscent of Ann Hutchinson, Margaret Fuller, or Mother Ann Lee, the pronouncement seems falsetto. Hawthorne's "new revelation," which seems (so far as I can understand it) not very new, is certainly not feminist but feminine and familial.[4]

Here he falters. He introduces the right names—but fails to notice that Hester does not exactly replicate any of their positions and may indeed be new—and feminist. Ann Hutchinson's antinomianism and her insistence on exercising a powerful and intelligent female voice are, as Colacurcio shows, clearly relevant. And Margaret Fuller's "great lawsuit" of Man *versus* Men, Woman *versus* Women equally clearly bears on Hester's case: "Those who would reform the world must show that they do not speak in the heat of wild impulse; their lives must be unstained by passionate error; they must be severe lawgivers to themselves."[5] Even more to the point is Mother Ann, foundress of the Shakers. It seems to be their insistence on celibacy that is remembered, while the theology behind that insistence is usually forgotten. The immediately relevant points are these: God is a dual person, male *and* female. Adam likewise necessarily had in himself both sexes, being created in the image of God. Christ appeared first in the person of Jesus, embodying the male order, and then in the person of Ann Lee, representing the female element. The day of judgement has begun with the establishment of the Shaker church, and will be completed with that church's full development.

If I understand Hester's coded statement correctly, she is going beyond any of these three prophetesses. (Mother Ann never claimed to be Christ come again: she merely represented the female element in God.)[6] Hester has come to believe that what is needed is a second Revelation of God to than—and woman. In other words, she looks forward to the Second Coming of Christ—only this time as a woman. Angel and Apostle indeed of a coming Revelation! Perhaps capitalizing Angel and Apostle is cheating slightly—but the choice of the two words, given their significant first letter and accompanied by the phrase "the destined prophetess" suggests that Hester has more in mind than just a very good female person. Cruden, in his *Concordance*, gives these definitions:

ANGEL signifies, A messenger or bringer of tidings, and is applied (1) To those intellectual and immaterial beings, whom God makes use of as his ministers to execute orders of providence ... (a) To Christ, who is the mediator and head of the church ... (3) To ministers of the gospel, who are ambassadors for Christ ... (4) To such as are employed by God as instruments for executing his judgments.

> APOSTLE signifies, A messenger sent upon any special errand ...
> It is applied (1) to Christ Jesus who was sent from heaven to
> assume our nature, with authority to exercise prophetical and all
> his offices, and to send forth his apostles to publish the gospel
> ... (2) To a minister immediately sent from Christ to preach the
> gospel.

The coupling of these words with "revelation"—a term that needs no
theological gloss—makes the millenarian nature of Hester's prophecy quite
clear.

Whether Hawthorne approves or disapproves of this prophecy is not
an open question—if one is Austin Warren, who claims that the author
wrote the conclusion "in the voice of Hawthorne, the commentator, the
husband of Sophia." But even if one shares this confidence that the voice
of Sophia's husband was always a conservative and conventional one,
the announcement can hardly be dismissed as "not very new" and (by
implication) therefore not very important. There were plenty of claims
to be the especial Bride of Christ in both the seventeenth and nineteenth
centuries—as a reading of Christopher Hill's *The World Turned Upside* Down
shows for the seventeenth century, and J.F.C. Harrison's *The Second Coming*
shows for the late eighteenth and early nineteenth centuries. But there were
few (if any) who waited for the Second Coming expecting Christ to be a
woman—and such an expectation would make for a radical (but reasonable)
re-ordering of theological language.[7] (Incidentally, Mother Ann said that
"we are the people who turn the world upside down." "The world turned
upside down" was an old English song which she probably knew, though she
is, no doubt, principally thinking of Acts xvii, 6, where this is the accusation
levelled against the primitive church. Ironically it was the tune played by the
English army when Cornwallis surrendered at Yorktown—unintentionally
playing into the hands of those who would claim that America is indeed the
Redeemer Nation.)

If my interpretation of Hester's claim is accepted, it may at least help
Warren with another of his problems—the question of the paraphrasable
content of Dimmesdale's Election Sermon:

> That the preacher, about to declare himself an avowed sinner,
> cannot (like Cotton Mather) denounce his New England's sins,
> I can see; but why need he celebrate its high destiny? It would
> appear that Hawthorne, to whom the "subject matter" of the ser-
> mon does not seem to matter, has inserted and asserted, his own

strong regional loyalties. (42)

It may be that we should feel—with the New England world described in "The Custom-House" in mind—that this forecast of the region's "high and glorious destiny" is one of Hawthorne's fiercest ironies—or, at best, his own very patient prophecy. These glories *may* lie in New England's future—just as there *may* be a future revelation of a new truth which will make the relation between the sexes mutually happy. But these prophesied futures can hardly be said to have arrived by 1850—unless one has the optimism of a George Bancroft. (On the spine of my edition of his *History of the United States* are these words circling an eagle sitting on top of the world: "Westward the Star of Empire Takes its Way".) But, however these prophecies are to be evaluated, what is clear is that they are to be paralleled and compared as secular and religious prophecies—and it is a nice irony that the clergyman makes a secular prophecy while the laywoman makes a religious one.

What Hester had only, thought privately in chapter XIII, she can now speak (though not practice)—and what she desires, if it were to take place, surely would be to overthrow and rearrange "the whole system of ancient prejudice," "to undermine the foundations of the Puritan establishment" (259, 260). Nina Baym writes about Hester's return in a particularly disappointing, even surprising, way:

> Hester has in fact brought about a modest social change. Society expands to accept her with the letter—the private life carves out a small place for itself in the community's awareness. This is a small, but real, triumph for the heroine ... [H]er return to Boston and the consequent loosening of the community to accommodate her lighten the conclusion. A painfully slow process of social relaxation may, perhaps, be hoped for.[8]

Perhaps. But this liberalist gradualism is clearly not what Hester looks for or desires. It is (perhaps) the most that Hawthorne thinks can be achieved, but even if we define Hawthorne as a liberal gradualist, that doesn't answer the obvious problem that the small advances may only be generated by great expectations and demands. And—even if she can only cast herself as Jane the Baptist—it looks as though Hester expects a lot: the Second Coming. To be without sin, shame and sorrow is to be more than human. Hester prophesies a world when there will be no more marrying and giving in marriage, when the apostle/angel will transcend or at least radically define the sexual relationship. Perhaps celibacy is meant by "the truest test"—as might be indicated by the emphasis on "ethereal." Perhaps Hester has read Revelations—in company with other sexual radicals in a radical Protestant tradition such as William Blake—and particularly chapter XII like him, and awaits "the woman clothed with the sun."

But even the new historicist Sacvan Bercovitch will have none of this. He calls Hester's prophecies a "moment of reconciliation," tells us that Hester "*must* now make compromise the work of culture," suggests that Hawthorne "absorbs the radical energies of history into the polar oppositions of symbolic interpretation," and worries that a potential confrontation in the novel "endangers both symbolic process and narrative closure."[9] I fail to see how a desire for—expressed as a prediction of—a transformation of the relationship between men and women can be called "reconciliation" or "compromise." I have argued that Hawthorne has criticized symbolic interpretation in the name of "the radical energies of history." And I would further suggest that here, as in all of Hawthorne's longer fictions, his narrative forms resist closure. In this case, it remains deliberately open—open to the future. To argue that Hawthorne speaks from and celebrates an ideology of liberal consensus seems entirely wrong. A man recently fired for his political views is hardly likely to think that political consensus exists in his own political culture—and, as he quite gratuitously chooses to identify himself in "The Custom-House" however ironically as the Loco-foco Surveyor, that is, as a radical, an egalitarian Democrat, he is hardly trying to assimilate himself to a consensus position.[10]

Hawthorne, by giving Dimmesdale and Hester the role of prophet, brings the future into the sphere of the novel, so that readers are not (or at least should not be) trapped into conservatively dwelling in and on the past. With both characters, the reciprocal relationships between the public and the private spheres are stressed and developed throughout the course of the novel. (One reason for the inadequacy of the appeal to nature is that it can only speak to the private side of man's being.) The symbolic sign is, at the last, stripped of its various imposed meanings, and becomes simply the letter A, a dead letter. The true significance of the novel can be seen to lie in its creation of a structure based on the personal histories of the central characters interacting with the historical life of the new community of New England. Both in turn interact with the double history of the artist and with an imagined better future. *The Scarlet Letter* is an historical novel—one which takes past, present and future into consideration—and is at the same time political in that the future is presented as something that we have to struggle to make—a making based on desire corrected by our perspectives on the past.

NOTES

1. Cotton Mather, *Magnolia Christi Americana*, Books I and II, edited by K.B. Murdock (Cambridge, Mass.: Harvard University Press, 1977), p. 295. Peter Farb, *Man's Rise to Civilization as Shown by the Indians of North American from Primeval Times to the Coming of the Industrial State* (London: Seeker and Warburg, 1969), pp. 60–1.

2. R.R. Male, *Hawthorne's Tragic Vision* (New York: W.W. Norton, 1964), p. 114.

3. Michael Colacurcio, "Footsteps of Ann Hutchinson: The Context of *The Scarlet Letter*," *English Literary History*, 39 (1972), 459–94.

4. Austin Warren, "*The Scarlet Letter*: A Literary Exercise in Moral Theology," *The Southern Review*, 1, new series (Jan. 1965), 22–45.

5. Perry Miller (ed.), *Margaret Fuller: American Romantic* (New York: Anchor Books, 1963), p. 162.

6. "Shaker adventism was shown to be spiritual and not physical. 'As the substance of the first woman was taken from the body of the first man: so that Divine Spirit with which the second woman was endowed ... was taken from the Spirit of Christ.' Mother Ann thus became the 'Second pillar of the Church of God,' but the Shakers were careful to state they did not mean the 'human tabernacle' of Ann Lee. That was but the instrument for the expression of divine truth, which could not complete its work until all men had become spiritual." Alice Felt Tyler, *Freedom's Ferment: Phases of American Social History from the Colonial Period to the Outbreak of the Civil War* (New York: Harper and Row, 1962), pp. 146–7.

7. Jane Tompkins, however, draws attention to Isabella Beecher Hooker, Harriet Beecher Stowe's half sister: "This woman at one time in her life had believed that the millennium was at hand and that she was destined to be the leader of a new matriarchy." *Sensational Designs: The Cultural Work of American Fiction, 1790–1860* (New York: Oxford University Press, 1985), p. 122.

8. Nina Baym, *The Shape of Hawthorne's Career* (Ithaca and London: Cornell University Press, 1976), pp. 130, 134.

9. Sacvan Bercovitch, "Hawthorne's A-Morality of Compromise," *Representations*, 24 (Fall 1988), 1, 2, 10.

10. See John Ashworth, *'Agrarians' and 'Aristocrats': Party Political Ideology in the United States, 1837–1846* (Cambridge: Cambridge University Press, 1987), *passim* for democratic Democrats.

EMILY MILLER BUDICK

Hester's Skepticism, Hawthorne's Faith; or, What Does a Woman Doubt? Instituting the American Romance Tradition

Throughout *The Scarlet Letter* one particular question generates the action. It is the question on everyone's lips, spoken and unspoken, from beginning to end. It is the question asked the moment Hester steps onto the scaffold in the public square. It is reformulated in various ways not only by the different characters in the novel but also by the reader. Whose child is Pearl? This question does not express some trivial curiosity concerning Pearl's paternity. It also means, what kind of being is Pearl? From what immortal constitution, divine or demonic, does she derive? As such, it represents exactly that inquiry Puritan society must conduct in order to preserve its sense of itself as a chosen people, a new Israel reincarnated in a New England. The issue of Pearl's paternity, in other words, is as much a historical, theological, and philosophical concern as it is a moral and social one. It expresses the Puritans' desire to discover a single line of descent, moving directly from God, the Father, through the patriarchs of ancient Israel, to the (male) leaders of the American entity. The illegitimate (female) child threatens that historical continuity. Interrupting the lines of spiritual genealogy Pearl calls into question the principle of visible sanctity on which the American nation had founded itself. The question, then, Whose child is Pearl? exposes a problem of historical consciousness inextricably linked to an issue in skepticism, where by skepticism I mean the doubt whether one can

From *New Literary History* 22, no. 1 (Winter 1991), pp. 199–211. © 1991 by *New Literary History*, The University of Virginia, Charlottesville.

prove either one's own existence or that of the world, or move from one proof to the other. Through its federal theology and its principle of visible sanctity, the Puritan community tried to resolve any and all doubts concerning itself and the reality of its embodiment of the divine. By tracing in its history a clear-cut, unambiguous line of divine inheritance, it attempted to confirm a relationship between physical evidences and spiritual realities.

The strategy of *The Scarlet Letter* precisely opposes these tendencies in Puritan society. I have argued elsewhere that a defining feature of American historical romance, as practiced by male authors such as Hawthorne, Melville, Faulkner, Fitzgerald, Hemingway, Doctorow, and Updike, and as embodied in *The Scarlet Letter*, is its typical employment of nonmimetic modes of representation, at the same time that it insists on specified settings in place and time, in what we usually call history.[1] In so doing, American historical romance, I suggested, recognizes that words and events cannot possess determinate meanings. At the same time, it also affirms the necessity for acknowledging and assuming responsibility both for our words and the world they attempt to describe. In Hawthornean romance, doubt is the condition of our lives in this world. Faith is the willingness to entertain and keep alive our skepticism alongside our commitment to thinking and acting determinately. The medium of this reconciliation between private doubt and social commitment is, for Hawthorne and for other (male) writers in this tradition, a certain consciousness of history. History, in the romance tradition, stands outside the subjectivities of the individual imagination. At the same time, it incorporates the uncertainties which inevitably attend to the irrecoverable and hence unprovable evidences of the past.

In *The Scarlet Letter* Hawthorne explores, in relation to the specific issue of biological progeneration, patriarchy's abuse of history. This abuse evolves out of patriarchy's drive toward certainty, its efforts to authorize the past through a written record which is only a patrilineal genealogy. In Puritan patriarchy, as, perhaps, in all patriarchies, fathers would guarantee knowledge of their sons by regulating the terms and conditions of female sexuality. They would secure themselves against doubt through a legal fiction of family relations. This legal fiction secures history by writing history in the language of the repeating patrinomial. Hence the community's insistence on discovering, Whose child is Pearl? Hawthorne's manipulation of this question both exposes the false assumptions of Puritan patriarchy and promotes a system of community and history predicated upon the preservation rather than the settling of radical doubt. In Hawthorne's view, the question of paternity must be asked. How one answers that question, however, determines the difference between the repressive authoritarianism of the Puritans and the impulses toward liberal democracy contained within Hawthorne's romantic retelling of their story.

Yet the question, Whose child is Pearl? may be the one question that Hester, as mother, cannot ask. Hester knows, as only a mother can, beyond the shadow of a doubt, whose child Pearl is. Hester might well suffer considerable *doubt* about the child's essential constitution.[2] Theoretically, at least, she might doubt Pearl's paternity. She cannot, however, knowing that she is the biological mother, mean by the question exactly what the community means. For whatever else a mother might doubt, she cannot, under normal circumstances, doubt that the child reproduces her. As Stanley Cavell has recently suggested, female skepticism may not originate in the same biological realities as male skepticism.[3] Therefore, it may not represent the same questions, the same discontinuities in the processes of knowing, especially bodily knowing, exposed by male skepticism. Female skepticism, therefore, if such skepticism exists, may have to be seen as evolving from some other kind of uncertainty. The woman may have to pose to herself—and answer—some other question. And she may have to conduct and conclude her inquiry on some other, nonhistorical, grounds.

Nonetheless, Hawthorne has Hester ask the question, Whose child is Pearl? (for example, 116 and 121–22). In so doing, Hawthorne attributes to his female protagonist an intellectual depth unrivalled in nineteenth-century American fiction, until Henry James's *The Portrait of a Lady* forty years later. At the same time, however, Hawthorne fails to get inside a woman's doubt. Indeed, he may, even as he is ascribing to women a profound skeptical consciousness, be prohibiting them from entering into the philosophical and literary tradition he initiates. Hawthorne's *Scarlet Letter*, I believe, institutes the American romance tradition in terms which make it eminently inheritable by women romance writers a century later; at the same time it threatens to close the tradition to women, necessitating their reinstitution of it later on wholly other terms.

In Hawthorne's novel, the strict authoritarianism of Puritan patriarchy finds its object in the child Pearl, who, as the living "likeness" of the letter, "the scarlet letter in another form; the scarlet letter endowed with life?" (125), becomes the target of the Puritans' efforts to control both human sexuality and its literary, historical expression. *The Scarlet Letter*, in other words, dramatizes a relationship between issues of birth (Whose child is Pearl?) and questions of interpretation (What does the letter mean?). Indeed, one of the ways the text validates the centrality and legitimacy of the community's doubt about the child is by representing it as its own investigation into its major symbol. At first we might assume that the two kinds of inquiries exist in a relation of mutual opposition. We might feel that the equation between the questions, What does the letter signify? and, Whose child is Pearl? disallows the search for meaning because it reduces human issues to literary ones.[4] We need only recall the example of Chillingworth and other Hawthornean characters to realize how demonic the desire for knowledge of other human beings can be. Nonetheless, from Hawthorne's point of view, no less than from the Puritans', the necessity to discover Pearl's origins is inescapable. As Hester freely confesses to Chillingworth, she has sinned against him; and that sin has social (if not moral and theological) consequences. At the very least, Hester's adultery disrupts the social order. It leaves Chillingworth homeless and familyless, and it violates the lines of patrimonial inheritance. The odd twist of plot whereby Chillingworth decides to leave his inheritance to Pearl, who is his legal offspring, emphasizes the way in which Hester's adultery complicates historical coherence. This, coupled with Pearl's repeated insistence on knowing her father's identity and the painful repercussions of Hester's prolonged silence, suggests that, though it may be impossible to specify Pearl's nature, it is neither impossible nor irrelevant to discover the identity of her father.

Our desire to fathom the meaning of the scarlet letter is no less justifiable. In the romance tradition to which it belongs, *The Scarlet Letter* explicitly entertains the indeterminacy of the symbol and, beyond it, of the world. It does not do so, however, to revel in the lack of cosmic coherence which the isolated sign may betray. Rather, the letter, as letter, though the most indeterminate of symbols, is also the basic building block of all meaning, all language.[5] As such, it compels us to enter into the interpretive process, despite our inability to know or understand anything beyond the shadow of our doubt, and despite the danger we run that in combining these indeterminate units on which language depends we may only further complicate the meaning-making process. Though the A's meaning is uncertain, its consequences in the world, which are, in the first instance, no less than Pearl's birth, are decisive.

Hawthorne's gesture of taking the letter upon himself predicts and imitates Hester's similar action at the end of the story. It is a significantly parental gesture. The tradition Hawthorne wishes to establish involves the willingness to acknowledge the sign, to take it upon oneself and make it one's own, despite its somewhat "fictitious" (107), indeterminate meaning. The urgency behind this embrace is explained through the living likeness of the letter—Pearl. For the two are joined at the very origins of the *A*. In order to "grow up amid human joy and sorrow, nor for ever do battle with the world, but be a woman in it" (268), Pearl must learn what the *A* means. She must learn who her father is, who her two fathers are, her biological father and her legal father. Indeed, it is only when Pearl discovers her biological father that she gains her legal father as well. Pearl leaves New England to reestablish the lines of patrimony broken in Hester's and Chillingworth's departure from old England.

In representing Pearl's dual parentage, Hawthorne exposes the fundamental uncertainty of paternity, which patriarchy wishes to exclude. He shows us that patriarchies, like Puritan America, would eliminate doubts about who and what we are by constituting the self as a vehicle of legal, historical, even transhistorical, inheritance. At the same time, however, by making Pearl's future success contingent upon her rectifying the social implications of her mother's adultery, Hawthorne admits the need to deal with the doubts introduced by human sexuality. Patrilineage may be a legal fiction, but it is a response to a genuine problem. Like any fiction, it deserves, indeed demands, to be interpreted. Patrilineage errs, not in choosing to respond to the doubtfulness of our birth, but in the nature of its response. This is to assert itself as fact and deny itself as fiction.

Given his text's preoccupation with the question of Pearl's paternity, it is not surprising that the major focus of the prefatory "Custom-House" sketch is Hawthorne's own attempt to locate his paternal ancestry. A place of "great-grandsires" (42), a "patriarchal body" (43), the custom-house is quite simply "a sanctuary into which womankind, with her tools of magic ... has very infrequent access" (39). Feminist critics have taken the absence of a strong female presence in the "Custom-House" to signify Hawthorne's unrelenting male bias.[6] The maleness of Hawthorne's concern is not to be easily discarded. Indeed, it may be even more invidious than feminist critics have yet portrayed it. In the first instance, however, it functions as part of the intricate moral fiber characterizing Hawthorne's undertaking. For Hawthorne the world of the custom-house is no ideal repository of the ancestral past. In particular it fails to institute the customs Hawthorne craves. Its sterility, which is closely related to the major issue of the sketch, Hawthorne's inability to write, is a direct consequence of its exclusive maleness. To write, Hawthorne makes very clear, is not to inscribe words which locate one's social identity and establish one's place and rank in the custom-house. Taking up a position through political patronage, Hawthorne has already traveled the road of social and political conformity, and it has almost destroyed his creative potential. Therefore, Hawthorne must relocate himself in some more "domestic scenery" (64–65). He must abandon the "narrow circle" of the custom-house, with its minimum of "lettered intercourse" (57–58) and get on to what he calls the "second story of the Custom-House" (58). Here in this second story, which is also, I take it, from tradition's point of view, a secondary story, he discovers the manuscript of Surveyor Jonathan Pue with its very different kind of intercourse and its very different kind of letter(s). Hester introduces many things into the custom-house—emotionality, passion, motherhood. The most significant of her contributions, however, is her "labyrinth of doubt" (122). Hester unsettles patriarchy's attempt to certify and institutionalize knowledge, especially of its future. She weds history to fiction, the desire for continuity and even certainty to the acknowledgment that all knowledge is tentative, fictitious.

In order to become something more than a "tolerably good Surveyor of the Customs" (68) and "go forth a man" (70) Hawthorne must end his "term" of confinement (72) in the patriarchal custom-house. He must be born into the world. He must, in other words, discover his mother, which is to say, he must discover his origins in the uncertainties of sexual birth. Not accidentally, Hawthorne's novel begins at the moment that Hester, having reached the end of one term and having given birth to her baby daughter, is about to reach the end of another "term of confinement" (103), her prison sentence. The ending of Hawthorne's term and Hester's coincide. It is as if Hawthorne is born into the world as Hester's child.

Throughout the story, the affinities between Hawthorne and Pearl are striking. Like Pearl, Hawthorne is by his ancestors' lights "degenerate," "worthless," and "disgraceful" (41–42). Unlike the "father of the Custom-House," Hawthorne is not "a legitimate son of the revenue system, dyed in the wool, or rather, born in the purple" (47). Rather, like Pearl, he is the illegitimate child, perhaps even the noninheriting female child of the unaffiliated, unmarried mother, cut out of the cloth that is scarlet in hue. "'What is he?' murmurs one gray shadow of my forefathers to the other" (41), echoing the central question of the text: Whose child is Pearl? Given the precariousness of both their pasts, the onus for both Pearl and Hawthorne must be to discover who their fathers are in order to go forth into the world, as man or woman. For Hawthorne the further challenge is to discover his mother as well. Ironically, it is Hawthorne, not Pearl, who follows in Hester's footsteps (as Hester has followed in the footsteps of another woman). When Hawthorne, the male writer, discovers his mother, the result is that he, and not the daughter, will become her true heir. This has to do, in part, with what Hawthorne's Hester, as opposed to Pearl's, gives him in the way of mothering. For Pearl's mother does not teach her the meaning of language (the *A*), while Hawthorne's Hester-as-mother does teach him. It is also, however, related to Hawthorne's basic assumptions about history and philosophy.

One of the most curious aspects of Hawthorne's tale is this substitution of himself for the child of Hester's adulterous union, the child of doubtful origins who, as the letter's double, raises the problem of social inheritance and naming. In order to become a writer Hawthorne does more than discover his female progenitor. He traces his origins to the illicit union (which we are told is kept from the knowledge of the male's heirs) between an official surveyor of the customs and an adulteress, whose lettered intercourse transforms the pattern of male domination. As the sliding of my terms suggests, this official male surveyor is as much Surveyor Pue of "The Custom-House" as the minister Dimmesdale within the novel itself. Pearl's biological father is Dimmesdale; Hawthorne's spiritual father is this other "official ancestor" (64) with whom Hawthorne shares not a patrinomial but an official name, *Surveyor* Pue and *Surveyor* Hawthorne. What makes Pue different from the other custom-house officials, and therefore what legitimates the historical continuity he inaugurates, is that Pue is willing to acquaint Hawthorne with his maternal "predecessor." Even more, he exhorts him to his "filial duty" (64), which is to take up her forgotten, purloined letter.[7] Hester Prynne, Surveyor Pue, and Surveyor Hawthorne constitute a peculiar family at best. But this reconstruction of the family suggests the critical importance for Hawthorne of family itself, of two-parent, heterosexual descent, as the basis on which moral history proceeds: a father who determines the "official" lines of inheritance (by providing a name) and a mother who will insure that the official will never depart from the "fictitious," from the doubts which names cannot dissolve any more than language can and which therefore become the basis for the other-directedness of moral-historical process.

In order to write Hawthorne must recover the letter. Simultaneously he must recover his female "predecessor" in order to know that writing both names our relationship to a past encoded in words and names and raises doubts about it. Discovering his origins in sexuality, the son confronts the fact that knowledge of the father (and hence of history) can never be certain; that fathers may be official ancestors rather than biological ones. In this way the son entertains the doubts of paternity, and thus of identity, which patriarchy tries to banish. He comes to consider the possibility of the illegitimacy of his birth; and hence the illegitimacy of history. *The Scarlet Letter*, in which Hawthorne retrieves a lost American history, is itself what we might call an illegitimate text. It is explicitly founded upon the illicit activities of prowling in the attic of the custom-house and snooping into sexual secrets. More important than this, as a fiction it represents, in Hawthorne's cultural context, a somewhat suspicious activity, made even more suspect by Hawthorne's bastardization of form in a work which is both history and romance. Bastard writer of a bastard text, Hawthorne magnificently defines an American tradition of cultural subversion and hence freedom.

Hawthorne's objectives in recovering the mother could not be more moral—either for history or for writing. Yet Hawthorne's substitution of himself for the daughter constitutes an act of aggression difficult to ignore.

I cannot fully explore this aggression here. It has to do with processes of identity formation, which are a crucial aspect of the novel's subject, and which have to do with skepticism as a vehicle of self-definition. But Hawthorne's male takeover of one of his major characters also figures his inability, despite his fondest wishes, to exceed his own male prejudice. What is at stake for Hawthorne is the very issue of the future; and this issue, Hawthorne believes, must remain within a paradigm of history which, for all Hawthorne's attempts to wrestle it out of the hands of patriarchy, is nonetheless male dominated, both imaginatively and substantively. It is important in this context that in Hawthorne's view, the patriarchal custom-house, though sterile and dead, still contains the "forgotten" letter, the letter that has been kept from the "knowledge of [its] heirs" (61). Even (or especially) patriarchal society contains the knowledge which both men and women need, though this knowledge has, as it were, been purloined by history. The letter, Hester's mark, contains the secret of the very loins concealed in the title of the Poe story to which Hawthorne's *Scarlet Letter* may well be alluding. Poe's story, critics have noted, also has to do with sexual secrets, and with the relationship between those secrets and the mysteries of writing.

In the final analysis, Hawthorne is more concerned in *The Scarlet Letter* with facilitating processes of historical inheritance than with reconstructing the idea of history itself. Despite his recognition of the Puritans' abuse of history, through their repression of women, Hawthorne, as male writer, proposes the same male solution that informs most of his other romances. At the end of the novel Hester rejoins public history. She assumes responsibility for history. Indeed, she becomes history: Hawthorne's history, his reader's, the history of America itself. From one point of view, Hawthorne's incorporation of Hester into American history, *as* American history, is an important gesture toward opening the tradition to women. Living on the outskirts of history, on the margins of civilization, Hester, like Ishmael in *Moby Dick*, or like the black McCaslins (Beauchamps) in Faulkner's *Go Down, Moses*, embodies a history that has been lost or marginalized. This is the history that defies the covenantal authority of white Anglo-Saxon males, who would prevent women, blacks, and others from entering American society. To adapt Walter Benjamin's thinking, we may say that Hawthorne restores to conscious memory a history that the dominant culture has repressed. This, in itself, establishes the book's centrality in the current discussion of textual openness and the literary canon. But in order to thus reinstate Hester's history (and thereby women's history), Hawthorne can only reinstitute history itself, the public record of social events, as the place in which human beings will work out the differences between them. Hawthorne expands the concept of history as far as he can in the direction of those who have been excluded from history. Yet he cannot get beyond the terms of his own masculinity. He cannot get beyond history itself.[8]

Even more problematic, Hawthorne defines the skepticism upon which the knowledge and enactment of a free, moral history depend in terms which may foreclose for women themselves the possibility of a full skeptical consciousness, and hence of full participation in the historical process. For Hawthorne has Hester ask the question she cannot ask, Whose child is Pearl? Skepticism and history may not be joined for women as they are for men. Indeed, unlike a man, whose doubts about his own past can assist him in dealing with his uncertain feelings about present and future and become a basis for freeing his own children from himself, a woman may find no aid for her relationship to her children in her doubts about her parents. The community's question, Whose child is Pearl? reproduces the child's own question, Who is my father? It can stand, therefore, for the basic inquiry into self-identity; and hence it can serve as Hawthorne's own question, Who am I? There is a perfect symmetry between the father's inability to know his child and the child's inability to identify his father—or, for that matter, his (or her) mother. The "shifting scenes" of Hester's first thoughts as she stands on the scaffold in the public square, thinking back on old England, suggest that this symmetry does not exist for the woman; and this may in part explain why or how Hawthorne substitutes himself for Pearl. Hawthorne realizes that only the male child can use the question, Who are my parents? in order to assert his children's independence from him: my children have had other roots, he tells us in the "Custom-House," and they will have different destinies. Not only is a woman's relationship to her biological offspring different from a man's, but it represents an asymmetry in her own experience of the world. This asymmetry has specifically historical implications. Still on the scaffold, Hester reveals that her reality consists exclusively of the letter and the child. The past has "vanished" (86).

Feminist criticism has been unnecessarily hard on Hawthorne. Nonetheless, the questions it raises have opened Hawthorne's novel to new and different scrutiny. The strength of Hawthorne's book lies in its ability to continue to respond to the questions we put to it. Indeed, *The Scarlet Letter* not only withstands contemporary investigations, it benefits from them. For even in the area of female skepticism, contemporary feminist romance has something to learn from Hawthorne's novel. Granted Hawthorne's major concern in *The Scarlet Letter* is not the women's cause (which he vehemently denounces in his sketch of Ann Hutchinson and in the figure of Zenobia in *The Blithedale Romance*). It is, however, the tendency, expressed in all human beings, regardless of gender, to convert history into the repetition and reflection of self. It is here that Hawthorne's aesthetics outdistance his philosophy. Even though Hawthorne has Hester formulate her skepticism in the possibly inappropriate male question, he has her enact the problems inherent in the mother's knowledge that the child does reproduce her. Again and again Hester dramatizes the ungendered human instinct to make the world into a mirror of self, thus identifying the source of patriarchy's own attempts to control history. Throughout the text, Hawthorne inverts the scheme of patriarchal progeneration and inheritance. He turns the tables on the Puritan patriarchy and proposes in its stead an alternate matriarchal scheme, which will not name the father. Yet matriarchy proves no more nurturing, no more capable of establishing human freedom, than patriarchy. Though the novel's elaboration of the matriarchal alternative is pervasive, I will not go into it here. My point is that for Hawthorne parenting itself causes the problems of social coercion and authoritarianism. The parthenogenesis implicit in patriarchy or matriarchy reveals the desire of all human beings, regardless of sex, to replicate themselves infinitely into the future.

Instead of going this route, Hawthorne tries to discover in the dynamics of family relationship and cultural interrelations forces to oppose the all-consuming egos of women as well as of men. Throughout the book Hawthorne tests varying family arrangements: the single-parent, single-sex family of Hester and Pearl, for example; or the nuclear family defined biologically by Dimmesdale, Hester, and Pearl; or legally by Chillingworth, Hester, and Pearl. He finds all of these family units wanting, because none of them break the tyrannical force of the individual's desire for self-replication. Yet family is crucial to Hawthorne's larger historical goals. Therefore he constructs an ideal family, consisting of himself, Hester, and his spiritual father and her spiritual lover, Surveyor Pue. Significantly the resolution of the problem of the family occurs, not within the present moment of the novel, but through the communal reconstitution of the family, over time, in history.

What Hawthorne intuits but cannot formally argue is that to know the world beyond the shadow of a doubt will not release us from the desire to make the world into self. Indeed, it may even complicate and retard the evolution of a meaningful skeptical consciousness. Hawthorne recognizes that all of us—men and women—must cultivate our doubts, entertain them Emersonian-fashion. In reclaiming the mother Hawthorne reintroduces the doubts patrimony dissolves. In imagining himself, first as Pearl, and finally as Hester, Hawthorne, for all his inability to escape certain stereotypes of the woman, demonstrates his own ability to imagine himself as totally other. Insofar as Hester and Pearl are his creative offspring, they represent a futurity (like his own biological progeny) which the author intentionally releases into a future which, like the past, must be seen as indeterminate and doubtful. Hawthornean historical romance constitutes a gesture toward dispossessing even the fictive mirrors of self. Hawthorne does not even simply fabricate a female self. He reconstructs her out of the historical Ann Hutchinson. He does not invent Surveyor Pue; he inherits him. In finding himself in the ancestral mirror that he does not create and by accepting the fact, simultaneously, that these ancestral reflections defy his attempts wholly to discover himself, Hawthorne performs vital gestures of creative inheritance, which he bequeaths to a tradition also free to discover and invent. Every effort of his story is to resist the self-reflection that is nonetheless inevitably part of the perceptual, creative condition. Hawthorne inserts himself as writer between past, present, and future, all of which must be acknowledged, though none can be possessed. And like the *w* he inserts into his patrinomial,[9] he finds his unique, personal signature in the lettered intercourse, which, raising our doubts, generates our hopes as well.

NOTES

1. See Emily Miller Budick, *Fiction and Historical Consciousness: The American Romance Tradition* (New Haven, 1989). Behind this book are readings of the American Puritans by Sacvan Bercovitch, such as *The Puritan Origins of the American Self* (New Haven, 1975), and ideas about skepticism and writing developed by Stanley Cavell in, for example, *The Claim of Reason: Wittgenstein, Skepticism, Morality, and Tragedy* (Oxford, 1979) and *The Senses of Walden* (New York, 1972).

2. See Nathaniel Hawthorne, *The Scarlet Letter* (Harmondsworth, 1984), pp. 116, 119, 122; hereafter cited in text.

3. See Stanley Cavell, *Disowning Knowledge in Six Plays of Shakespeare* (Cambridge, 1987), esp. pp. 15 ff. and 193–221.

4. This is David Van Leer's claim in "Hester's Labyrinth: Transcendental Rhetoric in Puritan Boston," in *New Essays on The Scarlet Letter*, ed. Michael J. Colacurcio (Cambridge, 1985), pp. 57–100.

5. As Charles Feidelson already suggested, long before semiology and its offspring had taken hold of the literary subject and necessitated such responses: "As a single letter, the most indeterminate of all symbols, and first letter of the alphabet, the beginning of all communication, Hester's emblem represents a potential point of coherence within a manifold historical experience" ("*The Scarlet Letter*," in *Hawthorne Centenary Essays*, ed. Roy Harvey Pearce (Columbus, Ohio, 1964], p. 37). For a deconstructive reading of the *Letter*, see Millicent Bell, "The Obliquity of Signs: *The Scarlet Letter*," *The Massachusetts Review*, 23 (1982), 9–26. Bell nonetheless concludes that Hawthorne means for us to try to interpret the letter. See also Earl H. Rovit, "Ambiguity in Hawthorne's *Scarlet Letter*," in *Studies in The Scarlet Letter*, ed. Arlin Turner (Columbus, Ohio, 1970), pp. 120–32, who argues that "this novel is at last as much about the ambiguity of and impossibility of meaning, as it is about meaning itself" (p. 128).

6. For the case against Hawthorne see Louise DeSalvo, *Nathaniel Hawthorne* (Brighton, Sussex, 1987), who summarizes the salient criticism, for and against the novel, on pp. 24–38; see also Gloria C. Erlich, *Family Themes and Hawthorne's Fiction: The Tenacious*

Web (New Brunswick, NJ., 1984); David Leverenz, "Mrs. Hawthorne's Headache: Reading *The Scarlet Letter*," in *The (M)other Tongue: Essays in Feminist Psychoanalytic Interpretation*, ed. Shirley Nelson Garner, Claire Kahane, and Madelon Sprengnether (Ithaca, N.Y., 1985), pp. 194–216; Judith Fryer, *The Faces of Eve: Women in the Nineteenth-Century American Novel* (New York, 1976); and Neal F. Doubleday, "Hawthorne's Hester and Feminism," *PMLA*, 54 (1939), 825–28. Nina Baym defends the book from the feminist attack in "Thwarted Nature: Nathaniel Hawthorne as Feminist," in *American Novelists Revisited: Essays in Feminist Criticism*, ed. Fritz Fleischmann (Boston, 1982), pp. 58–77 and "Hawthorne's Women: The Tyranny of Social Myths," *The Centennial Review*, 15 (1971), 250–72. Some of Baym's ideas are reformulated in her book-length study of Hawthorne, *The Shape of Hawthorne's Career* (Ithaca, N.Y., 1976).

7. The root meaning of *purloin* is not to steal but to *put away* or *render ineffectual*. It may well be that Pue, who is spiritually united with the mother/woman, evokes another of Hawthorne's ancestors, Edgar Allan Poe. Playing as he is with letters and names Hawthorne would not have missed the convenient similarity between the names Pue and Poe. He further emphasizes the connection between the two by dwelling on Pue's "mental part and the internal operations of his head" (p. 60). Hawthorne's discovery of the story, he tells us, leads him to "a hundredfold repetition" that sets into motion further patterns of "remembering" (p. 64). If the death of Hawthorne's mother in 1848 prompted his desire to rediscover the mother, perhaps Poe's death in 1849, while Hawthorne was composing his *Scarlet Letter*, activated his search for an appropriate father. Certainly the title of Hawthorne's novel can be understood as alluding to the title of Poe's "The Purloined Letter."

8. In "The A-Politics of Ambiguity in *The Scarlet Letter*," *New Literary History*, 19 (1988), 629–54, Sacvan Bercovitch has discussed the ideological imperatives that seal Hawthorne's work against endless open-endedness. The present essay has benefited both from Bercovitch's recent work on *The Scarlet Letter* and from his useful comments on my own thinking in this matter.

9. For a discussion of Hawthorne's insertion of the *to* into his name, see John T. Irwin, *American Hieroglyphics: The Symbol of the Egyptian Hieroglyphics in the American Renaissance* (New Haven, 1980).

JANICE B. DANIEL

"*Apples of the Thoughts and Fancies*": *Nature as Narrator in* The Scarlet Letter

Even the most casual reader of Nathaniel Hawthorne cannot fail to notice his conspicuous and consistent focus on nature. Through his description of natural surroundings as well as his use of figurative language, he works into his fiction a place of special importance for nature. As a Romanticist who gives abundant literary attention to nature, as an individual writer who attempts to remain true to the vision of his own art, and as a human being who treasures the importance of nature in his own life experiences, Hawthorne gives distinct attention in his works to the natural environment. One of the first in the literary field to notice this propensity was his contemporary, Henry Wadsworth Longfellow, in his comments on the *Twice-told Tales*:

> But it is one of the high attributes of the poetic mind, to feel a universal sympathy with Nature, both in the material world and in the soul of man. It identifies itself likewise with every object of its sympathy, giving it new sensation and poetic life, whatever that object may be, whether man, bird, beast, flower, or star.... Of such is the author of this book. (329)

Another notable comment comes from Herman Melville who brings Hawthorne into dose metaphorical proximity with the natural world: "For

From *American Transcendental Quarterly* 7, no. 4 (December 1993), pp. 307–319. © 1993 by The University of Rhode Island.

no less ripe than ruddy are the apples of the thoughts and fancies in this sweet Man of Mosses" (241).

Actually, Hawthorne's recognition of the extraordinary attributes of nature stems from a quite personal viewpoint. The American Notebooks reveals his individual veneration for nature's handiwork:

> Man's finest workmanship, the closer you observe it, the more imperfections it shows.... Whereas, what may look coarse and rough in Nature's workmanship will show an infinitely minute perfection, the closer you look into it. The reason of the minute superiority of Nature's work over man's is, that the former works from the innermost germ, while the latter works merely superficially. (VIII:157–158)

On a literal level, this passage reveals a writer's admiration for his natural surroundings and his humble acknowledgment of his own human inadequacies. However, if we explore his focus on nature in his fiction, we understand what this writer has managed to accomplish. In his own "superficial" approach to his human "workmanship," he has incorporated an individual approach to the literary treatment of nature which becomes an "innermost germ" that grows vital to his art and to our appreciation of it.

One such "innermost germ" has received little critical attention, yet it marks Hawthorne's use of nature in fiction as being distinctly different from other writing of the times and enables the reader to study his work with new insight. This particular approach is his use of the rhetorical figure of personification of nature. In addition to his traditional usage of this figure to endow objects in nature with human physical traits, he gives conspicuous attention to the ability of nature to reveal emotion, feeling, and passion. For example, his trees groan in fear, his mountains become angry, his clouds weep, his winds are mischievous, and his waves laugh. This "literary" feature lends a more "human" aspect to Hawthorne's fiction which impresses the reader with a strong sense of voice as if the author wishes to have nature interact with his fictional characters. Because this feat is implausible, he utilizes nature personification as a device for narrative voice which provides disembodied, personal attitudes which would otherwise not be present. This voice can be sympathetic, judgmental, ironic, warm, or harsh; it may criticize, approve, question, or confirm. As Reuben leaves the dying Roger Malvin, for example, sensitivity is provided by "a gloom on Nature's face, as if she sympathized with mortal pain and sorrow" (X:345–346); or deference is displayed when Reverend Hooper's veil is never blown aside by a wind which "respected his dreadful secret" (IX:48).

Whatever the various particular slants, Hawthorne's use of personification as a narrative device displays both a pattern and a purpose. This imagery is a vehicle with which the author reveals to his reader the underlying message of his consistent theme of community—especially the communities of man and nature and he brings these two worlds into closer proximity than his critics have previously recognized. The words of his narrator in the essay "Snow-flakes" give some insight into his intentions: "Would it [the wind] might inspire me to sketch out the personification of a New-England winter! And that idea, if I can seize the snow-wreathed figures that flit before my fancy, shall be the theme of the next page" (IX:346). In fact, personification plays a crucial part in developing his theme of community in more than a few of his pages.

An analysis of *The Scarlet Letter* reveals an author who thematically juxtaposes the communities of humankind and nature. Pearl, who is ostracized from her community of humans, is received into nature's community by personified sunshine which is "glad of such a playmate" (I:184); and Hester, who likewise experiences isolation, finds approval in a natural environment where each green leaf is gladdened by "a sudden smile of heaven" reflected in the merry gleam of a little brook (I:203). In his article, "Personification and Community," Clifford Siskin explains how this rhetorical figure can be the appropriate choice for such a theme:

> The personification of human faculties or attributes requires the transplantation of a part from the body of the individual (e.g., each man's reason) to the body of the community (e.g., reason as a standard faculty shared by all). Personifying and generalizing are, in that sense, interrelated processes. In rhetorical terms, personifications of this sort function as a synecdochic affirmation of community; the parts personified stand for the uniformity of their wholes. (377)

Nature personification, for Hawthorne, is an effective vehicle with which to bridge the gap between the community of humankind and the community of nature, and through his figurative manipulation of nature's ability to provide additional perspective, Hawthorne finds an expression for his theme without making direct authorial comments.

Admittedly, many readers of his fiction have learned to be alert to an elusive authorial presence, but as we become more aware of the role of personification in his work, we discover that the authorial presence is not so much elusive as it is placed into another voice. Many studies of narrative support the idea that a disembodied voice can be an effective device which allows the narrator to have two differing perspectives. John D. Kalb explains that one type of appropriate narrator is one who has free access to the roles of both participant and spectator in an event. "Removal of oneself from the scene of that event is necessary for the clear and fruitful observation and understanding for the event and one's participation in it" (169), and the advantage is that the story may be experienced first-hand, yet the spectator's distance "allows and warrants observation, speculation, and evaluation from without" (170). Like the narrator in "Sights from a Steeple," who calls himself "a watchman, all-heeding and unheeded" (IX:192), personified nature has the similar vantage point of being both present yet inconspicuous. We sense an additional consciousness, for example, when Pearl's desperate shrieks, upon seeing her mother and the minister at the brook, cause the woods to reverberate around her "as if a hidden multitude were lending their sympathy and encouragement" (I:210). For the moment, authorial presence steps aside and lets nature provide appropriate reactions.

In addition, Gerard Genette's discussion of voice defines two narrative postures—the heterodiegetic narrator who is absent from the story and the homodiegetic narrator who can be present as a secondary character (243–247). While Hawthorne does not project natural objects as characters into his fiction, his use of personification closely approaches a combination of Genette's two definitions: as narrating author, he is absent from the events, but he often hands over narrative perspective to nature which becomes a temporary secondary entity. When Hawthorne, as narrator, relates the tenuous encounter between Hester and Dimmesdale in the forest, but at the same time provides additional perspective from groaning old trees above them, he distances himself from the situation yet provides effective emotional commentary.

In the plentiful amount of modern critical theories of narrative technique, there appears to be an absence of a consideration of nature imagery as a possibility for additional perspective. Wayne Booth's analysis of distance and point of view suggests one type of narrator which closely approaches what Hawthorne accomplishes with personification. He describes the "implied author" who amounts to the author's "second self" which "is usually a highly refined and selected version, wiser, more sensitive, more perceptive than any real man could be" (175). Although Booth is exploring the field of human voices, this second self is apparent in Hawthorne's transferral of perspective to the natural environment in which his characters enact their human dramas.

The human dramas which transpire in Hawthorne's fiction have long been recognized as those in which he develops his theme of the importance of community. In *The Scarlet Letter*, Hester's entire ordeal begins with her ostracism from participation in the mainstream of mankind, but as she turns her face toward the assembly of humanity in the marketplace, she senses "that whatever sympathy she might expect lay in the larger and warmer heart of the multitude" (I:64–65). Ironically, the most pronounced sensitivity emanates, not from the human community, but from the natural environment. Whereas Hawthorne's theme of community characteristically plays itself out in his works with the interactions of humans, in this novel and on another level he further emphasizes his message by depicting nature in a community of its own, in an existence parallel to humankind's emotional and intellectual world. No emotional or intellectual interactions with humans occur; however, nature's close proximity to humans allows it to supply an additional perspective on the human dilemmas. The two communities are juxtaposed as occupying the same physical spaces, but no interaction takes place. Frequently, Hawthorne's use of personification hints at nature's desire to reach out to humans, to make attempts at bringing the two worlds closer together; but, for the most part, humankind's community and the natural community are separate, parallel entities, with personification of nature becoming the narrative voice which establishes this situation and yet bridges the gap. In Hawthorne's parallel arrangement of the worlds of nature and humans, he allows his reader to experience them both together as he uses both to enhance theme.

This process begins immediately in Chapter One, "The Prison Door":

> But, on one side of the portal, and rooted almost at the threshold, was a wild rose-bush, covered, in this month of June, with its delicate gems, which might be imagined to offer their fragrance and fragile beauty to the prisoner as he went in, and to the condemned criminal as he came forth to his doom in token that the deep heart of Nature could pity and be kind to him. (I:48)

Hawthorne promptly establishes a voice which expresses a commentary in the form of sympathy and kindness, attitudes which are absent from the human element in the scene. The rose bush is nature's means of communicating these feelings, and personification is the author's means of speaking to his reader. As he proceeds to narrate his "tale of human frailty and sorrow" (I:48), he consistently employs personification of nature as a special narrative device which provides a voice in addition to—or in place of—his own. Using this rhetorical figure provides an additional strategy with which he can be the elusive author who lets not a character but nature provide additional perspectives. One point of view may be from a forest whose heart rejoices at

Hester's temporary separation the letter; another may be voiced by a brook which mournfully laments an ominous future event; or yet another may be one of approval from sunshine which favors Pearl rather than her mother. When these various voices, perspectives, attitudes, or moods are examined, they consistently draw attention to nature as a community juxtaposed to the community of humans.

Many times in the novel, the human community is broken into two separate entities—the macrocosm of the Puritans of Boston and the microcosm of the alienated characters—a dichotomous arrangement which reinforces the pattern of nature's separate and parallel situation to man. From the very beginning, Hester's world is one which is separate from the community of humans around her. As she emerges from the prison to face the crowd, the townspeople gaze as if they are seeing a stranger for the first time, and the letter produces the effect of taking "her out of the ordinary relations with humanity, and inclosing her in a sphere by herself" (I:54). Another noticeable lack of restraint to treat Hester as "different" is evidenced in the behavior of the children who "turn their heads to continue to stare in her face" (I:54). Later, when Pearl is older, it is the children again who gather around her and her mother and "not unfrequently reviled them with their tongues" because they "had got a vague idea of something outlandish, unearthly, or at variance with ordinary fashions, in the mother and child" (I:94).

The children are representative of a community which severs from itself two other human beings who are forced into an ostracized community of their own. "Mother and daughter stood together in the same circle of seclusion from human society" (I:94), a narrow sphere which takes them into the same wide physical spaces as other humans (religious services, the market place, the city sweets) but without emotional, intellectual, or social interaction. Walks through the city streets, for example, present them with a populace which "Pearl saw, and gazed intently, but never sought to make acquaintance" (I:94). They are forced into a community of two which is separate from, yet in parallel existence to, the people of Boston, and Hawthorne's use of personification often provides voices from nature's community which is likewise present but separate.

For example, while Hester continually finds herself the target of ostracism by comments from ministers, citizens of Boston, and children in the streets, nature shares the knowledge of her shame yet provides a certain restraint that is absent from the actions of the humans. The natural community recognizes Hester's shame but does not choose to voice it aloud: "... all nature knew of it; it could have caused her no deeper pang, had the leaves of the trees whispered the dark story among themselves,—had the summer breeze murmured about it,—had the wintry blast shrieked it aloud!" (I:85). The narrator is providing an additional perspective—an understanding silence from nature's community—which gives balance to the vocal reproofs of the human community.

With a comparable balance, Hawthorne introduces the adjoining forest, a region where he concentrates our attention on nature as a world which is also separate from, yet parallel to, the world of humans in nearby Boston. The "personality" of this environment assumes various identities. For the nearby civilized community, it is "the wild, free atmosphere of an unredeemed, unchristianized, lawless region" (I:201): a realm for the Black Man, a meeting place for his followers, a habitat for the savages, and a locale for sin. At a time when the early colonists have recently separated themselves from the Old World and all that is civilized, this "precinct of the Devil and his American counterpart, the Indian" (Fossum 6) carries connotations of all that is associated with evil and implications that this evil influence will filter into their territory. Theirs is "a story set at the rough edge of civilization. The dark forest is still ominously near, and the dark dangers from foreign servants, untamed children, stubborn heretics, idle Indians, or hell-bound witches seem to threaten the progress of Puritan civilization's sacred new orders" (Herzog 7).

One would expect the temperament of this natural world to be hostile to any positive associations with humans; however, quite the opposite is true. This environment affords Pearl safe surroundings in which to roam and play with the freedom and abandonment of childhood; it offers Hester a kindred association for her innate passion and sense of independence; and it furnishes the lovers with a free atmosphere in which to ignore the confines of a judgmental society. It is to the persona of this natural world that Hawthorne many times gives a voice or an attitude in order to provide additional perspective to an emerging theme of closeness between the separate worlds of nature and humans.

The forest, for example, in a world separated from civilization, is where two lovers are allowed to be alone for the first time in seven years without the frowning disapproval or condemnation of their human peers. Hawthorne uses the reactions of a personified nature to portray a more benevolent view than would be issued from the human element:

> All at once, as with a sudden smile of heaven, forth burst the sun-
> shine, pouring a very flood into the obscure forest, gladdening
> each green leaf, transmuting the yellow fallen ones to gold, and
> gleaming adown the gray trunks of the solemn trees. The objects
> that had made a shadow hitherto, embodied the brightness now.

> The course of the little brook might be traced by its merry gleam afar into the wood's heart of mystery, which had become a mystery of joy. (I:202–203)

Sunshine, leaves, trees, brook, and woods are not interacting participants in the human drama but have a vantage point in close proximity to the action. For a short while, Hester and Pearl's community of two has increased to three, and the disembodied voices of nature furnish the narrator with an additional perspective with which to underscore for the reader the importance of intimate communion. This method of additional perception closely resembles the narrative figure which Genette recognizes in his analysis of internal focalization; he identifies one type of focalizer as a point of view character—a character other than the focal character who provides incidental information about a scene that the latter is not able to see (197). As Susan Lanser explains, "One voice is narrating while another consciousness is responsible for the perceptions, thoughts, feelings, or orientation to the scene that the narrator, in turn, relays" (142). In light of this theory, Hawthorne does not present nature as a character but as "another consciousness," in this case emanating from nature in a forest region which accepts rather than rejects its human counterparts.

This additional voice manifests itself in undisguised commentary during the reunion between Hester and Dimmesdale. The story's narrator fills in the details of the couple's gloom, the obscure forest, and the dreary forest track; but it is personification of nature which provides the human element of sympathy as "one solemn old tree groaned dolefully to another, as if telling the sad story of the pair that sat beneath, or constrained to forebode evil to come" (I:195). In one of the most emotional scenes of the novel, Hawthorne distances himself and yet makes indirect comments to his reader through the use of this effective narrative device which implies sympathy as well as dread.

The reader's sympathy is not directed solely toward the novel's lovers; it is elicited for other characters and for other reasons. When Pearl sees her mother with the minister, she reacts with violent gestures and contortions accompanied by wild, piercing shrieks "which the woods reverberated on all sides; so that, alone as she was in her childish and unreasonable wrath, it seemed as if a hidden multitude were lending her their sympathy and encouragement" (I:210). Again, the narrator supplies the description of Pearl's reactions, and personification provides commentary and focus on the fragility of relationships. Just as Pearl senses that her community of two is threatened, nature lends the appropriate element of human reaction in an environment which is void of humans outside her limited community.

In fact, it is Pearl with whom the parallel community of nature reacts most animatedly and with the most striking intent to communicate. As the child plays alone near the stream, the great forest becomes her playmate: it offers her partridge berries; its wild denizens are not afraid; a pigeon utters "a sound as much of greeting as alarm"; a squirrel chatters; a fox looks inquisitively; a wolf offers "his savage head to be patted by her hand"; and the flowers whisper to her to adorn herself with them. "The truth seems to be, however, that the mother-forest, and these wild things which it nourished, all recognized a kindred wildness in the human child" (I:204–205).

She is, after all, "a Child of Nature" whom Darrel Abel describes as one who can "discover conscious and valuable affinities with the natural world and enjoy an active and formative relationship with it" (192). She has been produced by a natural act of passion, and like the rose by the prison door, she is wild and organic, a human child who "could not be made amenable to rules ... whose elements were ... all in disorder; or with an order peculiar to themselves" (I:91). Pearl's sense of order gravitates toward the natural environment where she is more at ease than with humans. As Abel explains, "Her relationship with Nature was intensified by her ostracism. Her dwelling with Hester on the verge of the forest, at the outskirts of the town, symbolized her more intimate association with nature than with the human community" (195). It is important to remember that Pearl's interaction with her natural surroundings remains on the physical level; there is no emotional or intellectual bonding. Instead, she reflects the untamed qualities of her primitive environment. She is perhaps even closer to the elements of the forest than its savage denizens who come to share the holiday at the end of the story: "She ran and looked the wild Indian in the face; and he grew conscious of a nature wilder than his own" (I:244).

Pearl is therefore more successful than the other characters in being receptive to nature's efforts to achieve some level of rapport with humans. She is alert to the sound of the forest stream, "a babble, kind, quiet, soothing, but melancholy," and asks it to "Pluck up a spirit, and do not be all the time sighing and murmuring!" (I:186). She senses that the little brook has something to say, and her mother suggests that the message would be about a sorrow if Pearl were capable of having one. Pearl is determined to "mingle a more lightsome cadence" (I:187) with the brook's voice, but this voice is just as determined to communicate with the reader concerning imminent events in the story:

> But the little stream would not be comforted, and still kept telling its unintelligible secret of some very mournful mystery that had happened—or making a prophetic lamentation about something

that was yet to happen—within the verge of the dismal forest.
(I:187)

In this case, nature's sympathy is tinged with dread or foreboding, and Pearl is
the one who notices even though she misunderstands. Perhaps she is capable
of being more receptive because of her own "natural" position. Hawthorne
does not fully humanize her until the final moments of the story; therefore,
having been "exiled from the concrete world of human sympathy," she does
not experience "either the limits or the possibilities of the concrete human
life" (Feidelson 75–76) and is thus more prone to discourse with nature.

Some of the novel's characters are not as cognizant as Pearl in perceiving
nature's efforts to establish contact, but Hawthorne's personification indicates
that the efforts are present, nonetheless, and that they are sometimes directed
toward minor characters. Governor Bellingham's garden has sprouted a
pumpkin vine which

> ... rooted at some distance, had run across the intervening space,
> and deposited one of its gigantic products directly beneath the
> hall-window; as if to warn the Governor that this great lump of
> vegetable gold was as rich an ornament as New England earth
> would offer him. (I:106–107)

This diminutive detail might appear insignificant until we understand, a few
pages later, that the Governor's inability to nurture this plant or to heed its
"warning" to recognize something of value parallels his lack of appreciation
for Hester's plight. Also, the tenacious vine might well represent Hester's
determination at this point in the story not to lose her child. Regardless
of any symbolic intent, Hawthorne again depicts nature existing in an
untamed world parallel with the human civilized one and again provides a
voice in addition to the narrator's to comment on the situation. In its own
community, nature tends to be uncivilized and undomesticated; indeed, in
this novel, nature is present as a forest and as a sea. There are no meadows,
yards, farms, or fields, and the only garden (with the exception of the
graveyard) is inhabited by a wild, uncultivated vine. In Hawthorne we see no
"precarious semantic distinction between wild nature and tame nature. All
nature, for Hawthorne, is wild" (Bell 184).

As Hester and Pearl are forced by a "civilized" community of humans
to form a community of their own, the mother also develops an affinity
for the natural elements and exhibits a wildness of her own. In her life
on the boundaries of town and in parallel daily existence with the Puritan
community, she develops an "estranged point of view at human institutions,

and whatever priests or legislators had established; criticizing all with hardly more reverence than the Indian would feel" (I:199). Hawthorne personifies nature to reveal the mother's recognition of a similar erratic quality in her daughter's naturalness. She compares the child's personality to "the waywardness of an April breeze; which... will sometimes, of its own vague purpose, kiss your cheek with a kind of doubtful tenderness, and play gently with your hair, and then be gone about its other idle business" (I:179). Hawthorne's fusion of Pearl's disposition with a natural object underscores his recurring depiction of nature's potential for human emotion.

The use of sunlight plays a dominant role in this novel, and Hawthorne's personification of it provides commentary on his characters and communication with his readers. Richard Fogle's well-known interpretation of Hawthorne's imagery emphasizes that much of it is in the form of things being transfigured and that sunshine is the light of nature which is indispensable as a tool for the author's intention toward denoting reality (36–40), but the role of sunlight in its approval of Pearl and its avoidance of Hester also provides the reader with Hawthorne's reality of a balanced perspective of two differing viewpoints. The light lingered about the lonely child, as if glad of such a playmate, until her mother had drawn almost nigh enough to step into the magic circle too" (I:184). Not only does the narrator give the sunshine the capacity to "play," but he lets Pearl voice the personification of its attitude: "'Mother,' said little Pearl, 'the sunshine does not love you. It runs away and hides itself, because it is afraid of something on your bosom'" (I:183). Consequently, personification fuses with Pearl's comments in order to underscore the author's intent to bring attention to the parallel entities of nature and humans.

Of noticeable significance is the fact that Hawthorne's use of personification in *The Scarlet Letter* focuses almost entirely on only two of the four main characters—the mother and her daughter—because their world, like the one of nature, is parallel to that of society. The forest and the sea exist on the boundaries of the town just as these two characters are "placed" in a cottage on the boundary of their fellow humans. Just as neither of them can interact with their human community, so nature cannot interact with the world of humans.

However, through the use of figurative language, the novel's natural environment can provide additional perspective for purposes of narrative and theme. With a consistent pattern of nature's perspective on the fictional situations, Hawthorne achieves the romancer's artistic distance from human experience and, in addition, provides his reader with a better understanding of what the narrator furnishes. He transfers his authorial presence onto natural objects which are allowed to observe or to speak for him.

Therefore, Hawthorne's personification of nature is artistically intentional and not merely an occasional or superficial exercise in figurative language for descriptive purposes. His focus on nature is by design and is not to be associated with the extravagant imagery which was popular with many of the century's writers of sentimental fiction—"nature samplers" who indulged in glorifying nature and touching up its qualities to accommodate mood and who "tossed off sentiments like these by the candyboxful" (Branch 145–149). Hawthorne does not "toss off" figurative language; he uses it artistically as a recognizable and purposeful device.

He is a writer who rejects the artificialities of popular fiction and, instead, calls upon the imagination of his audience to collaborate with him in bringing his artistic creations to life (Quirk 224–225). By way of comparison, we remember the dilemma of the showman in "Main-street" when the critic complains that in the diorama, "The trees look more like weeds in a garden, than a primitive forest." The showman's answer may well reflect Hawthorne's request of his readers in accepting personified nature: "Human art has its limits, and we must now and then ask a little aid from the spectator's imagination" (XI:52). Hawthorne's fiction demands a special type of reader whose imagination can be involved in creative interplay with the author in order to give life and meaning to his narratives (Idol 334).

Nor is his imagery to be dismissed as a tendency toward the pathetic fallacy, as it is neither presented in a too-impassioned false emotionalism nor carried to the point of absurdity. As he claims in "The Old Manse," "I have appealed to no sentiment or sensibilities, save such as are diffused among us all" (X:32–33). Whereas Ruskin viewed the pathetic fallacy as stemming from "an excited state of feelings, making us, for the time, more or less irrational" and producing "a falseness in all our impressions of external things" (148), Hawthorne seeks to produce in his reader a cognitive understanding of logical concepts which he presents in his fiction. If we dismiss his use of this valuable rhetorical figure as merely a contrivance, we may discover ourselves in the same situation as the inhabitants of Ernest's village in "The Great Stone Face": "True it is, that if the spectator approached too near, he lost the outline of the gigantic visage, and could discern only a heap of ponderous and gigantic rocks, piled in chaotic ruin one upon another." But, as we likewise step back to acquire a more objective view, the larger picture comes into focus. Just as the villagers begin to perceive a form which seems "positively to be alive" (XI:27), so do we discern Hawthorne's use of personification as an intentional artistic device.

Hawthorne is a writer who does not use imagery as convenient analogy but who goes beyond the pathetic fallacy into using what

Edward H. Davidson has identified as the symbolic spectrum—a means of viewing the world as animate and as capable of having mind—in which "the reader, not the characters themselves, is required to see the ever-continuing drama of these two orders, the natural and the human" (492–493). Hawthorne's effort to bring these two worlds into clearer focus surfaces in his fiction in the form of personification of nature a device which serves him well in shaping his narrative and in sharpening his theme.

WORKS CITED

Abel, Darrel. *The Moral Picturesque: Studies in Hawthorne's Fiction*. West Lafayette, Indiana: Purdue University Press, 1988.

Bell, Michael Davitt. *Hawthorne and the Historical Romance of New England*. Princeton: Princeton University Press, 1971.

Booth, Wayne. "Distance and Point of View: An Essay in Classification." *Essentials of the Theory of Fiction*. Eds. Michael J. Hofman and Patrick D. Murphy. Durham, North Carolina: Duke University Press, 1988. 170–189.

Branch, Douglas. *The Sentimental Years, 1836–1860*. New York: D. Appleton Century Company, 1934.

Davidson, Edward H. "Hawthorne and the Pathetic Fallacy." *The Journal of English and Germanic Philology* 54 (1955): 486–497.

Feidelson, Charles, Jr. "The Scarlet Letter." *Hawthorne Centenary Essays*. Ed. Roy Harvey Pearce. Columbus, Ohio: Ohio State University Press, 1964. 31–77.

Fogle, Richard Harter. *Hawthorne's Imagery: The "Proper Light and Shadow" in the Major Romances*. Norman, Oklahoma: University of Oklahoma Press, 1969.

Fossum, Robert H. *Hawthorne's Inviolable Circle: The Problem of Time*. Deland, Florida: Everett/Edwards, Inc., 1972.

Gennette, Gerard. *Narrative Discourse: An Essay in Method*. Trans. Jane E. Levin. Ithaca, New York: Cornell University Press, 1980.

Hawthorne, Nathaniel. *The Centenary Edition of the Works of Nathaniel Hawthorne*. Vols. I, VIII–XI. Eds. William Charvat et. al. Columbus: Ohio State University Press, 1974.

Herzog, Kristin. *Women, Ethnics, and Exotics: Images of Power in Mid-Nineteenth-Century American Fiction*. Knoxville: University of Tennessee Press, 1983.

———. "Critical Reflections." *Studies in the Novel* 21 (1989): 332–38.

Kalb, John D. "The Anthropological Narrator of Hurston's Their Eyes Were Watching God." *Studies in American Fiction* 16 (1988): 169–180.

Lanser, Susan Sniader. *The Narrative Act: Point of View in Prose Fiction*. Princeton: Princeton University Press, 1981.

Longfellow, Henry Wadsworth. "Hawthorne's Twice-told Tales." *Nathaniel Hawthorne's Tales*. Ed. James McIntosh. New York: W.W. Norton and Company, 1987. 328–330.

Melville, Herman. "Hawthorne and His Mosses." *The Piazza Tales and Other Pieces, 1839–1860*. Chicago: Northwestern University Press and The Newberry Library, 1987. 239–253.

Quirk, Tom. "Hawthorne's Last Tales and 'The Custom-House.'" *ESQ: A Journal of the American Renaissance* 30 (1984): 220–31.

Ruskin, John. *Modern Painters*. Vol. III. London: J.M. Dent and Sons, 1929.

Siskin, Clifford. "Personification and Community: Literary Change in the Mid and Late Eighteenth Century." *Eighteenth Century Studies* 15 (1982): 371–401.

MICHAEL T. GILMORE

Hawthorne and the Making of the Middle Class

I

The currently fashionable triad of American literary studies, race, gender, and class, a triad born of the egalitarian dethroning of the white, male, largely Anglo-Saxon canon, contains its own tacit hierarchy and rests on its own unenunciated principles of exclusion and privileging. Disagreements abound over whether race or gender should occupy the top tier in the new cultural ranking, but about the subordination, even the effacement, of class, there can be no doubt. Few working-class authors have been recuperated— George Lippard, author of *The Quaker City* (1845), is a notable exception from the antebellum period—and no programs in class and its multifarious manifestations have entered college curricula to compete for students with women's studies and African American studies. Class as a thematic or formal consideration, once the obligatory nod has been made, usually recedes to the background, if it does not vanish altogether, while the critic goes about the business of interpreting *Uncle Tom's Cabin* (1852), *Clotel* (1853), or *Pierre* (1852) in the light of racial and feminist concerns.

One might speculate about the reasons for this omission. It could be argued that the assimilation of the children of working-class parents into the white-collar professoriate has dulled academic sensitivity to the reality of socioeconomic difference. Or it might be claimed that the historic

From *Rethinking Class: Literary Studies and Social Formations*, edited by Wai Chee Dimock and Michael T. Gilmore, pp. 215–238. © 1994 by Columbia University Press.

dominance of the middle class in the United States has produced a relatively homogeneous society in which class conflicts have been muted to the point of unimportance. Or if one balks at the notion of an ideological monolith, a related hypothesis offers itself. One might still hold that the United States, in contrast to the stratified nations of Europe where social and economic alterity erupted into armed combat in 1848, subsumes its class divisions under the sign of gender and/or race. What we find in nineteenth-century American writing, goes a version of this argument, is not economic struggle but a clash of gender styles, not a confrontation between social groups but the displacement of a patrician ideal of masculinity by an entrepreneurial or marketplace model.[1]

This paper takes issue with the critical consensus that relegates class to the margins of antebellum American literature. It does so not by examining the novels of a certified labor activist like Lippard, but rather by turning to a familiar and much-analyzed classic of the American Renaissance, *The Scarlet Letter* (1850). Nathaniel Hawthorne, perhaps our most "canonical" nineteenth-century novelist, the writer, indeed, in whom the canon is given birth, maps the emergence of middle-class identity and simultaneously reveals the self-contradictory and unsettled nature of the new configuration. Behind this claim lies the work of historians and students of gender and the family who have shown, convincingly to my mind, that the period when Hawthorne was writing saw the appearance of the middle class in its recognizably modern form. These scholars dispute the idea of an unbroken ideological or class hegemony in the United States. They recount the development of a social formation that declared itself, in part, through gender arrangements, the separation of public and private spheres, and the substitution of naturalism for historical contingency. Their work suggests not so much that class was submerged in gender but rather that gender and the family were imbued with the determinants of class.[2]

Yet Hawthorne's text complicates the findings of these scholars. *The Scarlet Letter* points not simply to the development of an American middle class but also to the highly ambiguous character of that construction. It makes clear that the category of class, at least as the category arises in the Age of Jackson, does not march under the banner of essentialism. Hawthorne's masterpiece amounts to a warning that, in rescuing class from erasure, we must dispel any notion of its being a self-consistent entity.

The social indeterminacies of *The Scarlet Letter* problematize the current view of Hawthorne as an important figure in the formulation of a conservative brand of liberal individualism. According to the interpretation put forward most forcefully by Sacvan Bercovitch, Hawthorne contributed to the building of an ideological consensus that complemented the middle class's coalescence.[3] But the class loyalties knitted into *The Scarlet Letter* seem altogether too unstable to authorize so unambiguous a cultural function for the narrative. And recognizing the textual vacillations fosters a certain skepticism about the critical method of reasoning by analogy or homology. The case for Hawthorne's "liberalism" often seems to rest on structural resemblances between literary and social states of affairs, a mode of demonstration that commonly suppresses evidence of dissimilarity.[4] The resemblances are undeniably there in *The Scarlet Letter*, but the differences are no less real, and Hawthorne's text can be usefully studied to bring out the historical and gender oppositions concealed within literary-social congruity.

It remains true that *The Scarlet Letter* participates in the project of shaping middle-class identity. The novel registers the exfoliation of a socially specific way of life. It encodes the deep structures of the middle class within its discursive patternings and to some degree labors to win consent to that class's dominance by validating its claims to universal legitimacy. But at the same time *The Scarlet Letter* obscures the boundary lines it seems to posit as impermeable. The book undoes its own synchronizations of gender roles, private and public spaces, and socioeconomic categories. Hawthorne's notion of what constitutes middle-class personhood turns out to be internally beleaguered. Patterns of male and female behavior, as pictured in the novel, slide into inversions of themselves, and the tale's image of the present is disrupted by pressure from the past and foreshadowings of the future. To borrow the terminology of Raymond Williams, we might say that Hawthorne's middle class incorporates both residual and proleptically oppositional elements,[5] but because gender is so integral to middle-class character as it crystallizes in the text, sexual ambiguation necessarily accompanies ideological and vocational exchange. The middle-class mother assumes a relation to the social like that of a free-market individualist, while the middle-class father embraces feminized sentiment. Hawthorne's new class threatens to come apart even as it comes into being.

Doubtless these inconsistencies can be traced in part to Hawthorne's own anomalous class position, a matter to which I will return at the end of this paper. But insofar as Hawthorne can be taken as an influential maker and articulator of nineteenth-century American culture, it is possible to generalize from the inconstant allegiances of his greatest work. The reversals and impasses of *The Scarlet Letter* betoken not merely his own unsettled status as an impoverished patrician trying to earn a livelihood by literature. They attest to the instability, the persistent vulnerability, of the ideological closure of the antebellum middle class.

II

Like the word *adultery*, the name of the middle class is never mentioned in *The Scarlet Letter*. The only socioeconomic groupings Hawthorne refers to are the rich and the poor, or, in the antiquated vocabulary the novel sometimes adopts, the high and the low. Hester Prynne is said to receive abuse equally from the poor on whom she bestows her charity and from the "dames of elevated rank" for whom she plies her needle.[6] The mass of Puritans are distinguished from their rulers only by being designated "the people," with little detail provided about their material condition.

Yet like the act of adultery, the middle class occupies a crucial position in Hawthorne's narrative. Following Roland Barthes—who defined the bourgeoisie as the class "which does *not want to be named*"—one might see the avoidance of nomination as the proof of textual centrality.[7] Hawthorne's labeling of those who are presumably neither rich nor poor as "the people" would be in keeping with this universalizing or self-excising impulse. Fortunately, there is more to go on than deletion. Hawthorne writes that the Puritan order supplanted the "system of ancient prejudice" associated with "nobles and kings" (164). He invites us to view the inhabitants of seventeenth-century Boston as the precursors of post-feudal—that is, bourgeois—civilization. But historical commonplace dissolves into anachronism, and anticipation gets conflated with actuality as the Puritan past merges into the American present. For Hawthorne presents colonial Boston as a preindustrial settlement sheltering a contemporaneous middle class, and he inscribes his major characters, above all Hester, with attitudes and modes of behavior that did not become normative until the entrenchment of commercial and industrial capitalism in the nineteenth century.

It might be useful to summarize some of the salient features of that emergent social and economic organization. Perhaps most important for *The Scarlet Letter* is the increasingly rigid segregation of work from the household, a divorce accelerated by the decline of domestic production and by the rise of factories and offices. Along with this change came a revaluation of female personality. Excluded from the public and male preserve of "productive" labor, women began to be identified with, and supposedly to derive their nature from, the private space of the home. They shed their traditional image as lustful and socially disruptive and were now believed to find fulfillment in moral purity, self-sacrifice, and caring for others. This revision, it should be emphasized, centered on middle-class women, who have been pictured—by, among others, Mary Ryan in history, and Nancy Armstrong in literature[8]—as the principal makers of middle-class lifestyle. The dominant values obviously penetrated working-class culture as well, but many laboring people retained residual or eighteenth-century perspectives on work and the family. Working-class women, for instance, were slower to assimilate domestic ideology because they typically sought employment in manufactories or carried paid work into the home.

The Puritan commonwealth depicted in Hawthorne's early chapters, and at various subsequent moments throughout the text, looks decidedly premodern in its emphasis on hierarchy and patriarchy and in its blurring of the boundaries between public and private. It is a community of rulers and ruled, of ministers, magistrates, and soldiers exercising authority over a deferential and largely undifferentiated people. Hawthorne says that seventeenth-century Boston takes its character from "the stern and tempered energies of manhood, and the sombre sagacity of age" (64). He distances its customs from his own time by observing that the Puritan elders regularly intervene in the most intimate details of moral and family existence. This patriarchal world antedates the Victorian model of domesticity and assumes the primacy of fathers in governing the family. Governor Bellingham, the Reverend Mr. Wilson, and other civil authorities contemplate removing Pearl from Hester's care because they assume the public's right to oversee the socialization of children. And just as the public intrudes into what came to be seen as a private and female enclave, so Puritan women in the novel think nothing of "stepping forth into the public ways" and loudly proclaiming their opinions of Hester's misdeed. For these New England matrons, writes Hawthorne, "the man-like Elizabeth"—not, one might add, the modest and sentimental Victoria—"had been the not altogether unsuitable representative of the sex" (50).

Although Hester emerges out of the seventeenth-century past, her Elizabethan qualities belong mainly to the narrative's prehistory. Hester the sexually sinful female, exemplar of traditional womanhood, seems outdated when the action commences. Her refusal to identify her lover in the marketplace reveals the heroine as someone who is already in transition toward a post-Puritan order that guards the private from public exposure. Dimmesdale is also revealed in this opening scene as a Janus-like figure with one eye on a future respectful of the separate spheres. He tells the Reverend Mr. Wilson, much to the older man's bewilderment, "that it were wronging the very nature of woman to force her to lay open her heart's secret in such broad daylight, and in the presence of so great a multitude" (65).

The later pages on Hester's psychological metamorphosis are read too narrowly if we make out in them only the account of one unhappy woman's accommodation to repression. The celebrated descriptions of Hester's change "from passion and feeling, to thought," of her once sensual but now forbidding aspect "that Passion would never dream of clasping in its embrace" (163–64), condense into the span of a few years and a single chapter the reconstruction of feminine nature that required roughly a century to complete. Hawthorne dissolves the transgressive, appetitive Eve into her sexless opposite, replacing concupiscence with the condition that Nancy Cott has accurately labeled "passionlessness" and that underwrites the age's ascendent ideal of self-negating motherhood.[9] He historicizes, as it were, the dark lady/fair lady split in classic American literature by portraying Hester as a dangerous adulteress recasting herself into a model Victorian saint. In the course of the story, she assumes all those mother-related callings available to nineteenth-century middle-class women, winning the people's reverence for her selflessness as a volunteer nurse and self-ordained "Sister of Mercy." The townspeople forget the "original signification" (161) of Hester's letter because that original meaning—of woman as fallen Eve—has been eclipsed historically by middle-class woman's role as self-sacrificing dispenser of nurturance.

Just as Hester is a woman in transition, so *The Scarlet Letter* itself can be understood as a text mutating from one generic category to a second, historically posterior, literary form. The tale, like the heroine, appears anachronistic at first, an eighteenth-century seduction story that has somehow strayed into the age of *Uncle Tom's Cabin* and *The Wide, Wide World* (1850). But Hawthorne's narrative quickly shows its hybrid character as a contemporaneous sentimental novel superimposed upon that obsolete seduction plot. It is remarkable how much of the book approximates the fiction of the "scribbling women" Hawthorne famously disparaged in his correspondence. The structure of the antebellum middle-class family is replicated, or rather disfigured, in the novel's central human reality, the mother and daughter who spend all their time together while the father absents himself at work. The many scenes involving Hester and Pearl parallel the sometimes affectionate, sometimes troubled, mother–daughter relationships familiar to readers of domestic literature. Hawthorne admits that the wearer of the letter behaves more like a mother from the permissive present than from the rigid Puritan past. Loving her daughter "with the intensity of a sole affection," she lacks the resolve to discipline Pearl severely and expects little return for her tenderness other "than the waywardness of an April breeze" (179). This domestic Hester almost lives up to Hawthorne's description of her as "the image of Divine Maternity" (56).

But Hester, even in her maternal avatar, is not, or not merely, the Victorian angel in the house, the woman Dimmesdale hails as his "better angel" (205). The proto-feminism into which her alienation modulates is, in Hawthorne's treatment, the corollary to her solitary mothering and doing of good. Thrust into a modernized family arrangement by her infraction,

Hester experiences as compressed personal history the gradual sundering of realms—public disjoined from private, male separated from female—that by the mid-nineteenth century constituted middle-class existence. One need only contrast the gawking, vociferous matrons who surround the scaffold in the early chapters with the mother and daughter who retire into the background while Dimmesdale delivers his election sermon. The now fully modern heroine, clinging to the margins of the marketplace, feels overwhelmed by a sense of her lover's remoteness "from her own sphere." Despite their private interview in the forest, Dimmesdale seems to have no connection to her; in his public, professional capacity, he is "utterly beyond her reach" (239). Such stark compartmentalizing underlines the rigid genderization against which antebellum feminism rebels but that simultaneously empowers feminist protest by making women cognizant of themselves as a separate human category and interest group. Hester is a female reformer two hundred years before her time because alone among the Puritans she is able to conceptualize "the whole race of womanhood" (165) as a branch of the human race apart from men.[10]

Dimmesdale is Hester's male counterpart as middle-class father and "new man" emancipated from the paradigms of an earlier cultural system. Unlike the Puritan patriarchs, he expresses admiration for Hester's unwillingness to speak in public: what for them is a failure of religious and civil duty is for him the mark of true womanhood. The split between public and private defines masculine identity for Dimmesdale, too. He internalizes the fundamental rupture of modern social life as a division between his inner and outer selves. The self he displays in public to his parishioners is sharply differentiated from—it is the contradiction of—the private self that the reader knows to be Pearl's unacknowledged father and Hester's soulmate. The minister is tortured by "the contrast between what I seem and what I am" (191) and struggles to take his place beside his "wife" and child before the public gaze. But every attempt to confess, to overcome the breach between family and workplace, founders on his fear of the consequences of exposure. As we shall see, Dimmesdale does succeed in mediating between the private and the public, but he does so in ways that controvert his characterization as middle-class male.

Dimmesdale is further set apart from Boston's ruling elders by his having risen in the community through ambition and ability. "It was an age," Hawthorne writes, "when what we call talent had far less consideration than now, but the massive materials which produce stability and dignity of character a great deal more" (237). Dimmesdale has acted the part of a Jacksonian man on the make and pushed ahead of his seniors through assiduous cultivation of crowd-pleasing verbal skills. The homology to

Hawthorne's own situation as a professional author trying to win fame and affluence through his linguistic gifts is evident enough.

Indeed, Dimmesdale's curious dwelling arrangements both highlight his post-Puritan professionalism and epitomize the text's enforcement of gender sequestration. The minister lives not with his "family" but with Hester's former husband, Roger Chillingworth, a man who, like himself, has a university education and practices an intellectual calling. Their lodgings resemble a workspace or office building more than a home. In one half is Dimmesdale's library, crammed with "parchment-bound folios" and writing materials, in the other the physician has installed his "study and laboratory," and the "two learned persons" daily settle down to their specialized vocations, at the same time "bestowing a mutual and not incurious inspection into one another's business" (126). Hawthorne has written into the narrative a graphic image of male professionals "married" to their work in the era after family production, when mental and manual forms of labor were segregated almost as sharply as men and women. Or better yet, he has given us a picture of the intensifying rivalry between the two great healing professions of the nineteenth century, the clerical attendants of the soul and the medical doctors of the body. Only Hester, in her gendered and unpaid role as charity worker, is entitled to treat spiritual as well as physical ailments.

Hawthorne is able to render the world of middle-class professionalism so vividly because he endeavors to enter it. His ambition to write for a livelihood, to become that invention of modernity, an independent author, gives him sympathetic understanding of his two male characters even as it figuratively places him in competition with them for status and income. As a young man about to matriculate at Bowdoin College, Hawthorne already pictured himself as a professional; in a well-known letter to his mother, he weighed the pros and cons of a career in law, medicine, and the ministry, ending with the question, "What would you think of my becoming an Author, and relying for support upon my pen?" As a writer who specialized in character analysis, Hawthorne did not flinch from rivalry with the other professions but positively cultivated it, as he ventured into territory traditionally reserved for clergymen and doctors. Reviewers, repelled or amazed by his psychological penetration, regularly compared him to a preacher, a Puritan, or an anatomist. "[H]e shows the skillful touches of a physician in probing the depths of human sorrow," exclaimed an admirer of the tales, and a reader of *The Scarlet Letter* was uttering a commonplace when he remarked that "of all laymen he [Hawthorne] will preach to you the closest sermons."[11]

Just as Hawthorne the novelist would lay claim to professional standing, so his novel apes the mores of the white-collar paradigm. *The Scarlet Letter* is formed by the same structural divisions that beset Hawthorne's principal characters. The book reproduces the separation of spheres most palpably in the line isolating "The Custom House—Introductory" from the ensuing narrative. The preface encloses the reader in the public and male domain of the Salem customhouse, "Uncle Sam's brick edifice" (15) symbolizing government and commerce. Here Hawthorne introduces us to his fellow workers, all of them men, describes his duties as Surveyor of the Revenue, and sets forth a kind of professional primer for writers, a detailed account of the genesis and composition of his romance. This sketch abuts but does not encroach upon the family romance of Hester, Pearl, and Arthur. Affective life quarantines itself in the tale of frustrated love, with its copious notation of female domesticity and private suffering. Holding in tension the oppositions endemic to nineteenth-century capitalism, the text as an entirety organizes itself as an instantiation of middle-class experience.

A similar splitting operates on a smaller scale within the romance proper, once the opening scene of Hester's punishment on the scaffold has run its course. Thereafter, imperceptible lines of gender division radiate throughout the plot and give the tale its exemplary character as a kind of microcosm of the divergent forms of antebellum American storytelling. Chapters track Hester and/or Pearl on the one side, and Dimmesdale and/ or Chillingworth on the other; mother and daughter inhabit one fictional space, the two males work and reside in another. When gender intersections occur, they do so outside society or in highly privatized settings that do not disturb the developing barrier between the familial and the public—places such as a jail cell, the scaffold at midnight, the seashore, or the forest. *The Scarlet Letter*'s spatial demarcations point to its double character as feminized domestic tale and canonical "drama of beset manhood."[12] The novel's divisions miniaturize respectable—that is, middle-class—literary culture's bifurcation into the two subgenres of sentimental fiction and the fiction of male bonding and competition.

III

Thus far we have been concerned with the parallels or homologies between Hawthorne's fictional universe and the historical details of middle-class formation. *The Scarlet Letter*, according to the argument, reinscribes the spatial and gender divisions constitutive of middle-class identity in the era of its rise. A change of focus is now in order, for it will bring to light some of the dark spots that concentration on similarity has ignored. The "dark spots" are complications and contradictions whose effect is to destabilize the particular alignments posited between textual and historical patterns. A first step toward correcting these occlusions would be to note that the gendered locus of class membership wavers in the novel and that Hester and Dimmesdale change places by donning the other sex's social characteristics.

The Scarlet Letter, for example, contains an American Adam figure who bears comparison to other Adamic heroes of nineteenth-century male sagas, heroes like Natty Bumppo, Ishmael, and Henry David Thoreau. This character, writes Hawthorne, "roamed as freely as the wild Indian in the woods" and criticizes the institutions of Puritan Boston "with hardly more reverence than the Indian would feel for the clerical band, the judicial robe, the pillory, the gallows, the fireside, or the church" (199). The character conceptualizes freedom and autonomy as qualities existing apart from the social order. For Hawthorne's Adam figure, the individual is defined not as a member of some larger unit but primarily in opposition to community; he is self-made and owes allegiance only to his own values and interests.

The character, of course, is Hester, but Hawthorne's account of her fierce independence suggests less Victorian womanhood than the Jacksonian individualist. It is appropriate to use the pronoun "he" in describing such a person because to Hawthorne's contemporaries, the solitary subject was necessarily a man. Ralph Waldo Emerson's representations stand as typical. In that most famous of treatises on the mid-century summons to autonomy, "Self-Reliance" (1841), the seeker after independence is always gendered as male. The iterated nouns and pronouns do not mask but instead proclaim the cultural exclusions. "The nonchalance of boys who are sure of a dinner, and would disdain as much as a lord to do or say aught to conciliate one, is the healthy attitude of human nature." Emerson's masculine insistences implicitly invert the clauses in his declaration, "Whoso would be a man, must be a nonconformist."[13]

In actuality, this virile nonconformist conformed to the social practices of his time. He was more entrepreneur than Transcendentalist or sourceless Adam. Karl Marx's comments in *The Grundrisse* on Robinson Crusoe, a literary avatar for the Adam myth, are illuminating not just about Hawthorne's tale but about the disjunction between the individual and civil society generally, a separation that provides so recurrent a feature of American masculine writing. Marx explains that the presence in eighteenth- and nineteenth-century literature of the isolated, apparently presocial individual—a figure he himself likens to Adam or Prometheus—entails a massive forgetting or ignorance. Entering the novel "not as a historic result but as history's point of departure," the Robinson Crusoe character reverses the actual circumstances of his appearance. He belongs to, and can only arise in, a "society of free competition" where "the individual appears detached from the natural bonds etc. which in earlier historical periods make him the accessory of a definite and limited human conglomerate."[14] Some of the bonds Marx has in mind, like clans or feudal hierarchies, never existed in America, but Hawthorne's rendering of the Puritan commonwealth reminds us that on this continent, too, the human community involved a dense network of responsibilities and connections. The autonomous individual who dominates antebellum narratives of male rivalry and maturation is a corollary to the acceleration of market capitalism in the Age of Jackson, not a reflection of humanity unencumbered by history but a product of the breakdown of republican commitment to the common welfare and its displacement over the century by laissez-faire ideology. The bearer of this historical change was Jackson's man-on-the-make, vocal opponent of customary restrictions on economic development and building block of the new middle class. But in *The Scarlet Letter*, paradoxically enough, this quintessential individualist and free-thinking pioneer in regions forbidden to women is herself a woman and otherwise the antithesis of Jacksonian man.

Hester's dissident side, as noted earlier, associates her with antebellum feminism. Recent critics have construed Hawthorne's strictures on his heroine as a repudiation of the movement for women's rights that was gathering force while he composed his romance, less than two years after the Seneca Falls Convention of 1848.[15] While this may be an accurate appraisal of Hawthorne's conscious purpose, it slights the historical volatility of his characterization of Hester. The heroine's assumption of masculine traits— which Hawthorne obviously intends as a disparagement—encodes a shadowy hint of future developments in female reformism. For a brief moment at the end of the story, Hester appears to overshoot, as it were, the domestic feminism of Hawthorne's own day and to verge on the androgynous "New Woman" of the post–Civil War period.

As Carol Smith-Rosenberg has pointed out,[16] the feminism of the late nineteenth and early twentieth centuries thrived outside conventional social arrangements. It broke with the ideology of domesticity. The "New Woman" differentiated herself from her mother's generation by rejecting marriage and opting for a career. She braved the charge of "Mannishness" by choosing a life not in the traditional family but in female institutions like women's colleges and social settlements, the best-known example of which was Hull House in Chicago, and she strove to cultivate autonomy in a nondomestic environment.

Hester's denial of her (hetero)sexuality can thus be viewed not simply as a de-eroticizing but as a prefiguration of the Gilded Age woman reformer. Such a reading would be patently anachronistic, but my point is that Hawthorne's portrait of Hester as self-reliant individualist converts her, in the novel's "Conclusion," into a prophecy of supercession. She never remarries after Arthur's death and, upon returning to New England from Europe, assembles around her a community of women who console and advise each other in the face of masculine oppression. In this liminal, nonfamilial setting, Hester creates an alternative institution to patriarchal structures. Her stated message, in which she assures her followers of a "brighter period" when "the whole relation between man and woman" will be established "on a surer ground of mutual happiness" (263), is far less radical and less meaningful than her example. Hester endures as an independent being who separates herself from the prevailing social order—her cottage lies on the distant periphery of the Puritan settlement—and who finds fulfillment in the company of other females. The image of her in the book's final pages seems as much a historical postscript as a textual coda to the action.[17]

Just as Hester undergoes a series of social and sexual mutations, so Dimmesdale, exemplar of mid-century manhood, alchemizes into a communal being who looks remarkably like a sentimental novelist. The minister, according to Hawthorne, could never join Hester—or the Deerslayer, or the hermit of Walden Pond—in "the hardships of a forest life." His "culture, and his entire development" as a man of the cloth forbid it (215). Standing at "the head of the social system," Dimmesdale derives his very identity from its framework; he internalizes the community's "regulations, its principles, and even its prejudices" (200). Whereas Hester discovers her authentic self in isolation from the Puritan colony, Dimmesdale—to revert to Marx's formulation—knows himself to be "the accessory to a definite and limited human conglomerate." He is a residual presence in the commercial and industrial middle class, a product as much of the eighteenth or seventeenth century as of the Age of Jackson and Hawthorne. The minister can be seen as demonstrating the accuracy of Hawthorne's historical imagination—he is supposed to be a Puritan, after all—but more interestingly, his portrayal underscores the persistence in the text of loyalties and assumptions about individuality that clash with the ideology of liberalism. As a man, Dimmesdale is an anachronism from the past, as Hester as a woman is a potential anachronism from the future.

But Dimmesdale is not just a man; he also completes Hawthorne's fictionalization of middle-class womanhood. From the outset, he is delineated in terms that typify nineteenth-century femininity more than conventional maleness. First beheld on the balcony during Hester's punishment, he has "large, brown, melancholy eyes," a "tremulous" mouth, and a "nervous sensibility." His diffidence ill suits public office and causes him to feel most at ease in "shadowy by-paths." Dimmesdale is said to keep himself "simple and child-like" and to retain "a freshness, and fragrance, and dewy purity of thought" that affect many people as the manner of "an angel" (66). It would appear from his description that the angel is domestic, the pure and retiring homemaker of Victorian ideology.

Besides physically resembling a woman—much as Hawthorne does in surviving daguerreotypes—Dimmesdale is identified with the female realm of the emotions. His feminine qualities tally with his (residual) immersion in the social; he and Hester swap positions dramatically in this respect. Hawthorne, speaking in his most naturalizing mode, observes that her years of isolation have stripped Hester of the capacity for affection and passion, the preservation "of which had been essential to keep her a woman" (163). But what Hester has temporarily forsaken, Dimmesdale, nominally a man, has possessed all along. The feeling evident in his voice when he addresses the Puritan populace works so powerfully on the hearts of his auditors, that the minister's words weld them "into one accord of sympathy" (67).

Dimmesdale's skill at deploying and manipulating sentiment enables him, like the popular women novelists of the 1850s, to bridge the gap between private affect and public occupation. The young preacher is conscious of the rift between the two realms, an awareness that certifies his modernity and places him apart from the Puritan patriarchs, who act as though the closet and the marketplace are synonymous. Dimmesdale's attempt to surmount the division rhetorically, through the mediation of language appealing to the emotions, inflects his nineteenth-century contemporaneousness toward the feminine and allies him, as an artist figure, with Stowe or Warner rather than Cooper or Melville. For the minister's sermons, delivered "in a tongue native to the human heart" (243), constitute a sentimental literature; they validate and make public—they publish—the inner feelings that the text denominates as female or domestic. Hawthorne tropes the heart as a chamber or residence, a space that only a woman can humanize and make inhabitable. He has Chillingworth observe to Hester, "My heart was a habitation large enough for many guests, but lonely and chill, and without a household fire" (74). Dimmesdale's "Tongue of Flame" suffuses the public world with affectivity; he feminizes culture by lighting a hearth fire in the popular heart.

Dimmesdale's volte-face, from rising male professional to domestic novelist reaching out from the private sphere to engage "the whole human brotherhood" in the language of sentiment (130), alerts us to the fact that the neat structural divisions of Hawthorne's own novel tend to lose their resolution upon closer scrutiny. Hawthorne himself is a male fiction writer redoing the seduction formula as a domestic love story of mother, daughter, and missing father. Moreover, the partition between public and private, male and female, encapsulated in the break between "The Custom-House" and the romance proper, inverts itself with a slight alteration of perspective. Hawthorne terms the preface an indiscreet surrender to the "autobiographical impulse" (3). Not only does he lay out his theory of romance, he divulges intimate details about his struggles with a writer's block. He gives an account of his personal affairs, including his resentment at being dismissed from office—the kind of washing one's laundry in public that Hawthorne well knew would create a stir. He even conducts the reader into a chamber of his home, with its "little domestic scenery" of doll, child's shoe, and hobby-horse (35). The tale that follows, on the other hand, is an impersonal commodity contrived for sale on the literary marketplace. Hawthorne, who addressed his readers as "I" in the introduction, now extinguishes the private self and assumes the mask of omniscience as a third-person narrator. The pigeonholing on which the text seemed to rest its articulation of social life under expanding capitalism proves impossible to maintain. *The Scarlet Letter*'s formal separation into preface and narrative operates to exhibit *and* to dissolve the structures of middle-class existence.

These migrations demonstrate the lability of structural parallels between text and history. They testify to the overflow or supplement that class brings to gender. Hester is a female denizen of the private sphere, but she is also an isolated individualist whose stance toward the social mimics laissez-faire doctrine rather than the cult of domesticity. Dimmesdale is an absent father and male co-worker, but he is also a domestic author. Both characters, in both their avatars, inhabit positions in the middle class—positions that did not emerge as ubiquitous until that class jelled in the Jacksonian era. Yet the two characters hold those places as occupational and ideological transvestites.

Class refuses to be permanently absorbed into gender in Hawthorne's text. For while gender style is always tethered to class, class exceeds the capacity of gender to contain it. The refusal of fixed gender roles returns upon class, as it were, to advertise a problem in Hawthorne's attitude toward middle-class identity. The mid-century middle class proscribed the very gender ambiguity he sponsors in his novel. To be a "masculine" woman was to veer toward the attributes of the working class; to be a feminized male was to ape the manner of the social aristocracy. Hawthorne's sense of occupational and gender mutability connotes a refusal to abide by the dominant class's sexual and spatial requirements. The novel's constant shifting of boundaries betrays authorial doubts about the middle-class ethos. The shifts intimate, not Hawthorne's collusion in the liberal consensus, but rather his indecision about a historical emergence that his art commemorates but simultaneously chafes at as stultifying.

IV

The ending of Hawthorne's novel precipitates a last effort to confront the compartmentalizations of market culture. The ending can be read in either of two ways, as an undoing of middle-class conventions or as their apotheosis. The final tableau on the scaffold, with Dimmesdale joining Hester and Pearl as he had failed to do at the beginning, reconstitutes the intimate nuclear family. T. Walter Herbert, in an influential article on gender in Hawthorne, calls this scene a recreation of "essential manhood and essential womanhood."[18] And there is no doubt that the last chapters contain some of the narrative's most ideologically sanitized pronouncements. A consolidating of gender stereotypes and cultural boundaries appears to signal Hawthorne's complete capitulation to middle-class ideals. He projects the fissures of his time into the afterlife. Not Hester and Dimmesdale, he suggests, but Dimmesdale and his male rival, "the old physician," will find themselves reunited in the "spiritual world," their "antipathy transmuted into golden love" (260–61). Pearl's shedding of tears at her father's dying kiss is construed, in the best sentimental fashion, as "the pledge" that she will cease to "do battle with the world, but be a woman in it" (256). The reader learns that Hester's hope of reforming gender relations will have to wait upon an "angel" of unblemished character, "a woman indeed, but lofty, pure, and beautiful"; and capable of "showing how sacred love should make us happy, by the truest test of a life successful to such an end!" (263). Though Hester delivers this prophecy to a community of women, Hawthorne's words imply that his heroine's feminist longings are to find fulfillment in the dream of a perfect marriage.

If at moments the ending strives to naturalize the doctrine of pure womanhood, however, it never does so without equivocation. Pearl's defection to Europe, where she reenters the gentry from which her mother's family descended, hints at a persistent and unmastered distaste for the confinements of middle-class life. The same impatience hovers behind Hawthorne's disclosure, in the tale's final paragraph, that on the tombstone of his ill-starred lovers "there appeared the semblance of an engraved escutcheon" beating a heraldic device (264)—feudal and aristocratic residues that affront middle-class closure. Moreover, Hester's insistence on reassuming the scarlet letter, on advertising her youthful sinfulness, acts as a reminder of the pre-modern understanding of woman's character. The letter reminds us that nineteenth-century female essentialism is a temporally bounded, post-Puritan construct, not an eternally existing ideal. Contemporaneous gender roles can be thought of as universally desirable only by repressing the historical differences that the tale itself has documented.

To put this more positively, Hawthorne seems as intent on rending the barriers of Jacksonian culture as he is on legitimating its norms. The scaffold scene, with its reuniting of the middle-class family unit, illustrates the point. The apparent essentialism of this episode is qualified, not to say undermined, by the physical setting of its occurrence. Hawthorne brings together the Victorian trinity of mother, father, and child in the very site where domestic ideology proscribes it: before the stares of the multitude in the marketplace or public stage. Understood in this way, the building of the entire narrative toward the climactic reconstruction of the family indicates a wish on Hawthorne's part, not to uphold, but to challenge nineteenth-century binary logic. The scaffold scene marks a trespassing of the industrial order's boundaries, a reversion to older patterns of behavior and an anticipation of future struggles to insert familial or domestic issues into the political sphere.

A glance at Hawthorne's own circumstances, and another look at Hester's standing in the community, may help to elucidate his oscillations. The author of *The Scarlet Letter* occupied a highly irregular class position. As he impresses upon us in "The Custom-House," he was descended from one of New England's most distinguished families. The Hathornes (spelled without the "w") were long-standing members of the Massachusetts elite and perhaps the closest thing the non-slaveholding states boasted to an aristocracy. The novelist's ancestors journeyed to the New World with the first wave of Puritan immigrants. They were prominent jurists and magistrates whose deeds—or rather, misdeeds—were recorded in histories of the country's earliest settlement. But like Poe's mythical Ushers, the line's fortunes have declined precipitously. When the future novelist was a child of three, his own father, a merchant, died at sea, and he was raised on the charity of relatives. As an author, he has not escaped dependency. He has continued to receive hand-outs to support his family; indeed, as we know from the preface, he has failed so miserably as a writer that he has had to accept employment as a government functionary. Little wonder that he imagines his forefathers dismissing him as a mere "writer of story-books! ... Why the degenerate fellow might as well have been a fiddler!" (10).

Like his fictional minister, Hawthorne the dependent patrician seemed to have an equivocal sexual identity that inclined toward the female. Many contemporaries commented on his extraordinary good looks, Elizabeth Peabody (the sister of his wife) pronouncing him "handsomer than Lord Byron"—another aristocratic figure renowned for almost feminine beauty. Reviewers detected "a large proportion of feminine elements" in the work—to quote Henry Wadsworth Longfellow—and heaped up adjectives like quiet, passive, pure, arch, delicate, lovely, and sensitive. They called the novelist "Gentle Hawthorne" in recognition both of his genteel roots and demeanor and of his womanly tenderness. Hawthorne's celebrated reclusiveness reinforced these impressions. The description of Dimmesdale as lingering in "shadowy by-paths" can be applied to the notoriously shy and aloof creator who withdrew into his mother's home for a decade after graduating from college. And of course Hawthorne's lack of financial independence cast him in a feminized position. Like women throughout history, he had to rely on others to provide the money for his family's maintenance.[19]

Compounding the feminizing of aristocracy, Hawthorne's pauperism highlights the mutability of his location in the social order. He represents a notable instance of antebellum declassing: he is an impoverished scion of the American patriciate, an aristocrat driven to subsist on public charity. But he is also, precisely as the author of the text we are reading, on the verge of redefining his social position as a member of the rising professional class. He aspires to, and with this fiction finally attains, the economic independence that comes from appeal to the marketplace and not to a patron. He belongs to the first generation of self-supporting writers in the nation's history, the men and women of the 1850s who proved it possible to live by the pen. Hawthorne is at once a professional male, an erstwhile aristocrat, and a failed laborer at literature reeling from the loss of his government sinecure. Ideological uncertainty and ambivalence toward the new middle class seem hardly surprising in his case. He stands within the emergent social formation, but he stands above it and below it as well.

And Hester shares his categorical instability as *déclassé* aristocrat. When first forced to mount the scaffold, she thinks back to her paternal English home, "a poverty-stricken" dwelling over the portal of which hangs "a half-obliterated shield of arms ... in token of ancient gentility" (58). Convicted of adultery, required to wear the badge of shame, Hester's regal bearing nevertheless invests her with an aristocratic air. The servant who admits the heroine to Governor Bellingham's mansion is so struck by her manner, and by "the glittering symbol on her bosom," that he imagines she must be "a great lady in the land" (104). But in fact Hester's sexual transgression only completes her family's social collapse, arguably into the laboring class. She ekes out a subsistence for herself and Pearl with her needlework, a Puritan forerunner of the nineteenth century's favorite emblem of downtrodden womanhood, the seamstress.

Seen from a different angle, Hester evokes the middle class in the making, but, like her creator, she stands outside as well as within the nascent configuration. Her ties to the working class are particularly significant in this regard. For the Jacksonian working class was both residual and sexually problematic in its behavior; its female members were mannish and unfeminine, as well as old-fashioned, by bourgeois standards. They departed the family for workshops or toiled in the home for wages at the very moment when the middle-class dwelling was becoming equated with leisure and with exemption from the rapacity of the marketplace. Female laborers approximated women of the past or men of the present more than the wives of antebellum lawyers, retailers, and manufacturers. Hester's erasure of her femininity and adoption of free-market attitudes may thus stem as much from the ambiguities of her class status as from the sliding of her gender position and historical specificity.

But these ambiguities do not negate the evidence linking Hester and Arthur to middle-class formation. As much as the overt allegiances, the instabilities in their respective characterizations announce the entrance into American literature of a new historical phenomenon. For the slippages are not unique but were in actuality common to the antebellum middle class. It is hardly a coincidence that the novel's version of that class materializes as a consequence of sin. To Hawthorne, middle-class emergence is a fraught difficulty, not a matter for congratulation. His two principal actors reflect his own, and presumably many other people's, incomplete incorporation into, and continuing uneasiness with, the social revolution of his time. Hawthorne's lovers proclaim the circumstance that at a time of profound sociological dislocation, Americans who were acquiring middle-class values and lifestyle were by no means unanimous about the process. Some retained older loyalties and patterns of behavior that could generate internal disaffection; others developed commitments that could lead to open resistance. Hester and Arthur's permutations bespeak the still fluid nature of an ideological ascendancy that hardened into dominance only after the Civil War—and did so, moreover, in relation to an increasingly restive and militant working class.

Gender and race have been rightly reinstated at the center of American literary history. We have learned, thanks to the insights of feminists and African-Americanists, to revise our thinking about the supposedly essential qualities that determine those two rubrics. It is now accepted that gender and race are social constructions with indeterminate boundaries that fluctuate over time and are shaped by historical circumstances rather than by anything innate. In the case of class, the situation in the United States has traditionally been the reverse. Americans have long taken for granted the proposition that there was no such thing as class in the country's past; unlike gender and race, it simply didn't exist. If this reading of *The Scarlet Letter* accomplishes nothing else, it is meant to suggest that here, too, change is necessary. Class, no less a social construction than gender and race, has been just as fluid and difficult to ascertain exactly. But its existence has been just as real, and it is time that we admitted its importance in the making of our cultural inheritance.

NOTES

1. I refer here specifically to the formulation of David Leverenz. See his book, *Manhood and the American Renaissance* (Ithaca: Cornell University Press, 1989). The elision of class, usually in favor of gender or race, is so pervasive in criticism on antebellum literature that to illustrate the practice, one could simply call the role of leading Americanists: Jane Tompkins, Philip Fisher, Lawrence Buell, etc. Some "second generation" New Historicists have argued for greater attention to class, although their own writing tends to marginalize it. See, for instance, Gillian Brown, *Domestic Individualism: Imagining Self in Nineteenth-Century America* (Berkeley and Los Angeles: University of California Press, 1990). A recent article that attempts to recuperate class more centrally in relation to several Hawthorne short stories is Nicholas K. Bromell, "'The Bloody Hand' of Labor: Work, Class, and Gender in Three Stories by Hawthorne," *American Quarterly* 42 (1990): 542–64.

2. Of the many writers who could be mentioned here, I would single out Stuart Blumin, *The Emergence of the Middle Clan: Social Experience in the American City, 1760–1900* (New York: Cambridge University Press, 1989); Bruce Laurie, *Artisans into Workers: Labor in Nineteenth-Century America* (New York: Noonday Press, 1989); Mary P. Ryan, *The Cradle of the Middle Class: The Family in Oneida County, New York, 1790–1865* (New York: Cambridge University Press, 1981); and Eli Zaretsky, *Capitalism, The Family, and Personal Life*, rev. ed. (New York: Harper and Row, 1986). On the English side, see Leonore Davidoff and Catherine Hall, *Family Fortunes: Men and Women of the English Middle Class 1750–1850* (Chicago: University of Chicago Press, 1987).

3. Bercovitch has developed his position in essays published over a number of years and drawn together in *The Office of "The Scarlet Letter"* (Baltimore: Johns Hopkins University Press, 1991). A somewhat similar interpretation of Hawthorne's novel as a document of ideological compromise has been advanced by Jonathan Arac in "The Politics of *The Scarlet Letter*," which appears in Bercovitch and Myra Jehlen, eds., *Ideology and Classic American Literature* (New York: Cambridge University Press, 1986), 247–66.

4. This form of argumentation has become identified with the New Historicism and is illustrated, in criticism on Hawthorne, by Walter Berm Michaels's essay "Romance and Real Estate," reprinted in his *The Gold Standard and the Logic of Naturalism: American Literature at the Turn of the Century* (Berkeley and Los Angeles: University of California Press, 1987), 85–112. On the totalizing character of Michaels's book, see Brook Thomas, *The New Historicism and Other Old-Fashioned Topics* (Princeton: Princeton University Press, 1991), 117–50.

5. See Williams, *Marxism and Literature* (Oxford: Oxford University Press, 1977), esp. 108–27.

6. *The Scarlet Letter*, volume 1 of *The Centenary Edition of the Works of Nathaniel Hawthorne* (Columbus: Ohio State University Press, 1962–), 84. Subsequent page numbers given in the text refer to this edition.

7. See Barthes, *Mythologies*, trans. Annette Lavers (New York: Hill and Wang, 1972), 138.

8. I refer to Ryan's *Cradle of the Middle Class* and to Nancy Armstrong, *Desire and Domestic Fiction: A Political History of the Novel* (New York: Oxford University Press, 1987).

9. See Cott's essay, "Passionlessness: An Interpretation of Victorian Sexual Ideology, 1790–1850," in Nancy Cott and Elizabeth H. Pleck, eds., *A Heritage of Her Own* (New York Simon and Schuster, 1979), 162–81.

10. I should perhaps qualify this statement by noting the conspicuous seventeenth-century exception (that proves the nineteenth-century rule?) of Anne Hutchinson. On the continuities between Hutchinson and Hester, see Amy Lang, *Prophetic Woman: Anne Hutchinson and the Problem of Dissent in the Literature of New England* (Berkeley and Los Angeles: University of California Press, 1987).

11. Nathaniel Hawthorne to Elizabeth C. Hawthorne, letter of March 13, 1821, in *The Letters, 1813–1843*, volume 15 of *The Centenary Edition*, 139; see the reviews collected in J. Donald Crowley, ed., *Hawthorne: The Critical Heritage* (New York: Barnes and Noble, 1970). Quotations are from 78, 193.

12. I am paraphrasing the title of Nina Baym's article, "Melodramas of Beset Manhood: How Theories of American Fiction Exclude Women Authors," *American Quarterly* 33 (1981): 123–39. *The Scarlet Letter* is fairly unique among the classics of the American Renaissance in encompassing both male and female domains.

13. The quotations are from *Essays: First Series*, volume 2 of *The Collected Works of Ralph Waldo Emerson* (Cambridge, Mass.: Harvard University Press, 1971–), 29.

14. References are to the selection from *The Grundrisse* reprinted in Robert C. Tucker, ed., *The Marx-Engels Reader*, 2d ed. (New York: W. W. Norton, 1978), 222.

15. See Bercovitch, *The Office of "The Scarlet Letter"*, 106.

16. See particularly the essay "The New Woman as Androgyne: Social Disorder and the Gender Crisis, 1870–1936," in her *Disorderly Conduct: Visions of Gender in Victorian America* (New York: Oxford University Press, 1985), 245–96.

17. This is not to suggest that the argument for a nondomestic feminism wasn't made in Hawthorne's day; Margaret Fuller's *Woman in the Nineteenth Century* (1845) is a case in point. But as a widespread cultural movement, the phenomenon belongs to the latter third of the century.

18. Herbert, "Nathaniel Hawthorne, Una Hawthorne, and *The Scarlet Letter*: Interactive Selfhoods and the Cultural Construction of Gender," *Proceedings of the Modern Language Association* 103 (1988): 285–97; quotation from 289.

19. Peabody is quoted in James R. Mellow, *Nathaniel Hawthorne in His Times* (Boston: Houghton Mifflin, 1980), 6; the Longfellow review appears in Crowley, ed., *Hawthorne: The Critical Heritage*, 80–83 (quotation from 81). Although I invert his emphases, I wish to acknowledge here the work of David Leverenz on types of antebellum masculinity. See *Manhood and the American Renaissance*.

LELAND S. PERSON

The Dark Labyrinth of Mind: Hawthorne, Hester and the Ironies of Racial Mothering

> If a pastor has offspring by a woman not his wife, the church dismiss him, if she is a white woman; but if she is colored, it does not hinder his continuing to be their good shepherd.
>
> —Harriet Jacobs, Incidents in the Life of a Slave Girl

"Explicit or implicit, the Africanist presence informs in compelling and inescapable ways the texture of American literature," argues Toni Morrison. "It is a dark and abiding presence, there for the literary imagination as both a visible and an invisible mediating force. Even, and especially, when American texts are not 'about' Africanist presences or characters or narrative or idiom, the shadow hovers in implication, in sign, in line of demarcation."[1] In this essay I want to accept the challenge Morrison issues to American literary scholars and to explore the "dark labyrinth of mind," as Hawthorne calls it, that constitutes Hester Prynne's subjectivity and subject position in *The Scarlet Letter*.[2] With some uncanny inspiration from the epigraph I have taken from Harriet Jacobs's *Incidents in the Life of a Slave Girl*,[3] I want to examine Hester within a historical context formed by the intersection of motherhood and race and to ask some questions about how discourses of motherhood, slavery, miscegenation, abolition, women's rights, child custody, and so on contend with one another at the site of Hester's character. Hawthorne referred to the importation of slaves as a "monstrous birth," and

From *Studies in American Fiction* 29, no. 2 (Spring 2001), pp. 33–48 © 2001 by Northeastern University.

in this essay I wish to see how and what Hester's maternal behavior signifies within a racial context of "other," if not monstrous, mothering.[4]

Hester Prynne's adulterous behavior and the scarlet letter that initially represents it also deform her motherhood. Examined within a nineteenth-century context, moreover, Hester's deviant mothering can be understood more particularly within a framework of slave motherhood. Sociologist Patricia Hill Collins, for example, describes a "distinctly Afrocentric ideology of motherhood" that slave women adapted to the oppressive conditions of slavery: community-based childcare, informal adoption, reliance on "*othermothers*"—traditions, she emphasizes, rooted in very different life experiences from the prevalent cult of true womanhood, with its dependency on a world of separate male and female spheres.[5] Hazel Carby points out, in this respect, that Harriet Jacobs's *Incidents in the Life of a Slave Girl* contradicts and transforms an ideology of true womanhood and motherhood "that could not take account of her experience."[6] Linda Brent abandons her children in order to save them—convinced that they have better chances of survival and success with "others." In Carby's view, "Jacobs developed an alternative set of definitions of womanhood and motherhood in the text which remained in tension with the cult of true womanhood."[7] Deborah Gray White, furthermore, documents cases from the 1830s and 1840s of slave mothers who actually killed their children. Some "claimed to have done so because of their intense concern for their offspring." One mother claimed that "her master was the father of the child, and that her mistress knew it and treated it so cruelly that she had to kill it to save it from further suffering."[8] Whether or not a mother actually commits infanticide, as Cassy does in *Uncle Tom's Cabin* or as the slave mother does in Frances Harper's poem of that title, slavery radically altered motherhood—inverting or ironizing it.[9] "I made up my mind," Stowe's Cassy explains. "I would never again let a child live to grow up! I took the little fellow in my arms, when he was two weeks old, and kissed him, and cried over him; and then I gave him laudanum, and held him close to my bosom, while he slept to death."[10] Converting the maternal breast into a source of poison rather than nourishment—being a good mother in the deforming context of slavery can actually mean killing, not nurturing, one's child. Killing the child to save it, giving it up to ensure it a better life: both forms of ironic mothering suggest a perverse inversion—what Jean Wyatt, referring to Sethe's murder of Beloved in Toni Morrison's novel, calls the "ultimate contradiction of mothering under slavery."[11]

If not quite in such terrible terms, the question of bad and even infanticidal mothering arises in *The Scarlet Letter*. After the opening scene in the market place, when Pearl is newborn, Hester returns from the scaffold "in a state of nervous excitement that demanded constant watchfulness, lest she should perpetrate violence on herself, or do some half-frenzied mischief to the poor babe" (*CE* 1:70). Later, at the Governor's Hall, when Pearl is three, Hester vows to kill herself before allowing the magistrates to remove Pearl from her care (*CE* 1:113). Later still, when Pearl is seven, a "fearful doubt strove to possess [Hester's] soul, whether it were not better to send Pearl at once to heaven, and go herself to such futurity as Eternal Justice should provide" (*CE* 1:166). This last thought proceeds directly out of the "dark labyrinth of mind" in which Hester has wandered during her seven years of ostracism from the Puritan community, and this infanticidal impulse leads directly into Hawthorne's observation that the "scarlet letter had not done its office" (*CE* 1:166). Among other features of her character, in other words, Hawthorne makes Hester's motherhood and its deviant tendencies—over the entire seven-year period of the novel—issues for careful observation.

Hawthorne could have found numerous examples of infanticidal mothers in the Puritan sources from which he composed *The Scarlet Letter*, including several that occurred during the period that comprises the novel's historical setting. Peter Hoffer and N. E. H. Hull cite the case of Dorothy Talbie of Salem, who was hanged in 1638 for murdering her three-year-old daughter. Recording this incident in his journal, John Winthrop noted that Talbie was "so possessed with Satan that he persuaded her (by his delusions, which she listened to as revelations from God) to break the neck of her own child, that she might free it from future misery."[12] Winthrop's explanation and the motive he attributes to Talbie anticipate Hester's thoughts of saving Pearl and herself from earthly pain. In another case Allice Bishop was executed in Plymouth in 1648 for murdering her four-year-old daughter, whom she had apparently conceived in an act of adultery.[13] In the same year another Massachusetts court condemned Mary Martin to death for killing her newborn daughter. The circumstances of the case bear some similarities to those in *The Scarlet Letter*. As recorded by Winthrop, Mary Martin's father had returned to England without arranging for proper supervision for his two daughters. Mary, the elder, promptly committed adultery with the married Mr. Mitton of Casco and, "her time being come, she was delivered of a woman child in a back room by herself." Martin attempted to kill the child by kneeling upon its head and then ultimately "put it into the fire."[14] Abandonment by a father (Martin) or father-like husband (Chillingworth), followed by adultery, the birth of an "illegitimate" child, and thoughts of infanticide—the resemblances seem compelling. Cotton Mather, moreover, preached two sermons inspired by the execution of Margaret Gaulacher, an Irish servant who had murdered her illegitimate newborn child. Mather cared less about the details of Gaulacher's case, which he scarcely mentioned, than about the frequency of bastard neonaticide. "I cannot but think," he concluded, "That there is a *Voice of God* unto the Country in this Thing; That there should be so many Instances of Women Executed for the Murder of their *Bastard-Children*. There are now Six or Seven such unhappy Instances."[15]

One of the most striking was the case of Esther Rodgers of Kittery, Maine, who confessed to being "defiled by a *Negro* Lad" at the age of seventeen, to murdering the resulting child, and to giving it a "Private Burial in the Garden."[16] Some time after committing this infanticide, which she did "in Secret" and without being caught, Rodgers moved to Newbury, where she repeated the crime. In her own words:

> And there I fell into the like Horrible Pit (as before) *viz.* of Carnal Pollution with the Negro man belonging to that House. And being with Child again, I was in as great concern to know how to hide this as the former. Yet did not so soon resolve the Murdering of it, but was continually hurried in my thoughts, and undetermined till the last hour. I went forth to be delivered in the Field, and dropping my Child by the side of a little Pond, (whether alive, or still Born I cannot tell) I covered it over with Dirt and Snow, and speedily returned home again. (124)

Rodgers was caught immediately and ultimately executed (on July 31, 1701) for both crimes, and the remainder of her brief confession, like the three sermons John Rogers preached upon the subject of her sinfulness, recounts her repentance and conversion. I cannot tell if Hawthorne knew this text, but Esther Rodgers' situation certainly bears some similarities to Hester's. Rogers emphasizes Rodgers' public presence in and for the Puritan community—the visitors she receives in prison, the round of visits she makes to "private Meetings of Christians in the Town" (131), the freedom and openness with which she discusses her situation (132), the "invincible Courage" she maintains on the verge of her execution (144), the public spectacle of the execution itself, which draws a crowd of 4,000–5,000 (153), and even her insistence to the High Sheriff that she be allowed "the liberty to walk on Foot" to the gallows rather than being carried in a cart (143). In his preface to Rodgers' "confession" Samuel Belcher calls her a "poor wretch, entering into Prison a Bloody Malefactor, her Conscience *laden with Sins of a Scarlet Die*" (italics added, 118). Whether or not this scarlet Esther inspired Hawthorne's Hester, Esther Rodgers' case does evidence an Africanist presence in the seventeenth-century background of *The Scarlet Letter*. Whereas Rodgers resorts to infanticide, of course, Hester Prynne rejects that final solution and chooses instead to raise Pearl by herself.

Nineteenth-century as well as seventeenth-century materials comprise Hester's character, of course. While these seventeenth-century examples of fornication, adultery, and infanticide offer important evidence that Hawthorne had ample material to underwrite the Puritan features of Hester's maternal situation, the most striking examples of maternal infanticide in nineteenth-century literature involve slave mothers killing (or some times simply abandoning) their children in order to save them from enslavement. *The Scarlet Letter* has increasingly been examined in its nineteenth-century context, and its participation in a conversation about slavery and abolition has become almost axiomatic. For the most part, however, critics such as Jonathan Arac, Sacvan Bercovitch, Jennifer Fleischner, and Deborah Madsen have revealed Hawthorne's historicism in order to confirm his conservatism—his failure to oppose slavery and embrace abolition. Arguing that Hester's scarlet A resembles the United States Constitution as a contested text, Arac, for example, considers the "indeterminacy" of the letter's meaning a strategy on Hawthorne's part for avoiding political action and change. *The Scarlet Letter*, he believes, is "propaganda—not to change your life."[17] Bercovitch makes a more abstract case, but he too considers *The Scarlet Letter* to be "thick propaganda," and he cites Hawthorne's "ironies of reconciliation" and laissez-faire "strategy of inaction" as key ingredients in the liberal ideology that sponsored numerous compromises with slavery, especially in 1850, the year of *The Scarlet Letter*'s publication.[18]

Jean Fagan Yellin has gone furthest in exploring the novel's inscription by slavery and abolitionist discourses and convincingly established Hawthorne's knowledge of anti-slavery feminism.[19] She has linked Hester iconographically to female slaves as sisters in bondage even as she stresses Hawthorne's refusal to let Hester function as a full-fledged anti-slavery feminist. "*The Scarlet Letter* presents a classic displacement," Yellin points out: "color is the sign not of race, but of grace—and of its absence. Black skin is seen as blackened soul." When "'black' is read as describing skin color and not moral status, the text of *The Scarlet Letter* reveals the obsessive concern with blacks and blackness, with the presence of a dangerous dark group within society's midst, that is characteristic of American political discourse in the last decades before Emancipation."[20] Even though she explicitly links Hester to slave womanhood, Yellin ignores one of the key parallels. She focuses briefly on Hester's single motherhood but only in order to link her to other "fallen women" in nineteenth-century life and letters.[21] Complaining of Hester's erstwhile feminism obscures her position on the "other" side of the slavery/

abolition equation—as a single mother whose racial identity helps illustrate the politics of racial mothering.

Jay Grossman offers an even more particularized reading of race in *The Scarlet Letter* by arguing that, in its fixation on the figure of the black man, the novel becomes "profoundly implicated" in "antebellum discourses of miscegenation." The "novel's depiction of miscegenation does not merely reproduce the terms of the Southern confrontation between a white master and a female slave," he argues. "Rather, the novel shifts the genders of that equation, with the effect ultimately of revealing the white fears that linked North and South: a shared belief in the unbridled sexuality of African men and the vulnerability of white women, a shared panic when confronted with the possibility of racial mixing."[22] In the allegorical terms that Grossman uses, Hester is a "victimized woman and Pearl the illegitimate child of a father-master"—Dimmesdale, whom the text obsessively figures as black.[23] Although he does not say so explicitly, Grossman seems to recognize the ambiguities, or doubleness, of Hawthorne's symbolic representation of race in *The Scarlet Letter*. Hester and Dimmesdale can be both black and white.

Similarly, I am not interested in identifying Hester Prynne as a slave mother or a black woman who has "passed" as white all these years. To be sure, our current critical interest in the representation of race and gender in literary texts provides a lens through which previously invisible textual features, such as Morrison's "Africanist presence," come to light. But the issue is not Hester's blackness or the Africanist "shadow" (to use another of Morrison's suggestive terms) that may "hover" over her character. The question is Hester's connection as a woman and a mother to other nineteenth-century female "characters"—in particular, to slave mothers and anti-slavery feminists. That connection is tricky. Hazel Carby, for example, has cautioned that "any feminist history that seeks to establish the sisterhood of white and black women as allies in the struggle against the oppression of all women must also reveal the complexity of the social and economic differences between women," so I want to be careful in examining how Hawthorne's representation of Hester as a mother engages and addresses contemporary issues of slave motherhood.[24] While Hester's motherhood, constructed discursively and intertextually, does link her with slave mothers, she also enjoys some privileges by virtue of her white racial identity. Insofar as she embodies racial identities, Hester represents an amalgam, or amalgamation. Hawthorne does link her situation closely enough with that of slave mothers that he tacitly invites us to discover an Africanist "presence" in her character. Describing the Puritans' expectations outside the prison door in the opening scene of *The Scarlet Letter*, Hawthorne observes that it might be that a sluggish bond-servant, or an undutiful child, whom his parents had given over to civil authority, was to be corrected at the whipping post. It might be, that an Antinomian, a Quaker, or other heterodox religionist, was to be scourged out of town, or an idle and vagrant Indian, whom the white man's fire-water had made riotous about the streets, was to be driven with stripes into the shadow of the forest. It might be, too, that a witch, like old Mistress Hibbins, the bitter-tempered widow of the magistrate, was to die upon the gallows. (*CE* 1:49)

Hawthorne's catalog makes clear the Puritans' conflation of various outlaw groups into a single figure of alterity—Hester herself. As an object of the Puritans' collective gaze, Hester embodies multiple forms of otherness, certainly including race. As a subject, therefore, Hester finds it difficult to escape her objectified being. Contemplating the "entire track along which she had been treading, since her happy infancy," she finds herself focusing on the scarlet letter and all that it signifies: "these were realties,—all else had vanished!" (*CE* 1:59).

This is not to say that Hester's objective status entirely eclipses her subjectivity—or, in the terms that concern me here, that her objectified status as an "other" woman colors her character completely in racial terms. Hester carries ambiguous racial markings, and I think Hawthorne exploits that ambiguity—the whiteness of her blackness—to shine an interesting and ironic light on the presumptions of white female abolitionists like Margaret Fuller and his sister-in-law, Elizabeth Peabody. In arguing the case for women's emancipation, for example, Fuller links women and slaves, effectively commandeering the subject position of black women for her own rhetorical and political purpose.[25] Elizabeth Peabody had long irritated Hawthorne with her abolitionist views. When she sent the Hawthornes an abolitionist pamphlet she had written, Hawthorne returned it to her without even showing it to Sophia. "No doubt it seems the truest of truth to you," he told his sister-in-law, "but I do assure you that, like every other Abolitionist, you look at matters with an awful squint, which distorts everything within your line of vision."[26] Three months later, after Peabody apparently sent him the same pamphlet, Hawthorne returned it again with a curt note:

I read your manuscript abolition pamphlet, supposing it to be a new production, and only discovered afterwards that it was the one I had sent back. Upon my word, it is not very good; not wor- thy of being sent three times across the ocean; not so good as I

supposed you would always write on a subject in which your mind
and heart were interested.[27]

This correspondence occurred in 1857 while the Hawthornes were living
in Liverpool and, thus, years after publication of *The Scarlet Letter*, but
the Hawthornes' arguments with Peabody over slavery and abolition were
Longstanding.[28] To whatever extent he was aware of it, then, Hawthorne
had personal reasons to criticize the feminist antislavery position and to
situate Hester Prynne within the ideological context that discourse created.
Considered as both subject and object, Hester occupies a symbolic position,
it seems to me, on the dividing line between black and white feminism—the
line that some white nineteenth-century feminists either ignored or erased.
Objectified in a way that associates her with slave mothers, Hester retains
some privileges of her status as a white feminist who, like Fuller and Peabody,
presumed to occupy the subject position of slave women.

When he referred to slavery as a "monstrous birth" in "Chiefly about
War-Matters," Hawthorne was playing upon the odd fact that, some time
after carrying the Pilgrims to Plymouth, the *Mayflower* had become a slave
ship. "There is an historical circumstance, known to few," he observed,
"that connects the children of the Puritans with these Africans of Virginia
in a singular way. They are our brethren, as being lineal descendants from
the May Flower, the fated womb of which, in her first voyage, sent forth a
brood of Pilgrims upon Plymouth Rock, and, in a subsequent one, spawned
slaves upon the southern soil;—a monstrous birth, but with which we have
an instinctive sense of kindred, and so are stirred by an irresistible impulse to
attempt their rescue, even at the cost of blood and ruin."[29] We "must let her
white progeny offset her dark one," Hawthorne concludes, and I would like
to speculate further on the black and white doubleness to which he refers by
suggesting that he had already explored the "singular" connection between
Puritans and Africans—that in Hester he had discovered a vehicle for letting
the "white progeny" of the *Mayflower* "offset her dark one." Hester Prynne
embodies the racial doubleness that Hawthorne cites. Objectively and
subjectively considered, she may be considered both black and white, and the
challenge Hawthorne poses for the reader is how to deal with the Africanist
presence (in Morrison's term) that shadows the white feminist subject.

Yellin has demonstrated conclusively that Hawthorne "became
intimately acquainted with the essential facts of chattel slavery, as well as
with the debate raging around it."[30] The Peabody sisters' Cuba Journals
describe the sexual exploitation of slave women, for example, and even the
frequency of infanticide—twenty or thirty deaths on the plantation where
they stayed.[31] Hawthorne's 1835 sketch "Old News" not only mentions the

slave population of Salem, but also includes the observation that "when the slaves of a family were inconveniently prolific, it being not quite orthodox to drown the superfluous offspring, like a litter of kittens, notice was promulgated of a 'negro child to be given away.'"[32] Although Yellin concludes that Hawthorne "deliberately avoided thinking about black slavery in antebellum America," I want to argue that, in identifying Hester with slave motherhood, Hawthorne interrogates and critiques the familiar identification of women and slaves—the conflation in nineteenth-century victimology of white mothers and slave mothers.[33] Illustrating the ironies of racialized maternal signification, Hawthorne undermines an anti-slavery feminist discourse that pretends to occupy the subject position of the slave woman and mother.

Dimmesdale's impregnation of Hester—after the "middle passage" that separates her from her husband—resembles a white master's miscegenetic coupling with a slave woman, at least in its analogous imbalance of power. Hester and Dimmesdale's action, even as it recalls the seventeenth-century predicaments catalogued by Mather and Winthrop, places Hester in a position that was beginning to register with nineteenth-century readers of abolitionist tracts and fugitive slave narratives. "Thou hadst charge of my soul," Hester reminds Dimmesdale at the Governor's Hall (CE 1:113), as she implores him to intercede with the Puritan magistrates and convince them to let her retain custody of Pearl. In *Incidents in the Life of a Slave Girl* (1861) Harriet Jacobs comments that "there is a great difference between Christianity and religion at the south.... If a pastor has offspring by a woman not his wife, the church dismiss him, if she is a white woman; but if she is colored, it does not hinder his continuing to be their good shepherd."[34] Much like a slave mother, whose only hope for keeping her child resided in her ties to white male authority, Hester must plead her case at secondhand. Harriet Jacobs maintains some leverage over Dr. Flint by threatening to expose his licentiousness to his wife and to the community. Similarly, Hester has gained leverage over Dimmesdale by refusing to name him as Pearl's father. According to a similar, absolute authority that separated slave mothers from their children and converted children into property subject to sale by the very fathers who denied their blood ties, Hester and Pearl remain subject to patriarchal law. Ultimately, however, Hester's feminist victory at the Governor's Hall offers a model that slave mothers like Jacobs were hard-pressed to emulate. Jacobs's many appeals to Mr. Sands, the biological father of her two children, repeatedly fall on deaf ears. Indeed, when she finally gets safely to New York, she is astonished to learn that, instead of freeing the daughter whose freedom she pressured him into buying, he has given Ellen to the daughter of a friend.

Like the mulatto children of slaveholders, Pearl follows the condition of her mother, and the parental triangle Hawthorne describes around Pearl resembles the common triangle on southern plantations if "Good Master Dimmesdale" occupies the position of the slave master, who fathers an illegitimate child upon one of his slaves, cuckolding her husband and then denying the child whom he fathers—even as, in his role as magistrate, he retains the power to remove her from her mother. In the terms that Hortense Spillers uses about fatherhood under slavery, "a dual fatherhood is set in motion, comprised of the African father's banished name and body and the captor father's mocking presence."[35] Not unlike a paranoid slave owner, determined to erase all traces of his miscegenetic paternity, furthermore, Dimmesdale worries about Pearl's maturing appearance. His refusal to acknowledge Pearl in any way, his dread that his "own features were partly repeated" in her face (*CE* 1:140), parallels the paradoxical relation between fatherhood and master-hood that writers such as Frederick Douglass and Harriet Jacobs describe. Douglass explains that slave women's children "in all cases follow the condition of their mothers," in order to make the slave-owning father's "wicked desires profitable as well as pleasurable; for by this cunning arrangement, the slaveholder, in cases not a few, sustains to his slaves the double relation of master and father."[36] And Jacobs tells the story of a Congressman who insists that his six mulatto children be sent away from the "great house" before he visits with his friends. "The existence of the colored children did not trouble this gentleman," she observes; "it was only the fear that friends might recognize in their features a resemblance to him."[37]

In the scaffold scene that opens *The Scarlet Letter* Hester seems uncannily linked to her sisters in bondage through a similar relationship to patriarchal power. Yellin notes the iconographic link to anti-slavery emblems of women on the auction block: "Hawthorne's book begins by presenting a woman publicly exposed, a figure made familiar by the abolitionists."[38] The narrator himself wonders before Hester's entrance if a "sluggish bond-servant" is about to appear (*CE* 1:36). Hester's stubborn refusal to name her child's father, furthermore, links her uncannily, if ironically, with slave mothers. Monika Elbert celebrates this refusal as a feminist gesture of defiance, a defiant "sin against patriarchy" along the lines Julia Kristeva marks out in "Stabat Mater."[39] The "Virgin assumes her feminine denial of the other sex (of man) but overcomes him by setting up a third person," Kristeva says: "I do not conceive with you but with Him."[40] For Hester, compared if "only by contrast" to the "image of Divine Maternity" (*CE* 1:56), denial of Dimmesdale promises transcendence—for Pearl—of the mother's condition. "My child must seek a heavenly Father," Hester insists; "she shall never know an earthly one!" (*CE* 1:68). Hester's refusal to name Pearl's father highlights the ironies of racial mothering, however, for in the inverted world of slavery, as Harriet Jacobs notes, "it was a crime for a slave to tell who was the father of her child."[41] While Hester's repeated refusals to name the father link her with the black sisterhood Jacobs identifies, such refusals signify very differently within different discursive and legal communities. The sort of heroic feminist action that Elbert celebrates signifies a slave mother's compliance with rather than rebellion against slave law. Parthenogenesis—Kristeva's feminist ideal, a male slaveholder's economic strategy. The condition and race of the mother make the difference.

While "Good Master Dimmesdale" may not be a *slave* master, his repudiation of Pearl resembles a slave master's behavior and subjects his daughter, as the Governor's Hall scene makes clear, to a similar patriarchal authority. Fatherhood, in Douglass's terms, gives way to "master-hood." Slave owners "controlled virtually all dimensions of their children's lives," Patricia Hill Collins observes; "they could be sold at will, whipped, even killed, all with no recourse by their mothers. In such a situation, simply keeping and rearing one's children becomes empowerment."[42] The Puritan magistrates, "Good Master Dimmesdale" included, claim a similar authority to dispose of Pearl. Hester claims a mother's power not to let them, and as her desperation increases in the face of her powerlessness her subjectivity and her subject position resemble those of nineteenth-century slave mothers like Harriet Jacobs. The "fact that slave society did not condemn 'illegitimacy' indicates the centrality of the mother role," observes Deborah Gray White, "a role which was presumed legitimate independent of the father's or husband's role."[43] Hester's situation in *The Scarlet Letter*, of course, tests the legitimacy of her maternal role. She does not commit infanticide, choosing heroically to live apart from her husband and to be the single mother of an "illegitimate" child, but she still confronts many of the same issues faced by slave mothers.

"What are a mother's rights," Hester asks Dimmesdale at the Governor's Hall, and "how much stronger they are, when that mother has but her child and the scarlet letter!"—that is, no husband/father and no political or legal standing (*CE* 1:113). Although Hester has successfully marked out a marginal space of her own in which to be a mother, the Puritan magistrates remind her that she mothers, so to speak, at the pleasure of the patriarchs; for they retain the power, in loco Parentis, to take Pearl away from her in much the same way that slave owners—fathers or not—possessed that absolute power. Michael Grossberg has shown that custody rulings in the nineteenth-century, however, "increasingly devalued paternally oriented, property-based welfare considerations and emphasized maternally biased child nurture ones."[44] Interpolating such changes anachronistically into his Puritan setting, Hawthorne conducts a "custody trial" (in Elbert's terms) at the Governor's Hall.[45] The Massachusetts legislature, in fact, enacted a law in the 1840s instructing the courts that "the rights of the parents to their children, in the absence of misconduct, are equal and the happiness and welfare of the child are to determine its care and custody."[46] As if quoting the statute—albeit for selfish as much as altruistic reasons—Dimmesdale argues that, "for Hester Prynne's sake, and no less for the poor child's sake, let us leave them as Providence hath seen fit to place them!" (CE 1:115). But even as the Governor's Hall scene dramatizes changes in nineteenth-century custody law, it addresses itself—if only in ironic contrast—to scenes of slave mothers begging for their maternal rights before intransigent slave owners, who had no legal obligation to care about the welfare of mothers or children. Harriet Jacobs, therefore, in contrast to Hester, must prevent her children from following their mother's condition—ironically, by giving them up or sending them away. "Poor little ones! fatherless and motherless!" she exclaims, as she bends over her sleeping children at the moment she leaves them for her solitary hiding place; "I knelt and prayed for the innocent little sleepers. I kissed them lightly, and turned away."[47]

Hester's admission to Mistress Hibbins that, had the magistrates taken Pearl from her, she would "willingly" have gone into the forest and signed her name—in her "own blood"—in the "Black Man's book" acquires an uncanny new meaning in this context, as if Hester acknowledges her racial difference, her narrow escape from the horrors of black slave motherhood—the privilege she has been granted, as it were, to pass as a white mother. Surely this scene and its threat to single motherhood might have struck a responsive emotional chord in a readership of anti-slavery feminists who might have appreciated the ironies of racial mothering Hawthorne highlights—the ironic signification of similar maternal acts. Following the condition of even the single mother means different things. In nineteenth-century America, Hawthorne instructs us, maternal differences are rooted in race.

Sacvan Bercovitch links the ending of *The Scarlet Letter* to the Liberian solution (the repatriation of slaves) promoted at the end of *Uncle Tom's Cabin*—largely, however, for its enactment of political gradualism or denial.[48] He might have found a more particularized similarity by following, if you will, the condition of the mothers. For like Linda Brent or Stowe's Eliza and George Harris, Hester flees America with her daughter. In the wake of the Fugitive Slave Law of 1850, Linda Brent feared that she and her children could be kidnapped on the streets of New York and returned to the South. Indeed, "many a poor washerwoman who, by hard labor, had made herself a comfortable home," she comments, "was obliged to sacrifice her furniture, bid a hurried farewell to friends, and seek her fortune among strangers in Canada.[49] Hester, too, considers a kind of Underground Railroad journey to freedom from white men's power. Deeper and deeper goes the path into the wilderness, she tells Dimmesdale, "less plainly to be seen at every step; until, some few miles hence, the yellow leaves will show no vestige of the white man's tread. There thou art free" (*CE* 1:197). After Dimmesdale's death, however, Hester seeks asylum in England, much as Jacobs—ironically— leaves New York for New England to avoid the likelihood of capture and then travels to England with her mistress's daughter Mary. "For the first time in my life," Jacobs observes, "I was in a place where I was treated according to my deportment, without reference to my complexion. I felt as if a great millstone had been lifted from my breast" and experienced for the first time "the delightful consciousness of pure, unadulterated freedom."[50] Even Pearl's inheritance from Chillingworth rather than from Dimmesdale makes a kind of sense—if Dimmesdale, with his exaggerated paleness, plays the role of slave-owning father. While Dimmesdale seems to acknowledge his paternity, his death enables Pearl's repatriation away from her father's world. She follows the condition of her mother. Linda Brent's children receive nothing from their white father, Mr. Sands. In bypassing her biological father in favor of her mother's legal husband, Pearl (despite her generous behavior to Dimmesdale on the scaffold) can be liberated from a "slave" economy and can return to her "step" father's estate—to a patrimony associated with the Black Man in the forest.

The case I have been making for reading Hawthorne's representation of Hester Prynne within a context of slave mothering does not mitigate recent criticism of his politics—his gradualist, providential views on slavery and its abolition. His interest in the experience and psychology of motherhood has its own political dimensions. If only through instructive analogy, Hawthorne situates Hester's maternal behavior within a context in which mothering signifies in racial terms. Refusing to name her child's father, resisting the efforts of the good masters to take her child away, planning an escape to freedom—Hester resembles slave mothers like Harriet Jacobs even as her actions signify and thereby underline the politics of racial difference. Situating Hester in a complex subject and object position in which slave motherhood and antislavery feminism come together, he represents the dangers of a presumption—the identification of black and white women's experiences and politics—that cuts as sharply today as it would have in the nineteenth century. Hester's abject dependence upon patriarchal sufferance for her mothering fights links her to her slave sisters, but her ability to mother at all marks her feminist difference from slave mothers like Harriet Jacobs. Hester Prynne is not a slave mother, but in representing her maternally, Hawthorne shows more sympathy and ironic understanding of the politics of her motherhood than his nineteenth- and twentieth-century detractors have allowed.

Notes

1. Toni Morrison, *Playing in the Dark: Whiteness and the Literary Imagination* (Cambridge: Harvard Univ. Press, 1992), 46–47.

2. Nathaniel Hawthorne, *The Scarlet Letter*, ed. William Charvat et al., *The Centenary Edition of the Works of Nathaniel Hawthorne*, Vol. 1 (Columbus: Ohio State Univ. Press, 1962), 166. Hereafter cited parenthetically by volume and page number.

3. Harriet Jacobs, *Incidents in the Life of a Slave Girl* (1861), ed. Jean Fagan Yellin (Cambridge: Harvard Univ. Press, 1987), 74.

4. Nathaniel Hawthorne, "Chiefly about War-Matters," *Miscellaneous Prose and Verse*, ed. Thomas Woodson, Claude M. Simpson, and L. Neal Smith, *The Centenary Edition of the Works of Nathaniel Hawthorne*, Vol. 23 (Columbus: Ohio State Univ. Press, 1994), 420.

5. Patricia Hill Collins, "The Meaning of Motherhood in Black Culture and Black Mother/Daughter Relationships," *SAGE* 4, no. 2 (Fall 1987), 3, 5.

6. Hazel V. Carby, *Reconstructing Womanhood: The Emergence of the Afro-American Woman Novelist* (New York: Oxford Univ. Press, 1987), 49.

7. Carby, 56. In Stephanie Smith's felicitous terms, Jacobs' "desertion will translate into devotion." *Conceived by Liberty: Maternal Figures and Nineteenth-Century American Literature* (Ithaca: Cornell Univ. Press, 1994), 146.

8. Deborah Gray White, *Ar'n't I a Woman? Female Slaves in the Plantation South* (New York: W. W. Norton, 1985), 88.

9. Frances Harper, "The Slave Mother," *A Brighter Coming Day: A Frances Ellen Watkins Harper Reader*, ed. Frances Smith Foster (New York: Feminist Press, 1990), 85:

> Then, said the mournful mother,
>   If Ohio cannot save,
> I will do a deed for freedom,
>   She shall find each child a grave.
>
> I will save my precious children
>   From their darkly threatened doom,
> I will hew their path to freedom
>   Through the portals of the tomb.
>
> A moment in the sunlight,
>   She held a glimmering knife,
> The next moment she had bathed it
>   In the crimson fount of life.
>
> They snatched away the fatal knife,
>   Her boys shrieked wild with Dread;
> The baby girl was pale and cold,
>   They raised it up, the child was dead. (ll. 41–56.)

10. Harriet Beecher Stowe, *Uncle Tom's Cabin*, ed. Elizabeth Ammons (New York: Norton, 1994), 318.

11. Jean Wyatt, "Giving Body to the Word: The Maternal Symbolic in Toni Morrison's Beloved," *PMLA* 108 (May 1993), 476.

12. Quoted in Peter C. Hoffer and N. E. H. Hull, *Murdering Mothers: Infanticide in England and New England 1558–1803* (New York: New York Univ. Press, 1981), 40.

13. Hoffer and Hull, 42.

14. Hoffer and Hull, 43.

15. Cotton Mather, *A Sorrowful Spectacle, in Two Sermons Occasioned by the Just Sentence of Death, on a Miserable Woman, for the Murder of a Spurious Offspring* (Boston: T. Fleet & T. Cramp, 1715), 90.

16. Esther Rodgers, "The Declaration and Confession of Esther Rodgers," in John Rogers, *Death the Certain Wages of Sin to the Impenitent: Three Lecture Sermons; Occasioned by the Execution of a Young Woman, Guilty of Murdering Her Infant Begotten in Whoredom* (Boston: Green and Allen, 1701), 122. Hereafter cited parenthetically.

17. Jonathan Arac, "The Politics of *The Scarlet Letter*," *Ideology and Classic American Literature*, ed. Sacvan Bercovitch and Myra Jehlen (New York: Cambridge Univ. Press, 1986), 251.

18. Sacvan Bercovitch, *The Office of The Scarlet Letter* (Baltimore: Johns Hopkins Univ. Press, 1991), 89, 109, 110. Fleischner also argues that *The Scarlet Letter* reflects an "ideology that is related to the belief in compromise toward slavery adopted by Hawthorne and other Northerners at mid-century who, although anti-slavery, were above all pro-union." See "Hawthorne and the Politics of Slavery," *Studies in the Novel* 23 (1991), 97. Deborah L. Madsen, "'A for Abolition': Hawthorne's Bondservant and the Shadow of Slavery," *Journal of American Studies* 25 (1991), 255–59, focuses on Governor Bellingham's bondservant to claim that Hawthorne "complicates the vision of American liberty by representing, in 'typical' form, the entire generation of Founding Fathers who were slave owners" (257).

19. Jean Fagan Yellin, "Hawthorne and the American National Sin," *The Green American Tradition: Essays and Poems for Sherman Paul*, ed. H. Daniel Peck (Baton Rouge: Louisiana State Univ. Press, 1989), 75–97, and *Women and Sisters: The Antislavery Feminists in American Culture* (New Haven: Yale Univ. Press, 1989).

20. Yellin, *Women and Sisters*, 138. Yellin goes on, however, to argue that Hester's refusal to become a prophetess at the end of the novel reflects Hawthorne's repudiation of the "antislavery feminists who were defying social taboos in an effort to move other women to action" (149).

21. Yellin, *Women and Sisters*, 142.

22. Jay Grossman, "'A' is for Abolition?: Race, Authorship, *The Scarlet Letter*," *Textual Practice* 7 (Spring 1993), 14, 15.

23. Grossman, 14, 17.

24. Carby, 53. See also Margaret M. R. Kellow, "The Divided Mind of Antislavery Feminism: Lydia Maria Child and the Construction of African American Womanhood," *Discovering the Women in Slavery: Emancipating Perspectives on the American Past*, ed. Patricia Morton (Athens: Univ. of Georgia Press, 1996), 107–26. Kellow concludes that the "discourse of independence and self-reliance as constructed by Child, crucial though it was to undermining the defense of slavery, had very little to do with black women" (113).

25. Fuller asserts, for example, that "there exists in the minds of men a tone of feeling towards women as toward slaves," and makes her case for women's emancipation by placing women in the same position as "Negroes": "As the friend of the negro assumes that one man cannot by right, hold another in bondage, so should the friend of woman

assume that man cannot, by right, lay even well-meant restrictions on woman," *Woman in the Nineteenth Century*, ed. Larry J. Reynolds (New York: Norton, 1998), 18, 20.

26. Nathaniel Hawthorne, *The Letters*, 1857–1864, ed. William Charvat et al., *The Centenary Edition of the Works of Nathaniel Hawthorne*, Vol. 18 (Columbus: Ohio State Univ. Press, [987), 89.

27. *The Letters, 1857–1864*, 115.

28. In his biography of Peabody, Bruce Ronda discusses the conflict between Hawthorne and Peabody, as well as Hawthorne's "hostility to antislavery advocates." See Elizabeth Palmer Peabody: A Reformer on Her Own Terms (Cambridge: Harvard Univ. Press, 1999), 265.

29. Hawthorne, "Chiefly about War-Matters," 420.

30. Yellin, "Hawthorne and the American National Sin," 76.

31. Yellin, "Hawthorne and the American National Sin," 84.

32. Nathaniel Hawthorne, "Old News," *The Snow-Image and Uncollected Tales*, ed. William Charvat et al., *The Centenary Edition of the Works of Nathaniel Hawthorne*, Vol. 11 (Columbus: Ohio State Univ. Press, 1974), 139.

33. Yellin, "Hawthorne and the American National Sin," 89.

34. Jacobs, 74.

35. Spillers, "Mama's Baby, Papa's Maybe: An American Grammar Book," *diacritics* 17, no. 2 (Summer 1987), 80.

36. Douglass, *Narrative of the Life of Frederick Douglass* (New York: Penguin, 1982), 49.

37. Jacobs, *Incidents in the Life of Slave Girl*, 142.

38. Yellin, *Women and Sisters*, 126.

39. Monika M. Elbert, "Hester's Maternity: Stigma or Weapon?" *ESQ* 36 (1990), 179.

40. Julia Kristeva, "Stabat Mater," *The Kristeva Reader*, ed. Toril Moi (New York: Columbia Univ. Press, 1986), 180.

41. Jacobs, 13. "The secrets of slavery are concealed like those of the Inquisition," Jacobs observes. "My master was, to my knowledge, the father of eleven slaves. But did the mothers dare to tell who was the father of their children? Did the other slaves dare to allude to it, except in whispers among themselves? No, indeed! They knew too well the terrible consequences" (35).

42. Collins, "Shifting the Center: Race, Class, and Feminist Theorizing about Motherhood," *Representations of Motherhood*, ed. Donna Bassin, Margaret Honey, and Meryle Mahrer Kaplan (New Haven: Yale Univ. Press, 1994), 66.

43. White, 159.

44. Michael Grossberg, "Who Gets the child? Custody, Guardianship, and the Rise of a Judicial Patriarchy in Nineteenth-Century America," *Feminist Studies* 9 (1983), 240–41.

45. Elbert, 194.

46. Grossberg, 241.

47. Jacobs, 96.

48. Bercovitch, *The Office of The Scarlet Letter*, 89.

49. Jacobs, 191.

50. Jacobs, 183.

RICHARD KOPLEY

The Matter of Form

This final chapter will focus on the pattern of threads in *The Scarlet Letter*—it will attend more to formal traditions and conventions, and less to specific source passages. The theme of sin and abiding guilt—evident in "The Tell-Tale Heart," "A Legend of Brittany," and *The Salem Belle*—is reflected in *The Scarlet Letter* in a structure involving Christian judgment. This chapter will argue that *The Scarlet Letter* offers a symmetrically framed Sun of Righteousness, Christ come in judgment, and a critical chiastic expression of that judgment.

The form of *The Scarlet Letter* has been amply studied. The novel has been variously understood to involve four, five, six, and seven sections.[1] A matter about which there seems little dispute, however, is that F. O. Matthiessen has observed, the novel's "symmetrical design is built around the three scenes on the scaffold of the pillory."[2] The first scaffold scene, involving the condemned Hester and her infant, Pearl, balances the third scaffold scene, involving the confessing minister, Hester, and Pearl. These two scaffold scenes frame the central scaffold scene, wherein the guilt-ridden Arthur Dimmesdale stands on the scaffold with Hester and Pearl at night. What warrants elaboration is the presence of the midday sun—or its midnight equivalent—in each of these scaffold scenes.

From *The Threads of* The Scarlet Letter, pp. 97–109. © 2003 by Rosemont Publishing and Printing Corp.

In the first of these scenes, Hester stands on the scaffold beneath "the hot, midday sun burning down upon her face and lighting up its shame; with the scarlet token of infamy on her breast" (1:63), the scarlet letter *A*, indicating the judgment of adultery. Hawthorne ironically reinforces the association of the sun and its judgment when John Wilson lectures the unresponsive Hester in the unadulterated sunshine" (1:65). In the last scaffold scene, the minister, Hester, and Pearl stand on the scaffold beneath "The sun, but little past its meridian" (1:254)—a sun that "shone down upon the clergyman" (1:254) while "God's judgment on a sinner" (1:255) is again revealed: the *A* upon Dimmesdale's breast, again the judgment of adultery. When some people doubt Dimmesdale's guilt, Hawthorne acknowledges "proofs" of that guilt "clear as the mid-day sunshine on the scarlet letter" (1:259).

The middle scaffold scene offers an extremely bright meteor at midnight—a meteor of "powerful ... radiance" (1:154). It would appear that, for this meteor, Hawthorne may have borrowed and modified another existing thread. In all likelihood, Hawthorne, an avid reader of newspapers, came upon the *Salem Tri-Weekly Gazette* on Saturday, 6 November 1847, where he would have noticed on the first page a long paragraph titled "Intelligence Office" (engaging because of his March 1844 sketch titled "The Intelligence Office")—and he would have read in the adjacent right column a short untitled paragraph:

> A very brilliant Meteor was seen last evening just before ten. Its course was from South to North, and passed very near the Pleiades. The light was so bright for the moment, as to light up the street. It left a bright train behind it.[3]

Perhaps Hawthorne had seen this meteor himself—in any case, he would surely have read this piece about it. Probably relying on this item, Hawthorne wrote in *The Scarlet Letter* that the meteor "showed the familiar scene of the street, with the distinctness of mid-day"—that it produced "the noon of that strange and solemn splendor" (1:154). The terms "midday" and "noon" intimate that Hawthorne's meteor serves as the midday sun. And taking the form of the letter *A*, the sun-like meteor also yields the judgment implicit in that letter—adultery.

The sun in the three scaffold scenes suggests a judgmental divine presence. And the association of sun and divinity was not anomalous for Hawthorne. He wrote in his 1837 sketch "Sunday at Home," "so long as I imagine that the earth is hallowed, and the light of heaven retains its sanctity, on the Sabbath—while that blessed sunshine lives within me—never can my soul have lost the instinct of its faith" (9:21). Additionally, when sending sunflowers as consolation to mourning neighbors, Hawthorne also sent the message, "the sunflower is a symbol of the sun, and ... the sun is a symbol of the glory of God."[4]

The framing of the middle scaffold scene by the first and last scaffold scenes is reinforced in *The Scarlet Letter* by the framing of the scene by symmetrical language. A sample of such language will clarify the pattern:

First half of *The Scarlet Letter*, forward

[one of the flowers of a wild rose-bush] may serve ... to symbolize some sweet moral blossom, that may ... relieve the darkening close of a tale of human frailty and sorrow. (1:48)

distil drops of bitterness into her heart (1:84–85)

Sometimes ... venerable minister or magistrate.... Again ... some matron.... Or, once more ... young maiden.... (1:87)

"O, I am your little Pearl!" answered the child. (1:97)

to the mansion of Governor Bellingham (1:100)

"one of those naughty elfs or fairies, whom we thought to have left behind us... in merry old England" (1:110)

taking his hand in the grasp of both her own (1:115)

a man ... emerging from the perilous wilderness, beheld the woman, in whom he hoped to find embodied the warmth and cheerfulness of home (1:118)

... he gathered herbs ... and dug up roots.... (1:121)

kindly, though not of warm affections (1:129)

"But wilt thou promise," asked Pearl, "to take my hand, and mother's hand, to-morrow noontide?" (1:153)

The great vault brightened.... It showed the familiar scene of the street, with the distinctness of mid-day, but also with the awfulness that is always imparted to familiar objects by an unaccustomed light. (1:154)

Second half of *The Scarlet Letter*, backward

[a herald's wording of a device on an engraved escutcheon] might serve for a motto and brief description of our now concluded legend, so sombre is it, and relieved only by one ever-glowing point of light gloomier than the shadow:—"ON A FIELD, SABLE, THE LETTER A, GULES." (1:264)[5]

drop into her tender bosom a germ of evil (1:219–20)

For instance.... hoary-bearded deacon.... Again.... old dame.... Again.... youngest sister.... (1:217–19)

... answered the child...... And I am thy little Pearl!" (1:211)

"to the house of yonder stern old Governor" (1:207)

"one of the fairies, whom we left in our dear old England" (1:206)

holding her mother's hand in both her own (1:180)

... he used to emerge ... from the seclusion of his study, and sit down in the fire-light of their home, and in the light of her nuptial smile (1:176)

He gathered here and there an herb, or grubbed up a root.... (1:175)

"kind, true, just, and of constant, if not warm affections" (1:172)

"Thou wouldst not promise to take my hand, and mother's hand, to-morrow noontide!" (1:157)

... the meteor kindled up the sky, and disclosed the earth, with an awfulness that admonished Hester Prynne and the clergyman of the day of judgment. (1:156)[6]

The intensely bright meteor that yields midday—the midnight equivalent of the sun, which offers judgment upon the guilty minister—is amply framed by both the visual and the verbal.

Critically, the scene in which this sun-like meteor appears is repeatedly linked to the Last Judgment. The connection to the Last Judgment is anticipated by Dimmesdale's response to Pearl that he will hold her hand, and her mother's, "At the great judgment day!" (1:153). He adds that "Then, and there, before the judgment-seat, thy mother, and thou, and I, must stand together!" (1:153). Thus, through Dimmesdale, Hawthorne alludes to Romans 14:10—"we shall all stand before the judgment seat of Christ"—and 2 Corinthians 5:10—"we must all appear before the judgment seat of Christ." The connection to the Last Judgment is evident again in Hawthorne's rendering of the meteor's effect: "They [the minister, Hester, and Pearl] stood in the noon of that strange and solemn splendor, as if it were the light that is to reveal all secrets, and the daybreak that shall unite all who belong to one another" (1:154). Hawthorne then discusses the Puritan belief in "meteoric appearances" "as so many revelations from a supernatural source" (1:154). And he refers to the meteor's warning Hester and Dimmesdale "of the day of judgment," and Roger Chillingworth's seeming to be "the arch-fiend," ready "to claim his own" (1:156).

In the eschatological context that Hawthorne creates—an earthly approximation of the Day of Judgment—the sun-like meteor seems an emblem of Christ come in judgment. And presumably the judgmental sun in the other scaffold scenes is such an emblem as well. The judgment in each case, the letter *A*, is a sign of Christ's recognition of the minister's guilt for adultery. In this regard, we should recall that *The Scarlet Letter* was almost called *The Judgment Letter* (16:308). But we should also note that Hawthorne would later write that he did not wish to see Christ at the Last Judgment portrayed as "inexorable" (14:214–15).[7]

The framed meteor, appearing in the central section of *The Scarlet Letter*, causing (like the sun) what seems to be "mid-day" or "noon," and serving as an emblem of the judgmental Christ, suggests a notable literary convention. *The Scarlet Letter*, a novel honoring a providential atonement, seems itself written in a providential form—that is, it offers symmetrical language framing a significant midpoint, a midpoint associated with the noonday sun, "the Sun of righteousness"—a biblical image taken to mean, in a Christian reading, Christ comes in judgment:

> For, behold, the day cometh, that shall burn as an oven; and all
> the proud, yea, and all that do wickedly, shall be stubble: and the

day that cometh shall burn them up, saith the Lord of hosts, that
it shall leave them neither root nor branch. But unto you that fear
my name shall the Sun of righteousness arise with healing in his
wings. (Malachi 4: 1–2)

Art historian Erwin Panofsky has traced the development of "the Sun
of righteousness" from both pagan and Christian origins to its articulation in
the late Middle-Ages by Pierre Bersuire:

Further I say of this Sun [viz, the "Sun of righteousness"] that
He shall be inflamed when exercising supreme power, that is to
say, when He sits in judgment, when He shall be strict and severe
... because He shall be all hot and bloody by dint of justice and
strictness. For, as the sun, when in the center of his orbit, that is
to say, at the midday point, is hottest, so shall Christ be when He
shall appear in the center of heaven and earth, that is to say, in
Judgment.... In summer, when he is in the Lion, the sun withers
the herbs, which have blossomed in the spring, by his heat. So
shall Christ, in that heat of the Judgment, appear as a man fierce
and leonine; He shall wither the sinners and shall destroy the
prosperity of men which they had enjoyed in the world.

Panofsky goes on to discuss Albrecht Dürer's famous 1498/99 engraving of
the Sun of Righteousness: a Christ with eyes of flame, who is seated upon
a lion and holding a sword in his right hand and a set of scales in his left
hand.[8] Ernst H. Kantorowicz has considered the Sun of Righteousness to be
suggested in the sixteenth canto of Dante's *Purgatorio* in its reference to "Two
Suns." Alastair Fowler sees the Sun of Righteousness, the *Sol iustitiae* (and
the *Sol oriens*, the rising sun) in the central stanza of John Donne's "Nuptial
Song," and he observes the Sun of Righteousness as Phoebus "in the central
position of sovereignty" in John Milton's "Lycidas." John Carey sees the
image of the Sun of Righteousness in the "greater Sun" of Milton's "Nativity
Ode." And Fowler writes that the image of the Sun of Righteousness is
intimated by the ascent of Christ in a chariot at the textual center of *Paradise
Lost*. Douglas Brooks extends the argument; he finds "the Christian notion of
the *Sol iustitiae* or Sun of justice (Christ come in judgment described in terms
of the midday sun)" at the center of Daniel Defoe's novel *Robinson Crusoe*.[9]

Defoe's novel was one of those books for which Hawthorne, as a boy,
"acquired a great fondness," and it became a part of his library. In subsequent
years, his young son Julian pretended to read it (8:407). Later, Julian and
sister Una play-acted Crusoe's story—what Julian Hawthorne termed "our

autobiography."[10] It is of note that Tappan and Dennet sold the E. C. Biddle children's edition of *Robinson Crusoe* in 1842 and 1843 and that the reviews of the book appeared immediately previous to reviews of *The Salem Belle* in the *Boston Evening Gazette* and the *Boston Miscellany*. But regardless of any possible association of the two books, Hawthorne, when preparing to write his first novel in 1849, would probably have turned to an old favorite that was, in fact, the first novel written in English—an inevitable part of any "artistic study" of novels. We may be encouraged in sensing his interest in Defoe by observing that in June of 1848 Hawthorne borrowed from the Salem Athenaeum Defoe's *Captain Singleton* and in June of 1849 Defoe's *Roxana*.[11] Of course, other works besides *Robinson Crusoe* were written with a providential form; we cannot claim more than is warranted for Defoe's classic. However, we can note that there is a formal affinity between *Robinson Crusoe* and *The Scarlet Letter*. And we can note that even as Hawthorne borrowed and transformed threads for his literary fabric, he also borrowed and transformed the design for that fabric.

Douglas Brooks shows that *Robinson Crusoe* has the symmetrical design typical of the providential form: "Adventures with Xury / Brazil // Island // Brazil / Adventures with Friday." And, relying on E. M. W. Tillyard and Frank H. Ellis, he points to the symmetrical verbal patterning in, the pre-island chapters and the post-island chapters. And at the center of the island section, and of the novel as a whole, is that critical moment when Crusoe discovers Friday's footprint—the moment of the Sun of Righteousness. Brooks sees the footprint as "a telling test of the strength of Crusoe's religious faith." He notes, "In Christian iconography the foot symbolizes humility and human fallibility; e.g., Ps. 94:18: 'When I said, My foot slippeth; thy mercy, O Lord, held me up.' In other words, the footprint should be understood by Crusoe as a warning against self-sufficiency and a reminder of God's Providence."[12] We may add that Crusoe acknowledged what he termed "my ORIGINAL SIN," his opposing his father's "excellent Advice" to accept his "middle State."[13]

As Brooks maintains, the warning footprint occurs "halfway through the novel," with notable markers. Defoe writes, in the paragraph before that concerning the footprint, "this was also about half Way between my other Habitation, and the place where I had laid up my Boat." And Defoe states, "It happen'd one Day about Noon going towards my Boat, I was exceedingly surpriz'd with the Print of a Man's naked Foot on the Shore." The focus on "Noon" emphasizes the centrality of the passage. And Brooks asserts, "there can be little doubt that Defoe alludes to the identification of the midday sun with the *Sol iustitiae* and the consequent interpretation of noon as a time of trial and judgment." Furthermore, Brooks observes, Crusoe "went up to a rising ground to look farther"—Defoe thereby acknowledges his working within "the iconographical tradition of elevation at the centre," indicative of "cosmic kingship."[14]

Initially, Crusoe fails the test, but over time, his faith grows. Crusoe comes to conclude "that God had appointed all this to befal me"; he comes to see that not only his suffering, but his prevailing, was providential. Indeed, as Brooks notes, Crusoe later states, "I frequently sat down to my Meat with Thankfulness, and admir'd the Hand of God's Providence, which had thus spread my Table in the Wilderness."[15]

Even as both *Robinson Crusoe* and *The Scarlet Letter* offer symmetrical action and language, both novels offer a significant midpoint (the appearance of a footprint or the letter *A*), occurring at noon, involving the implicit appearance of the sun—or the explicit appearance of a sun or sun equivalent—signifying the Sun of Righteousness. "Cosmic kingship" is suggested by an elevation—whether a hill or a scaffold—and the king implied is Christ, who has come in judgment. Though very different in myriad ways, the novels *Robinson Crusoe* and *The Scarlet Letter* both of which do, in fact, concern Original Sin, Divine Providence, and spiritual redemption—may be considered as homologous texts, distinct instances of providential form.[16]

Another instance of the providential form may be elaborated, and this American. Poe's novel *The Narrative of Arthur Gordon Pym*, directly influenced by Defoe's *Robinson Crusoe*, embodies such a form.[17] Although there is no evidence to suggest that Hawthorne read Poe's novel, its structural affinity with *The Scarlet Letter* should be noted.

The novel's providential form may be delineated briefly. Symmetrical events frame the center: most conspicuously, the destruction of a boat, the *Ariel*, by a ship, the *Penguin*, and the rescue of Arthur Gordon Pym and Augustus Barnard; the confinement of Pym in the hold of the ship *Grampus*; and the attack of the mutineers, in the first half, appear in reverse order in the second half with the attack of the Tsalalian natives, the confinement of Pym by the landslide, and the imminent destruction of Pym's canoe by the (encoded) *Penguin* and the rescue of Pym and Dirk Peters. The symmetry of events is reinforced by a symmetry of language. Such phrases as "were hurrying us to destruction" (*Collected Writings* 1:60), "of ultimate escape" (*Collected Writings* 1:60), "a loud and long scream or yell" (1:60), "drowned some thirty or forty poor devils" (1:64), and "death or captivity among barbarian hordes; ... a lifetime dragged out in sorrow and tears" (1:65) in the first half of the novel are reflected in the second half by such phrases as "being put to death by the savages ... dragging out a miserable existence in captivity among them" (1:185), "killed, perhaps, thirty or forty of the savages" (1:187), "screaming and yelling for aid" (1:187), "of ultimate escape" (1:198), and "were still hurrying on to the southward" (1:204). *Pym's* symmetry calls attention to its critical center. And at this center—in the middle of the middle chapter (chapter 13)—Pym's friend Augustus Barnard dies of his wounds. Poe writes,

> *August 1.* A continuance of the same calm weather, with an oppressively hot sun.... We now saw clearly that Augustus could not be saved; that he was evidently dying. We could do nothing to relieve his sufferings, which appeared to be great. About twelve o'clock he expired in strong convulsions, and without having spoken for several hours. (1:142)

The well-framed "oppressively hot sun" at "twelve o'clock," occurring at the midpoint of Poe's novel, represents the Sun of Righteousness. Pym's trial is the death of his friend Augustus—or, to speak of an allegorical meaning, Poe's trial was the death of his brother Henry (who did, in fact, die on August 1). That Pym/Poe successfully endured the trial is implied by the transcendent vision at the book's end—the white "shrouded human figure," suggesting Christ in Revelation. The providential form of the work enhances the providential theme, illustrated by the recurrent deliverance of Pym and intimated by Poe's reference in the novel to "the special interference of Providence" (1:62).[18]

Accordingly, the form of *Pym* anticipates the form of *The Scarlet Letter.* Both works feature symmetrical events and phrases framing a significant midpoint—the death of Augustus or the letter *A.* Associated with this midpoint in *Pym* is "the oppressively hot sun" at noon that represents the Sun of Righteousness; similarly, linked to the midpoint in *The Scarlet Letter* is the sun-like meteor that turns night to day—specifically, to "mid-day," "noon"—and that represents the same image, the Sun of Righteousness. The trial in Pym is the loss of the brother-like friend; the trial in *The Scarlet Letter* is the hidden sin of the guilt-ridden minister. Providentially, it would seem, Pym finds a new brother in the formerly savage Dirk Peters, and he will be reunited with Augustus/Henry in the afterlife, as promised by the final coded vision of Christ come to prophesy the New Jerusalem. Dimmesdale is permitted to atone for his sin and to confess it publically, thereby finding salvation and, perhaps, eventual reunion with Hester in the afterlife. Though one story is set on nineteenth-century shipboard and on a remote island in the South Seas, and the other is set in seventeenth-century Boston, the two works have a shared structure. The imagination of Poe and that of Hawthorne had an even greater affinity than we have formerly recognized. Hawthorne and Poe did share a common literary heritage, the providential form, which constitutes an important part of the design of two of their major works. In both Pym and *The Scarlet Letter*, "the Sun of righteousness" does "arise with healing in his wings."[19] According to Christian belief, man is redeemed from Original Sin by the Covenant of Grace, attained through Christ's sacrifice. It is fitting, then, that *The Scarlet Letter*, a narrative about Original Sin and redemption, is overseen by an emblem of a providential Christ. Hawthorne's tale of the unfortunate lovers is, after all, a tale of the Fortunate Fall.

Even as the brilliant meteor serves as the providential Sun of Righteousness in Hawthorne's novel, the significant midpoint is the letter that it forms—"an immense letter,—the letter A" (1:155). The symmetrical visual and verbal patterning of *The Scarlet Letter*, already discussed, frames a vital central chiasmus—a figure that warrants further inquiry.

The word "chiasmus" is drawn from the name for the Greek letter *X*, "chi." The figure of chiasmus involves symmetrical inversion—crossover—the pattern *ABBA*. (It had hitherto been known as "commutatio" and "antimetabole.") Chiasmus has been amply treated with regard to classical literature, the Old and New Testament, and British and American literature.[20] It has also been discussed specifically in terms of *The Scarlet Letter*.

In 1973, Raymond Benoit focused on the phrase "A letter, the letter A" (1:178) in chapter 15 of Hawthorne's novel, "Hester and Pearl"; he saw the letter as "one limb spirit and one limb matter, with Pearl, herself a symbol, the connecting link between these two." In 1990, Jon B. Reed noted the same instance of chiasmus in *The Scarlet Letter*, stressing the ambiguity of the letter. In 1995, Matthew Gartner speculated that perhaps the chiastic structure of the Book of Esther importantly influenced the structure of *The Scarlet Letter*.[21] This latter view may be valid, but many other chiastic models could have served. And we should observe that the chiastic pattern that Benoit and Reed address is found elsewhere. For instance, there is the language in "The Custom-House" introduction, "This rag of scarlet cloth ... assumed the shape of a *letter*. It was the capital *letter A*" (1:31; emphasis added here and below). And there is the language of the sexton to the minister at the close of chapter 12: "But did your reverence hear of the portent that was seen last night? *A* great red *letter* in the sky,—the *letter A*" (1:158). The three noted instances serve to underscore the well-framed central chiastic phrase in chapter 12, describing the appearance of the meteor to Dimmesdale:

We impute it, therefore, solely to the disease in his own eye and heart, that the minister, looking upward to the zenith, beheld

there the appearance of *an* immense *letter*,—the *letter A*,—marked
out in lines of dull red light. (1:155)

The significant midpoint with which the Sun of Righteousness is linked—its
judgment of the guilty minister—is the letter *A*, chiastically expressed.

And the phrase "looking upward to the zenith" calls attention to
the centrality of this passage, itself framed by the nearby previous passage
in which the minister "cast his eyes towards the zenith" (1:154) and the
imminent one in which the minister "gazed upward to the zenith" (1:155).
The notable proximity of the central *A* to the *z* of the repeated word "zenith"
may call to mind Hawthorne's biblical range, from Original Sin to Last
Judgment, as well as Christ himself, "Alpha and Omega, the beginning and
the end, the first and the last" (Rev. 22:13).

As chiasticist Max Nänny has thoroughly and ably demonstrated,
chiasmus is sometimes ornamental and sometimes functional. In the case
of *The Scarlet Letter*, the central chiasmus is clearly functional. The chiastic
phrase at the center of the novel—"an immense letter,—the letter A"—
suggests the verbal symmetry of the entire novel. *The Scarlet Letter* is folded;
its reading involves its unfolding. The evident verbal balance throughout
(suggested by the chiastic pattern *ABBA*) nicely underscores the thematic
balances—those between head and heart, law and love, sin and redemption,
justice and mercy, providence and free will. If there is an innovation in the
spatial chiasmus of Hawthorne's novel, it is that the outer elements—the rose
of the first chapter and the red letter of the last chapter—relate so closely
to the central phrase. We seem to find here a noteworthy correspondence—
even as the scarlet letter on Dimmesdale's chest is said to emerge from the
remorse in his heart (1:258–59), so, too, do the rose in the beginning and
the red letter *A* at the end emerge from "an immense letter,—the letter A,
marked out in lines of dull red light" at the heart of the novel.

Temporally, the central chiastic phrase relates to the changing
characters. Inasmuch as the inversion of chiasmus indicates an *X*, that central
phrase reflects the crossing paths of the protagonists. There is the changing
position of Hester and Chillingworth over seven years—her rising, his falling:
"She had climbed her way, since then, to a higher point. The old man, on
the other hand, had brought himself nearer to her level, or perhaps below
it, by the revenge which he had stooped for" (1:167). Her ascent and his
decline reveal the chiastic *X*. There is also the changing position of Hester
and Dimmesdale over seven years—the respected minister standing high
above the guilty woman in the first scaffold scene (1:64–69), the increasingly-
respected woman holding up the guilty minister in the final scaffold scene
(1:255–57)—he who has finally "stepped down from a high place" (1:67).[22]

Accordingly, the central chiastic phrase "an immense letter,—the letter A" is not only the powerful divine judgment upon the guilty minister, but also the controlling figure for both textual space and narrative time in the novel. Its resonance is rich, both morally and formally.

Notably, a central chiasmus may be found in other classic American works of Hawthorne's time. Edgar Allan Poe's "The Tell-Tale Heart" (again), Henry David Thoreau's *Walden*, and Harriet Beecher Stowe's *Uncle Tom's Cabin* illustrate the pattern well.

"The Tell-Tale Heart," so critical an influence on chapter 10 of *The Scarlet Letter*, offers a chiastic center concerning the old man's "Evil Eye." The "ray ... upon the vulture eye" and the "ray ... upon the damned spot" frame that center, a center that describes the provoking eye itself: "It was *open—wide, wide open*" (*Collected Works* 3:794–95; emphasis added). Poe's chiastic *X* marks "the spot." His chiasmus intensifies the horrific image of the "Evil Eye" and effectively serves to emphasize the centrality of that image to the story. And perhaps the double *d*s of "wide, wide" serve, as David Ketterer has noted regarding the double *d*s of "The Fall of the House of Usher," as Poe's signature, "Eddy."[23]

And Thoreau's 1854 masterpiece *Walden* features a chiastic center, as well. We may be directed there by Thoreau's remarking that, having repeatedly sounded Walden Pond, he found that "the number indicating the greatest depth was apparently in the centre of the map." Charles R. Anderson leads us to the center, too:

> At the very heart of the book lies Walden Pond, the central circle image. All paths lead into this chapter, "The Ponds"; all lines of meaning radiate from it. Here Thoreau found his ideal Self in that symbol of perfection which was the exact opposite of all those imperfections he had inveighed against in the life of society. The other ponds form a ring around Concord ... the circle of his endless saunterings. At their center lies Walden, and at its center Thoreau glimpses the end of his quest.

Thoreau writes about Walden Pond, at the center of "The Ponds," with a subtle chiasmus:

> It is a soothing employment, on one of those fine days in the fall when all the warmth of the sun is fully appreciated, to sit on a stump on such a height as this, overlooking the pond, and study the *dimpling circles* which are incessantly inscribed on its otherwise invisible surface amid the reflected skies and trees. Over this

great expanse there is no disturbance but it is thus at once gently smoothed away and assuaged, as, when a vase of water is jarred, the trembling circles seek the shore and all is smooth again. Not a fish can leap or an insect fall on the pond but it is thus reported in *circling dimples*, in lines of beauty, as it were the constant welling up of its fountain, the gentle pulsing of its life, the heaving of its breast. (emphasis added)

The chiastic phrases not only clarify the formal center of the work, but also delicately frame what may perhaps be "the end of his quest." The "trembling circles" becoming smooth are infinitely emblematic. They seem to suggest, among other possibilities, human consciousness attaining calm.[24]

Finally, in view of the Christian significance of Hawthorne's central chiasmus—it is the judgment on the minister by the Sun of Righteousness, Christ—we may consider a final instance of central chiasmus that also offers a Christian resonance, an instance appearing in Stowe's 1852 classic, *Uncle Tom's Cabin*. The work offers at its center (the beginning of the second volume of two volumes) a chiastic conversation. Little Eva has just heard from Tom about the death by starvation of a slave woman's baby, and, stricken, she refuses to be taken for a ride in her carriage:

> "Tom, you needn't get me the horses. *I don't want to go*," she said.
> "Why not, Miss Eva?"
> "*These things sink into my heart*, Tom," said *Eva*,—"*they sink into my heart*," she repeated, earnestly. "*I don't want to go*," and she turned from Tom, and went into the house.[25] (emphasis added)

Assuredly, this is no secular chiasmus. While indicating the center of the narrative, the *ABBA* pattern clearly frames Little Eva—Evangeline, the bearer of the good news of the redemption of the world through Christ. The chiasmus honors Eva's loving Christian spirit. And, indeed, in this case, the *X* may be the cross. Unmistakably, Hawthorne's central chiasmus in *The Scarlet Letter* concerns judgment and Stowe's in *Uncle Tom's Cabin*, love. But the judgment and the love are specifically those of Christ. And we may well wonder whether the central chiasmus in *The Scarlet Letter*—"an immense letter,—the letter A" (1:155)—also suggests the cross. In this regard, we might remember that, over time, Hester's "scarlet letter had the effect of the cross on a nun's bosom" (1:163).[26]

By virtue of the central chiasmus in each work, *The Scarlet Letter*, "The Tell-Tale Heart," *Walden*, and *Uncle Tom's Cabin* are akin. While Hawthorne,

Poe, Thoreau, and Stowe are diverse writers, whose works are examined and taught, in divergent ways, the formal relatedness of these works suggests a greater affinity than heretofore recognized. And, assuredly, there are a number of other examples of central chiasmus in American literature— examples warranting identification and interpretation. In this regard, Poe's canny chiastic statement, made in his comic short story "X-ing a Paragrab," may be aptly employed here: "*X*, everybody knew, was *an unknown quantity*; but in this case ... there was *an unknown quantity* of *X*" (*Collected Works* 3:1375; emphasis added).

Even as Hawthorne creatively transformed previous work for *The Scarlet Letter*—including "The Tell-Tale Heart," "A Legend of Brittany," and *The Salem Belle*—he also borrowed and reshaped formal conventions— including the Providential form and the central chiasmus. Thus, Hawthorne both hid and revealed. Even as *The Scarlet Letter* is made up of various knowable matching threads, muted for aesthetic concerns, those threads are stitched in a knowable design—evident, to varying degrees, in other literary works as well. To borrow again from Hawthorne regarding the scarlet letter, the "skill of needlework" in his masterpiece is indeed "wonderful"—but the "art" is not "forgotten" (1:31).

NOTES

1. Edward Dawson divided *The Scarlet Letter* into four acts based on the chronology of events, "Hawthorne's Knowledge," 74. Act 1 included chapters one through four (May 1642); Act 2 comprised chapters 7 and 8 (June 1645); Act 3 featured chapters 12, 14, and 16 through 19 (May 1649); and Act 4 offered chapters 21, 22, and 23 (Election Day, May 1649). (Nondramatic chapters were excluded.) Charles Ryskamp recapitulated this formulation ("New England Sources," 261). Focusing on the influential characters, John C. Gerber identified four parts to the novel: the first part, chapters 1 through 8, in which the community shapes the action; the second, chapters 9 through 12, in which Chillingworth shapes the action; the third, chapters 13 through 20, in which Hester determines the action; and the fourth, chapters 21 through 24, in which Dimmesdale precipitates the action ("Form and Content," 25). Gordon Roper restated this configuration (Introduction, xxxviii–xlii). Darrel Abel modified Gerber's view: the first part, the community's, includes chapters 1 through 3; the second part, Chillingworth's, includes chapters 4 through 12; the third part, Hester Prynne's, comprises chapters 13 through 19; and the fourth part—God's, not Dimmesdale's—comprises chapters 20 through 23 ("Hawthorne's Dimmesdale," 84–99). G. Thomas Tanselle also modified the Gerber configuration, giving chapter 20 to the fourth part of the novel, and Michael Clark restated Tanselle's view (Clark, "Another Look," 135). Alternatively, Malcolm Cowley ("Five Acts") considered *The Scarlet Letter* to be analogous to a Greek tragedy, with five acts: act 1 is made up of chapters 1 through 4; act 2 is made up of chapters 7, 8, and 10; act 3 is constituted by chapter 12 alone; act 4 includes chapters 14 through 19; and act 5 comprises chapters 21 through 23. Cowley's view may be considered a revi-

sion of Dawson's original four-act arrangement. Robert Stanton argued, in "*The Scarlet Letter* as Dialectic of Temperament and Idea," that *The Scarlet Letter* comprised six segments—two halves, each of which included three four-chapter sections, distinguished by philosophical stance. Finally, Leland Schubert, who considered the novel "not really suited to play form," saw seven components: A, chapters 1 through 3, "Hester on the scaffold"; B, chapters 4 through 8, "Hester and Pearl struggling"; C, chapters 9 through 11, "Chillingworth's progress"; D, chapter 12, "Dimmesdale on the scaffold"; E, chapters 13 through 15, "Hester and Pearl rising"; F, chapters 16 through 20, "Hester and Dimmesdale rise as Chillingworth falls"; G, chapters 21 through 23, "Hester, Pearl and Dimmesdale on the scaffold" (*Hawthorne, the Artist*, 140). (The introduction and the final chapter constitute the framework.)

2. Matthiessen, *American Renaissance*, 275.

3. See ["Very Brilliant Meteor"]. For an earlier account of a meteor turning night to day, see "Meteor," an article appearing in the Salem children's magazine, *The Hive*.

4. Perry, "Centenary of Hawthorne," 102.

5. The first corresponding phrases have been noted by Edward Stone in "The 'Many Morals' of *The Scarlet Letter*," 233–34. "Gules," of course, means "red"—the rose is matched by the red letter. For consideration of symmetry involving detail in the introduction and conclusion, including Surveyor Pue and the scarlet letter, see Alfred Weber, "Framing Functions." Additional verbal parallels include the "heraldic honor" and "the best and fittest of all mottoes for the General's shield of arms" (1:23–24), on one hand, and "armorial bearings" and "a herald's wording of which might serve for a motto" (1:264), on the other; and "Aged persons ... from whose oral testimony he had made up his narrative, remembered her" (1:32) and "the verbal testimony of individuals, some of whom had known Hester Prynne" (1:259–60).

6. It is intriguing to note the resemblance between the structure of *The Scarlet Letter* and the "long-disused writing-desk" (1:43) on which the novel was written: "This writing surface consisted of two lids, hinged at their junction in the centre" (Julian Hawthorne, *Hawthorne and His Circle*, 10).

7. Although Dimmesdale is seen as Christ-like in the second and third scaffold scenes (see chapter 2, note 61), he is finally a man, not a divinity. The judgmental sun—or sun-like meteor—represents Christ.

8. Panofsky, *Meaning in the Visual Arts*, 261–65; see also *Dürer*, 78–79.

9. Kantorowicz, "Dante's 'Two Suns,'" 329–30, 334–35; Fowler, *Triumphal Forms*, 73, and "To Shepherd's Ear," 177; Carey and Fowler, *Poems of John Milton*, 104, 442; and Brooks, *Number and Pattern*, 13.

10. For Hawthorne's early fondness for *Robinson Crusoe*, see Pearson, "Elizabeth Peabody on Hawthorne," 259–60. For Julian Hawthorne's characterization of *Robinson Crusoe* as "our autobiography," see *Hawthorne and His Circle*, 7.

11. Hawthorne's "artistic study" of novels is mentioned by Elizabeth Hawthorne (as noted in chapter 3) in Julian Hawthorne's *Nathaniel Hawthorne and His Wife*, 1:125. Hawthorne's borrowing *Captain Singleton* and *Roxana* is noted in Kesselring, "Hawthorne's Reading," 137–38, 178.

12. Brooks, *Number and Pattern*, 20–21, 38 n.

13. Defoe, *Robinson Crusoe*, 141, 5. For further discussion of Providence in *Robinson Crusoe*, see Hunter, *Reluctant Pilgrim*, 51–75; McFarlane, "Reading Crusoe"; and Zeitz, "Checker-Work of Providence."

14. Brooks, *Number and Pattern*, 20–21, 13.

15. Defoe, *Robinson Crusoe*, 68; Brooks, *Number and Pattern*, 25.

16. The providential form may also be evident in Samuel Taylor Coleridge's seminal romantic poem, "The Rime of the Ancient Mariner"—of which Hawthorne was "very fond" (Julian Hawthorne, *Hawthorne and His Circle*, 127). In the second part, occurring immediately after the mariner has shot the albatross, the seventh of fourteen stanzas reads:

> All in a hot and copper sky,
> The bloody Sun, at noon,
> Right up above the mast did stand,
> No bigger than the Moon. (50)

Perhaps, thus, Christ offers his intense judgment of the guilty mariner. Seven stanzas later, the albatross hangs on the mariner's neck.

Hawthorne was, of course, keenly sensitive to the influence of British literature on American literature, and he appreciated it. At a literary occasion in 1857 in England, he commented on American writers: "it gives me heartfelt happiness to think that we have returned something back of the great debt which we owe to England" ("Hawthorne's Speech," 209). Like Lowell, Longfellow, and Poe, Hawthorne was not especially sympathetic to the resistance to British models that was characteristic of the nationalistic literary group, Young America.

17. For Poe and *Robinson Crusoe*, see Poe's review in *Collected Writings*, 5:98–99, as well as Pollin, "Poe and Daniel Defoe."

18. The argument regarding *Pym* is developed in a series of articles by the author: Kopley, "Secret of *Arthur Gordon Pym*," "Hidden Journey of *Arthur Gordon Pym*," "'Very Profound Under-current' of *Arthur Gordon Pym*," as well as "Poe's *Pym*-esque." The argument is elaborated again in the new Penguin edition of *Pym*. Regarding the role of Providence in Poe's novel, see Fukuchi, "Poe's Providential Narrative."

19. The providential image of the Sun of Righteousness may be traced in early American literature, too. For example, it is mentioned by Anne Bradstreet in her "Meditations" (*Complete Works*, 50, 200, 202, 206, 207–8) and by Edward Taylor in *Preparatory Meditations* (see especially second series 21 [116–19]; 67A, 67B, 68A, 68B, 69 [200–209]; and 114 [290–91]). Taylor's work, of course, was not published in Hawthorne's lifetime. For a study of Providence in early American literature, see Hartman, *Providence Tales*.

For an instance of the appearance of the Sun of Righteousness in a Boston newspaper of Hawthorne's time, see Beveridge, "Sun of Righteousness." The passage originally appeared in "Thoughts upon the Appearance of Christ the Sun of Righteousness, or the Beatific Vision." It is interesting to see how Beveridge characterizes a man without faith in the Sun of Righteousness: "As if a man be born stark blind, though the sun shine never so clear about him, he sees no more than he did before, but lives in dark at noon-day as much as at midnight." In contrast, the Sun of Righteousness in *The Scarlet Letter* provides noon at night.

Ralph Waldo Emerson wrote a poem significantly related to the providential form—an 1816 elegy, long unpublished, on the occasion of the death of his cousin Mary Bliss Farnham (von Frank, "Emerson's Boyhood," 32). The seven-stanza poem, titled "Lines on the Death of Miss M. B. Farnham," offers a symmetrical frame comprising the first words of the first three and final three stanzas: "Come," "Here," "Lowly," and "Long" "Her," "Farewell." And at the center of the poem is the following revealing quatrain:

Her's was the brightness of the noonday Sun
Her fancy brilliant as his golden rays,
Judgement & Reason, mounted on the throne,
And pure Religion shone in all her ways. (*Collected Poems*, 286)

With this stanza, which offers such critical markers as "the noonday Sun," "Judgement," and "the throne," young Waldo extols his cousin, comparing her to the Sun of Righteousness. Experimenting with a literary convention, he offered his deceased cousin high praise indeed.

Herman Melville seems to have resisted the providential form. It is certainly not apparent in his greatest work, *Moby-Dick*. Furthermore, when Starbuck, the most devout character in *Moby-Dick*, confronts the doubloon with the "keystone sun," he says:

A dark valley between three mighty, heaven-abiding peaks, that almost seem the Trinity, in some faint earthly symbol. So in this vale of Death, God girds us round; and over all our gloom, the sun of Righteousness still shines a beacon and a hope. If we bend down our eyes, the dark vale shows her mouldy soil; but if we lift them, the bright sun meets our glance half way, to cheer. Yet, oh, the great sun is no fixture; and if, at midnight, we would fain snatch some sweet solace from him, we gaze for him in vain! This coin speaks wisely, mildly, truly, but still sadly to me." (*Writings*, 6:432)

Melville seems almost in dialogue with Hawthorne, who had rendered a nighttime Sun of Righteousness in *The Scarlet Letter*. Perhaps the doubting, defiant Melville forbore use of the familiar convention because it implied a faith he did not have. Although Melville did offer a fiction with a Christocentric form in "Bartleby the Scrivener," that work reveals Melville's characteristically dark vision: the returning Christ (Bartleby, "one of the least of these my brethren" [Matthew 25:40])—who appears at the story's midpoint, framed by symmetrical language—goes unrecognized and eventually dies (Kopley, "Circle and Its Center").

   20. The scholarly treatment of chiasmus is substantial; a brief selection will be mentioned here. For consideration of chiasmus in classical literature, see Welch, *Chiasmus in Antiquity*. For the assessment of the figure in the Old Testament, see Lund, "Chiasmus in The Psalms" and "The Presence of Chiasmus," and Levenson, *Esther*, 5–12; and in the New Testament, see Lund, *Chiasmus in the New Testament*, and Thomson, *Chiasmus*. For the examination of chiasmus in British literature, see Sanford Rudick, "Chiasmus"; Macandrew, "Life in the Maze"; Ralf Norrman, *Samuel Butler and the Meaning of Chiasmus*; and Olson, "'Soul's Imaginary Sight.'" Chiasmus in American literature is investigated by Djelal, "All in All"; Norrman, *Insecure World of Henry James's Fiction*, and *Wholeness Restored*; and Nänny, "Chiasmus in Literature," "Chiastic Structures," "Formal Allusions," "Hemingway's Architecture," "Hemingway's Use," and "The Reinforcement of Meaning."

   21. Benoit, "A Letter," 94; Jon B. Reed, "'A Letter,'" 79–80; Gartner, "The Scarlet Letter," 140. Chiasmus in the Book of Esther is explored by Levenson (5–12). Although he does not discuss chiasmus, Robert S. Friedman does discuss the symmetry of the letter *A* (63–67). And Christine Brooke-Rose sees the letter as reflective of Hawthorne's antithetical style.

   22. The crossing of Hester and Chillingworth and that of Hester and Dimmesdale anticipate the crossing of Lambert Strether and Chad Newsome in Henry James's *The*

Ambassadors (Norrman, *The Insecure World*, 138). However, James himself does not seem to have recognized the chiasmus at the center of *The Scarlet Letter* (Hawthorne, 118–19).

23. David Ketterer, "'Shudder': A Signature *Crypt*-ogram in 'The Fall of the House of Usher'" (197). Double *d*s figure at the center of other Poe works, as well: consider "The Man of the Crowd" ("As the night *deepened, so deepened* to me ..." [*Collected Works* 2:510; emphasis added]) and "A Tale of the Ragged Mountains" ("'You arose and *descended* into the city.' 'I arose ... as you say, and *descended* into the city'" [*Collected Works* 3:946; emphasis added]).

24. For Thoreau on his soundings, see *Walden*, 289. For Charles R. Anderson on the center of *Walden*, see *Magic Circle of Walden*, 222–23. See also Hocks, "Thoreau, Coleridge, and Barfield," 192. For the central passage itself, see *Walden*, 187–88. Richard Tuerk has suggested that Thoreau's reference to a "jarred" "vase of water" owes something to the first verse of the fourteenth canto of Dante's *Paradise*, which concerns the rippling water in a vase. Tuerk notes that Dante's relating his mind to the water tends to reinforce the association of Thoreau's mind with Walden Pond (*Central Still*, 59–60). For circles in *Walden*, see also Charles R. Anderson. For several literary instances of circles of rippling water, see Georges Poulet, *Metamorphoses of the Circle*, 7–8, 174–75, 236–37. For a fuller treatment of Thoreau's use of chiasmus in his greatest work, see Kopley, "Chiasmus in *Walden*."

25. Stowe, *Uncle Tom's Cabin*, 190. Notably, the number of the chapter that begins volume two of *Uncle Tom's Cabin*, "XIX," is symmetrical (as my daughter Emily observed).

26. For a consideration of chiasmus as suggestive of the Christian cross, see Tate, "Chiasmus as Metaphor." For a thoughtful contrasting of Hawthorne and Stowe, see Buell, "Hawthorne and Stowe" in his *New England Literary Culture*. For discussion of the scarlet letter as a cross, see Betty Kushen, "Love's Martyrs."

MARGARET REID

From Artifact to Archetype

Be these things how they might, [she], fair as she looked, was plucked up
out of a mystery, and had its roots still clinging to her.

—Hawthorne, *The Marble Faun*

At the end of *The Scarlet Letter,* the *A* reappears, and through its image
Hawthorne reminds readers that the artifacts generating (then framing
and containing) his story are inextricably bound in a symbolic vocabulary
within which the meanings of revolution have come full circle but without
closure, promising to regenerate yet again its own spontaneously variable
cycle. When we imagine the gravestone that Hawthorne tells us was carved
for Hester and Dimmesdale together, we remember the tattered cloth *A,*
still remarkably red after those many years. Here in this final scene, the
rediscovery of the letter takes on an eerie, if not sinister, aspect. In this
incarnation the letter stands out in sharp relief from the dark historical
memory of Puritan Boston. That obliquity of memory, still a part of
the Custom House attic in 1850, once again paradoxically enables the
inexplicable recurrence of a deeply foreboding sign of primal divisions—
images disquietingly relevant in a new way to Hawthorne's antebellum
America:

From *Cultural Secrets as Narrative Form: Storytelling in Nineteenth-Century America*, pp. 106–131.
© 2004 by the Ohio State University.

On a Field, Sable, The Letter A, Gules:

So the narrator describes the tombstone that looms over the "old and sunken grave" (262) of Hawthorne's tragic Puritan lovers.

With this final image of the novel—a herald's shield in red and black—Hawthorne raises the banner of revolution one more time. The story begins under the watchful eyes of the federal eagle of colonial revolution and the rippling shadow cast by the national flag flying at the Custom House door. It ends with Andrew Marvell's image of blood and war, now etched as a gravestone to commemorate fallen Puritans far from their British roots. Standing apart from—above—the bodies themselves, the letter (*A*, gules) and its given context (a field, sable) exist so saturated with histories that they continue to generate meaning to the "curious investigator" (262) who may wander through the burial ground and who is the last living presence Hawthorne imagines for us in the novel.

Hawthorne's readers, too, are compelled to reread the image. The marker records its own testimony, its weakness as a shield for the living, insofar as its endurance as an artifact engraved in stone marks an utter contrast to "the dust of the two sleepers" (262) buried below. And, no doubt there is further irony in the fact that it is a heraldic image put to work only as a memorial to the dead. As a monument, this stone's face is more than a testimony to those who have passed; it is, to be sure, the first American coat of arms, designed by history's accidents, for the family of the ever-enigmatic Pearl Prynne.

Despite—or through—the *A*'s dizzying array of meanings, it is clear that this symbol is not transcendent. It is created, maintained, and replicated from within its own material, historical existence and from the interplay of that existence with each interpreter's historically bound imagination. In the abundance of that interplay—which at every turn bears witness to history's power over the imagination—we ironically also see how such historical symbolism might appear transcendent in its seemingly boundless capacity for incarnation. There, in the boundlessness, is its revolutionary quality— the quality of language and meaning as *not* containable, even within the broader bounds of the narrative. However, the *appearance* of transcendence, boundlessness, here is a return to origins—origins of the text, the story, its language. The tombstone—that fragment of language standing outside of Hester's own time—returns the reader to that opening image, the worn yet magnificent *A*, both in its status as historical artifact and as a storyteller's talisman. It remains on the fringes of containment, edging ever toward the new, as we must remember when we recall that this object carried the power to mandate the birth of a historical imagination from even the most unpromising of candidates, the Custom House narrator. In that process the *A* has moved from artifact to archetype, or rather, its role as archetype has been layered onto its role as artifact. As archetype, it speaks to the powers of consolidation; as artifact, it bears witness to the lingering embers of history.

The process allowing for the preservation of the radical within the broader, new, cultural story offered by the romance plays itself out in large part through character interaction. When, through the narrative poetics of his romance, Hawthorne explores the crisis of the symbolic foundations of American language, the layers of storytelling within the romance construct a system of language and irony that first allows (or compels) Hester to regenerate the very conflict her penitential life is designed (by her town leaders) to dispel. Hester and her scarlet *A* are part of a symbolic vocabulary active within a dogmatic religious code as well as a democratic political code; indeed, she and her symbol together embody the enduring conflict that at first is the only connection between these codes.[1]

While Hester's town magistrates understand transgression and punishment in traditional, hierarchal terms, Hester's own experience as the transgressor is creative, innovative, and even obliquely prophetic. Thus, Hawthorne brings forth Hester in all of her contradiction and ambiguity as an example of the productivity of America's crisis in language and storytelling. Hester's complexity specifically mirrors the ambiguous roots of America's linguistic independence and the power of such ambiguity to effect both origin and union for a new modern culture, even a culture, like Hester's or Hawthorne's, divided. Noah Webster's vision of an American language promised an opportunity to examine national rhetoric, revise national self-definition without discarding the known, and be reminded that—especially in the early stages of a culture—the danger and power of language are never so far apart. *The Scarlet Letter* is an experiment in that tradition. In fact, because the romance itself enacts the culture's shift beyond a point of potentially revolutionary impasse, it is one of the most complex assessments of the history of the American language as it develops over the two centuries that separate Hawthorne's political and social world from his fictional setting.

In *The Scarlet Letter* Hawthorne directly addresses the foundations of language, the "story" within the rhetoric of national narrative. Suggesting danger in the "theoretical" nature of both Puritan rhetoric and nineteenth-century American symbology, he makes a progressivist's argument for a new infusion of history into theory. Michael Colacurcio describes the damaging results of "progressive history" as the reduction of "multiplicity to unity, not only in 'explanation' but in 'reality.' What is edited out from the past will not be available soon again."[2] Here we find an echo of "The Custom House" narrator's fears, as he is effectively "edited out" of what he sees as the story of national progress. *The Scarlet Letter's* historiographical progressivism, however, prevents Hawthorne's experiments with language from falling into the traps of reductionism. Through the romance's narrative voice and the ambiguously radical and yet often silenced consciousness of Hester Prynne, the novel provides a complex system of language theory dependent upon irony and, in so doing, establishes as a first priority the task of making available exactly that which progressive historiography had "edited out." Further, these recovered materials function in the service of a revised plan based on oddly familiar progressive sentiments, which in turn are strengthened through their newly appropriated material and knowledge.

From its initial appearance, the *A* itself first asserts revolutionary authority within Hawthorne's text. Clearly that scarlet letter is not only what it first appears. Although the narrator introduces it to us as if he can know it "It was the capital letter *A*. By an accurate measurement, each limb proved to be precisely three and one quarter inches in length" (34)—it is immediately clear that what Hawthorne calls the "deep meaning" of the "mystic symbol" is neither clear nor inviting, as it radiates the "burning heat" of a "red-hot iron" (34). At once too hot to hold and too oblique to read, then, the scarlet *A* is an aggressively material fragment of history.

Once found in the attic of the old Salem Custom House, it compels storytelling in a uniquely troublesome way: It is an artifact of cultural history, but it has not found a place in a museum or library; it is an emblem of personal experience, but it has not been protected within any familiar context, as, for example, a family heirloom. Instead, the place of the *A* in the Custom House attic and the vigor of its imaginative assault on the narrator demand that this material fragment be understood in its inadequate present context as the trace of something more—something out of its own temporal sphere. As an artifact, it hovers just at the outer reaches of the narrator's interpretive responsibility. The strangeness of the find ignites the storyteller's imagination, and the story to be told is, at this initial moment, dangerously open ended.

"The authenticity of the outline" (36) is all that the narrator claims to find in Surveyor Pue's attic papers, but the romance springs forth in full, with decidedly little to mark it as the work of the Custom House narrator as we have come to know him. Jarred from his life as a bored bureaucrat—watching over a "dilapidated wharf" (7) in rooms "cobwebbed and dingy" with only "venerable figures" for company, "talking ... in voices between speech and a snore" (9)—this narrator has been charged with much more than he knows. This story about life in the New World is a story distinctly larger than his own consciousness. Whatever the *A* signifies, that significance is beyond the common vocabulary of the narrative world, and yet it represents only the smallest fragment, the most basic experience, of the world from which it came.

To allow the emergence of this story into the narrator's consciousness and—through that—into cultural knowledge is to unleash a set of unfamiliar (and potent) forces, forces far removed from the narrator's—as well as the reader's—ordinary practices of everyday life. The narrator, then, somewhat unwittingly invites a total reconstruction of his epistemological and historical frames of reference. Reading the meaning of the *A* mandates a radical revision of the culture of Hawthorne's known interpretive world, from the elemental—that is, beginning with the first letter of the alphabet—to the most complex, the secrets of the past, of experiential history, now gone from human consciousness yet still vibrant within that scrap of red cloth. The *A* itself, as a material, historical, and linguistic fragment, overthrows the authority of the narrator ("decapitate[s]" [46] him, in his own terms[3]) and instantly begins to act the part of the revolutionary.

As I have been suggesting, *The Scarlet Letter* offers as a response to this violence the considered attention to the role (at once historical and theoretical) of language in the development of America, even the participation in the making of a national language. For Hawthorne, inheriting British empiricism, surrounded by transcendentalism, descending from Puritanism, and setting out to revitalize history, the manipulation of language into a reenactment of the moment of founding a language for the New World potentially promises the reaffirmation of America in new modern terms.[4] Here (as for Benjamin), storytelling means both preservation and transmission: Secrecy and speech are equal and mutually dependent, without division or impediment between them. Further, from this unlikely union of opposites the theory of national storytelling—first suggested by the coexistent and contradictory religious and political significations of the scarlet *A*—begins to cohere.

Hawthorne's manipulation of levels of language and communication in *The Scarlet Letter* reveals the fact that no character in Puritan Boston has either the ability or the desire to narrate history in its deepest communal sense. Nonetheless, the novel further demonstrates that such a history persists. The narrative voice of the romance, which is at one level a denial or suppression of history, turns on itself to become a vehicle for a kind of spontaneous eruption of the new American story. Only the narrator—and none of the characters—can see "how far removed ... hidden meaning [is] from revelation, and how close [it can] be brought by the knowledge of this remoteness."[5] The narrator in "Endicott and the Red Cross" defines "the policy" not only of his "ancestors" but also of himself and of the similar narrator in *The Scarlet Letter*. "It was the policy of our ancestors to search out even the most secret sins, and expose them to shame, without fear or favor, in the broadest light of the noonday sun."[6] In *The Scarlet Letter* Hawthorne suggests to his readers that now, with some distance, it may be the time to look back at what that light has exposed, at the bases for community interpretation. Moreover, to create a narrator who can put cultural history into transmissible form, not simply into the form of information or rhetoric, and who can at least attempt "to regain pure language fully formed in the linguistic flux"—is some triumph in itself; beyond that it is also direction and exhortation for the newly reviving program of an American language.[7] The paradoxical difficulties of storytelling, including the impossible goals of approaching pure language and truth, affect *The Scarlet Letter*'s narrator but do not render him powerless. Because removed from the story by several generations, this narrator is able to speak, to tell the story of a town in the New World: By looking back, he ensures that his words are neither purely rhetorical promise nor simple information. By his own admission, this narrator tends to write from an "autobiographical impulse" (3). He has less to lose, however—and also less to gain—through his storytelling than one of the original players would have had. Instead, the past becomes the present writer's story; his desire is to imagine "that a friend, a kind and apprehensive, though not the closest friend," is listening to his story, so that he "may prate of the circumstances that lie around us, and even of ourself, but still keep the inmost Me behind its veil" (4). As a storyteller he must be more than a man of mere instinct, as is the Custom House inspector, who is tied so closely to his homeland that he has "no power of thought, no depth of feeling, no troublesome sensibilities." In addition, like any authentic storyteller, this narrator wants to be creator and truth teller at once; he realizes that the way to do this is to tell what has never before been told but has long been true:

> Literature, its exertions and objects, were now of little moment in my regard. I cared not, at this period, for books; they were apart from me. Nature, except it were human nature, the nature that is developed in earth and sky, was, in one sense, hidden from me; and all the imaginative delight, wherewith it had been spiritual-ized, passed away out of my mind. A gift, a faculty, if it had not departed, was suspended and inanimate within me. There would have been something sad, unutterably dreary, in all this, had I not been conscious that it lay at my own option to recall whatever was valuable in the past. (25–26)

Thus this narrator "contend[s] for ... the authenticity of the outline" (33) but openly claims great liberty of invention; this narrative stance, in which the imagined truth of the past stands between and indeed binds literature and nature, is a type of perspective unavailable without a distancing of time and place. Hawthorne, too, is a storyteller at another remove. With the same theory of language, a lens of "suspended and inanimate" consciousness, he represents but does not define Hester Prynne. She in turn becomes the model of the unconscious promise in the evolution of a national vocabulary and language: The various imagined truths of Hester's past life also stand between—and bind—rhetoric and experiential history.

Though the autobiographically inclined narrator sees in retrospect "the true and indestructible value that lay hidden in petty and wearisome incidents and ordinary characters" of his own life, at no given time is he able to "diffuse thought and imagination through the opaque substance of to-day, and thus to make it a bright transparency" (37). Overt and conscious definition—maybe especially self-definition—eludes the storyteller precisely because it must be saved, condensed instead for future transmissibility: "[T]he page of life that was spread out before me seemed dull and commonplace, only because I had not fathomed its deeper import. A better book than I shall ever write was there ... only because my brain wanted the insight and my hand the cunning to transcribe it" (37). However, hope matches frustration in the narrator's response: If he can make, in his own mind, "a bright transparency" of his cultural past, then perhaps his own story will be as distinctly present to future readers as the *A* emblem seems to him. Perhaps the novel, like the adorned letter, will be transfigured for future readers; perhaps it will "turn to gold on the page" (37).

The depth of understanding implied in narrator, character, and fictional community in *The Scarlet Letter* bears a direct correlation to facility with language, and while "understanding" suggests social participation in a system of codes, facility is actually dependent upon distance, separation from the congregation, and an ability for nonrhetorical, truthful but creative, leadership. Despite the narrator's claims of distance, even he has difficulty extricating himself from the paradoxical webs binding the spoken and unspoken. He can no more say "adultery" than the town fathers can. It seems that he has inherited some degree of language deficiency—but in its reduced form, this language deficiency ironically also embodies the promise of a "bright[er] transparency" for future narrators of the culture's history.

As the narrative eye passes by a rosebush at the prison door, the narrator can "hardly do otherwise than pluck one of its flowers and present it to the reader" (48); this is a strange and jarring moment—another startling narrative symbol. No longer is the narrator so clearly removed from his story, nor is the reader safely distant. Narrative, tale-teller, and reader are here linked in an unsettling way: It is a gesture that implicates all three in the linguistic game that Hawthorne has begun to play. Interestingly, when the *North American Review* complained that "the master of such a wizard power over language as Mr. Hawthorne manifests" had wasted his talent on such a "revolting subject," it is specifically Hawthorne's most overt symbolism that seems most bothersome: "Fine writing [about adultery] seems as inappropriate as fine embroidery [on the scarlet letter]"; "the ugliness of pollution and vice is no more relieved by it than the gloom of prison is by the rose tree at its door."[8]

The rose blossom is in once sense as clear and familiar a symbol as is the *A*—either one can be read through context, tradition, and common intuition. Also like the *A*, however. the blossom is left with free-floating meaning, undefined by the narrator and the characters. Both symbols are too close to the storyteller (who makes a point of describing them tactilely) to be explicated, and similarly both are overly (even aggressively) accessible to the reader. Hawthorne provides in these symbols historical and imaginative links that preserve two opposing halves of their respective symbolic functions. Such connections put demands on the present moment—demands instinctively rejected by visions of history and symbolism that look for the "relief" of "ugliness" and "gloom" by beauty and new life, the cancellation of history through any alternative aesthetic. This narrator refuses such solutions and instead enters into the historical consciousness of New England Puritanism as Hawthorne would have it, even to the extent of recreating the ritual—now in the fulfilled linguistic form of the novel—that placed Hester and her sin before the community.

Through this ritual aspect of his novel, Hawthorne linguistically reenacts a moment of founding. Such a moment is necessarily unspeakable in its original nature but infinitely powerful as well. In order to represent the paradox of the founding moment, Hawthorne cannot have his Puritans give Hester a label reading "Adultery" or "Adulteress." From his own description it seems clear that if the narrator of "The Custom House" had found a cloth label of such specific kind, his historical imagination would have suffered reduction because of the label's specificity: The less concentrated form of language, the word or phrase, could not have cast the same imaginative spell; it would not have represented the "secret" sin. In the *A*, this narrator feels the preternatural power of an unspoken story, the "burning heat" as if of a "red-hot iron" (32). Both he and the seventeenth-century players in Hester's drama feel the danger and the power of that undefined idea—of a symbol as opposed to a label—and both intend to communicate meaning through that symbol.

Nevertheless, the meaning that Hawthorne, the narrator, and the fictional Puritans communicate is not definition; it is instead a sign of the entrance into the process of creating a new cultural language. Hester has suddenly embodied a transgression previously invisible to her community, and first efforts at language can acknowledge only importance, difference, and the need for attention—all indicating an intent to define later, once collective competence is achieved.[9] Like the New England regicides, Hester Prynne bears the extraordinary potency of the forbidden and the mysterious, but as Hester escapes that first instinct to define (and so to limit), she thus preserves the radical potential so quickly drained from the judges in their almost immediate cultural incorporation as symbolic figures.

In these first efforts toward communication, the town magistrates reveal their inability to differentiate between dangerous and otherwise powerful functions of language. Though she is bearer of their symbol, Hester alone can produce the freedom to think and to function in a nonsymbolic (that is, not *only* symbolic) realm. Her understanding and her use of language are based on—but not restricted to—the primary rational and empirical function of words.[10] In Hester, Locke's "arbitrariness" of the word or sign is counteracted by what emanates from that sign; within Hawthorne's work, the interplay of "sign" and "emanation" produce effective cultural symbolism. Hester is only another powerless Puritan woman destroyed by sin without the (ironic) gift of the imposed, dead letter of the law from the magistrates. With this gift, though, Hester begins to embody some interplay between sign and emanation (as between history and symbol); she thus revives her social order and a dying language—connects them to a future from which they are about to be ruptured—by becoming a living letter, that is, a letter of the emerging law.

As the latent promise of a second age, Hester's *A* is significantly unlike other Puritan forms of linguistic punishment, which were based on the principle of restricting language use.[11] In the language of both the fictional Puritans of Hawthorne's story and the historical Puritans of seventeenth-century New England, there is the consistent expression of a cultural hope—perhaps even a belief—that "they had captured the whole of reality in the texture of a rational language"; "word, thought, and thing were one" in this equation.[12] If language could be culturally monitored, then through organized education, controlled speech and literacy, and the use of only metaphors that would consistently refer to the biblical "Word," known to all, the leaders of the colony might blanket the population with a common morality.[13]

In "Endicott and the Red Cross," where an early figure of Hester Prynne first appears, the "Wanton Gospeller" reflected in Endicott's shield is one of Hawthorne's examples of language used in the service of controlled authority. He is defined, clearly and publicly, so that the community will immediately contextualize any of his "unsanctioned" "interpretations of Holy Writ" as "wanton."[14] Here "definition" ironically depends upon the vagueness necessary to cover a multitude of possible interpretations. This is the trick that escapes those punishing Hester: These Puritans clearly know that, in order to avoid being reductive, one's definitions must not confine in such a way as to be immediately obsolete. Metaphorical and symbolic language, ways of anticipating challenge and feeding imagination, are integral parts of Puritan thought.[15] However, the critique given through *The Scarlet Letter* points out an excessive reliance on the symbolic and the attending danger to the social structure. The conflicts within the romance show that although early America could count on importing rituals—of language, religion, or punishment—the interpretation of these rituals within the new context soon moved beyond predictability. In addition, this lost connection between sign and interpretation had eroded the primary function of ritual—social control—in the colony.

Ironically, the ritual nature of American language remained, though control of the ritual function had failed. In this world so conscious of language, the letter *A* on Hester's dress would stand for two untreated sentences: the biblical criminal sentence—death by stoning—waived in favor of the letter, and the sentence within the narrative that would name her sin. In these first days of the colony, however, one founded on the belief in a need for a new code of values, there are words for laws, but no words for broken laws. That is to say, there are laws to restrict activity and belief, but no clear understanding of the persistent existence of deviant behavior. In this context there is no way to harness the *positive potential* of deviance.[16] This leaves one simple reason that it seems as though no one within the story (including the narrator) can give even a capsule summary of Hester's sin: The necessary words—with the deviance they signify—have been deeply suppressed within the vocabulary of the colony, just as Hester's life story is so deeply buried under layers of narrative romance. Words within this society have either been tied too closely to actions in an excessively rational way or radically divorced from actions in an immediately symbolic way. In both cases words for sin—or any transgression, for that matter—are comprehensible only within the context of the negative imperative, in this case, the biblical commandment. By negating potential action and by making symbolic meaning explicitly referential, the commandment allows sin no existence of its own. Clearly the punishment of sin remains a ritual in structure, but an empty one—it is a ritual without function, without a defined nemesis.

Although this is a community for which "religion and law were almost identical" (50), they are not quite identical. In Hester's world as Hawthorne draws it, the faith systems of both religion and proto-national identity only coexist with—but do not match—a legal system that must address and work within lived history. Nonetheless it is true that both Puritanism specifically and laws generally are essentially reactionary: Both begin in restriction and dissent, thus acknowledging a dangerous power structure beyond themselves. If the conflict between the reactionary culture and the feared alternative identity is simply denied or artificially blanketed with an agreed-upon value system, then culture and power will never fuse into a "positive pattern" of social reality.[17] The narrative poetics of *The Scarlet Letter* suggests a different approach—a way to harness the easy route to self-definition guaranteed to the defensive party with the large-scale "positive pattern" available only to a potent culture that has moved beyond the language of negativity. Hawthorne represents all of this—the power of defense, establishment, conflict, and deviance—in the ironically empowering punishment of the scarlet letter.[18] Like Pearl, this letter has as its "principle of being" the "freedom of a broken law" (134).

In this model, Puritan Boston's town fathers are aware only of the first of language's powers, the ease of defensive self-definition based on contrast or negation. They acknowledge and even emphasize that Hester is different. They do not go back to this first step in communication to seek definition, however. Instead, they would prefer that she simply embody "difference," thereby encouraging the general, vague "conformity" of the rest of the town. Instead of banishing Hester, sending her like a true scapegoat into the wilds and thus acting as if she and her sin are closed off from society, this community chooses not only to keep her with them, but in fact to make her especially noticeable—to give both her and themselves a clear vision of her failing, to give visible form to the absence of a virtue.

As they lead Hester out of prison, the town fathers' one known purpose is to keep this transgression as part of Hester's identity for an unlimited time, whether with the scarlet letter or through the collective memory of her public confession. Working in part with "mercy and tenderness" (63), the magistrates want to help Hester achieve "an open triumph over the evil within [her]" (67). However, at least as strong is the community's motive of self-defense: It is as if these leaders, like Dimmesdale, think that a saturation of the community with the image of sin will be some ritual of purgation. But also like Dimmesdale, these men are manipulating language in such a way that they avoid the very core of its meaning: They suspend the demands of knowledge and transform the stigmatized Hester immediately into a cultural symbol. Depending upon the power of interpretation, but also with no means to control that power, the town magistrates set free a symbol that takes on a life of its own.[19]

Without the sanctioned codification of an explicitly spoken and positively asserted language, the Puritans have trouble controlling the meaning of the *A*. In this context—the tradition of sacrifice—it is significant that Hester is not only branded but also decorated, not only damaged but also adorned. However, the positive force of this punishment is an emblem of paradox, a demonstration that this sign still signifies only an abstract need for differentiation and not a definitive action or value. The absence of the *A* becomes a badge of honor and respectability: To be a member is not to wear an *A*—not to embody what the *A* symbolizes and not to know the experiential meaning of the *A*. Thus the strangeness of the sign, rather than any rational meaning fused with it, is the essence of the shame it conveys. While the terms of Hester's own integration require the active binding of experiential and rational with the symbolic—that is, the abandonment of a belief in definitive meaning as established in one realm or the other—society as a whole is still working too defensively to challenge the symbolic with the historical. In this colony, no affirmative statement of values can come about for those who do not wear the *A* because, as the narrative emphasizes, the entire response has been defensive rather than self-assertive: No purging of sin has occurred, no progress on a doctrine of ethics has been made, and—most specifically—no forward-looking codification of the transgression and punishment has emerged.

LANGUAGE IN HESTER'S WORLD

The promise given into Hester's charge is nowhere more evident than in her first emergence from prison. Walking out of the darkness into light, seen as a different person from the one who entered because she is now a mother and wears an *A*, Hester has been transformed as an image to the community. Nevertheless, instead of that transformation marking an end, it is surrounded with the images of beginnings—the baby, the first letter of the alphabet, the light. The town fathers believe that they can make of Hester what they will—for them that means to make her purely a symbol of sin— but in her historical life and in the empirical life of her fictional character, the important implicit gesture is an assumption that her personal past, including her adultery, is washed away in a ritual gesture of purification. The whole "ceremony," which was meant as a purification rite for the town—a transfiguration of the historical Hester into the symbolic Hester—empowers her not so much because she cares for their forgiveness but because it shows her that she is a presence threatening to her town, one too real to expel and—as yet—too strange to name. Hester thus acquires both the freedom and the burden of fusing her lived experience to a cultural symbol.

Wearing only the single letter, Hester is to flower into the grandest form of Puritan language, a "living sermon against sin" (63). As symbol and as sermon, she is to stand as the embodiment of the negative potential of every resident in her community. Like Dimmesdale's rhetorical assumption of this same role, Hester's involuntary assumption is outside of the realm of common speech. Although in Hester's case there is an assumed understanding of the message she wears and in Dimmesdale's case there is an assumed misunderstanding of the sermons he delivers, the two are connected in their knowledge of the "truth" and their status as perceived symbols. As symbols in the possession of the community, Hester and Dimmesdale are elusive and malleable: They are sacred and they are sinners, angels and humans, prophets and mutes; most importantly, they are the holy sermon whose subject is the unspeakable sin.[20]

The primary importance of one specific obligation—the commitment of the subject's experience and knowledge to the larger community—characterizes Benjamin's Storyteller and also governs the ranks and powers of characters in Hawthorne's world, as evidenced in his (at first apparently schematic) distribution of language abilities in the novel. In order to function most efficaciously as historical symbol, such a figure must allow the imposition of culturally chosen meanings; only Hester fulfills this political role.[21] All of the other characters within the fiction either elude or impede its progress. For example, Dimmesdale is a self-styled symbol. His manipulation of context, his tendency (whether conscious or not) to see to it that his words are inscribed within a situation he knows will be presumed "spiritual," makes the process of demystifying his symbolic character difficult for his congregation. Through an overdetermined rhetorical self-definition, Dimmesdale—like the colony itself—lives as if rational meaning is not only inaccessible but also obsolete. He thus severs his referential metaphors from his historical life.

Similarly—though in a less complex way—Chillingworth expresses himself only in ways that keep meaning at bay from the Puritan community; his primal passions are deeply out of place, and, in the eyes of this community, they are probably better placed among the Indians with whom he has spent recent time in captivity. Within these poles, however, is Hester. There is only the *A*, nothing elaborately rhetorical, nothing mythically prelinguistic; it is the familiar *A* of the hornbook. Whereas Dimmesdale and Chillingworth seem trapped in their respective symbolic modes, Hester is empowered by hers in a perverse sort of way. So simple and so clear, the import of Hester's symbol is thus the more strikingly undefined in speech. Boston's children can speak of her cultural meaning, but without comprehension: They utter "a word that had no distinct purport to their own minds, but was none the less terrible to [Hester]" (85). Thus the importance of Hester's story—its potential to help define the culture's values—coupled with its unspoken mystification, delineates the weaknesses of the emergent American language at mid-century and points to a vision (however remote) of a better way, of a language based upon the whole of experiential life.

Pearl, as part of the generation of children who are the only ones to be able to name—if not to understand—Hester according to her sin, shows a greater freedom with her language and thus implicitly offers a vision of a different future.[22] She is interested in learning meaning and applying it to the familiar people and things of her world; she asks questions that have never before been asked, questions embarrassing to her elders. Nevertheless, although Pearl has the desire absent from the older Puritans, she does not have the distance necessary for revelation. As the "living hieroglyphic" (207), Pearl can set in motion the impulse to speak in her world: She can question, but the answers, the language and stories that she may see latent in the *A*, can emerge only slowly, through a growing distance from New World culture; some of this distance—and its tempting claims to objectivity—the romance's narrator hopes to gain. Pearl, so often defined in criticism as the *A* embodied, is one version of that already-fulfilled living form, that transmissible essence, of Benjamin's theory. As that form, however, she is constrained in another way: She has no way of giving voice to the story that has created and encoded her, and so she too depends to a certain extent on the machinations of narrative.

The historically distanced narrator compensates for—and so implicitly comments on—Boston's inability to make sense of the transgression that Hester has committed. He sees and represents the town fathers' bungling of ritual, their failure to demand a foundation—a primary moment when language is bound to meaning—for the creation of their new cultural symbol; from this evidence, the narrator sees and represents also the ironic purification of Hester, gained only by way of ritual defilement.[23] Even though it is the suppression of story, the denial of conflict, and thus the maintenance of a utopia of sorts that is the job of the town's most powerful members, they are the ones calling for truth to be visible, to come out of the shadows. Hester's reply—a determined secrecy—thus undermines their decision and recoils upon their traditional strategy of the suppression of language: Now the suppression of language has been coopted by the town's outrageous transgressor.[24]

In this way, the shift in power to Hester Prynne begins the narrative's most extraordinary challenge to communal understanding, wherein Hawthorne's formal properties of narrative emphasize over and over the historical properties of the *A* and the irreducibility of this trace that stands for so many material facts of America's living record. The magistrates are not the only offenders in their narrowness of vision: Through these same errors, this blindly utopian project of submitting to the refusal of storytelling, the preacher and the doctor—two other individuals with roles centered on providing for the health and welfare of the community—fail as communicators within both their own social world and the world of the text.

At odds with Hester's cultural role of advancing society through a linguistic fusion of symbol and history is this utopian mode of rhetoric, which we might associate with the romance itself but for Hester's own vivid interruptions of its tone and function. It is a dysfunctional theory of language for which Dimmesdale and Chillingworth provide the frame. Together they fashion a model of the trap of language that both binds and sustains this community's present state: Dimmesdale replaces fundamental statements with rhetoric, and Chillingworth represses every essential fact of language. Both men manipulate their language to suppress their (threateningly transgressive) identities in order that they might blend into Boston, as members essentially the same as everyone else—Chillingworth in his "purposes to live and die unknown" (76), and Dimmesdale, who, because of his position in the community, must say to Hester, "I charge thee to speak out the name of thy fellow-sinner" with such passion that any observer would expect that the "guilty one himself ... would be drawn forth by an inward and inevitable necessity" (67–68). Purely symbolic communication—including Dimmesdale's celebrated rhetoric and Chillingworth's primal avoidance of the spoken or written word—is a literally empty symbolism. In both cases the substance (or the secret) that gives rise to symbolic language has been fully removed, and what remains is a shell, an outline of a truth once lived. Though overtly supportive of the status quo, such symbolism is all the more dangerous for its persuasiveness; in reality it threatens the culture with nothing less than a loss of foundational knowledge through its denial of the relevance of generative mystery within cultural symbolism.

Chillingworth's refusal to express himself verbally is clear in his defiance of the simplest duty of human language, the dissemination of information in the community. He obscures both of the primary facts of his life related to language, his name and his marriage vow; for all of these overt similarities, Chillingworth stands as a marked contrast to the New England regicides, whose dangerous silence was directed toward the abstraction of monarchical power and never (apparently) toward their own neighbors. Chillingworth, though, choosing to erase his prior self and become instead a "dark miner," waiting for "the soul" of his usurper Dimmesdale to "be dissolved, and flow forth in a dark, but transparent stream, bringing all its mysteries into the daylight" (124), indeed has emptied himself of all substance. "Without any intrusive egotism" or any "disagreeably prominent characteristics of his own" (124), he is the inverse of Dimmesdale, who has "extended his egotism over the whole expanse of nature" (155) in such a way as to leave the burden of his self-styled identity ironically on those around him. Chillingworth instead surrenders his individuality to the project of invading a consciousness outside of his own, and by doing so he forsakes both the promise and the integrity of his own mind.

Furthermore, what Chillingworth knows is certainly important. But by denying the existence of an active self (the potential storyteller) in favor of preying upon Dimmesdale's soul—by insisting, that is, on being a reader of another man's heart rather than writing the new and unique facts of his own heart—Chillingworth refuses to advance any cultural story. What he thinks and feels would surely be an important element, one that must be gathered into the collective knowledge of the new society as part of their memory of an early instance of a direct challenge to their own laws, their primary social bonds. From his story, the town could learn about whatever is most real, most human, in the consequences of sin as they understand it. If he played the role of King Arthur (for example), he could be wise and just, doomed to sorrow, nevertheless providing a real presence to the abstract notion of the betrayed and so embodying just what the Puritans need to see, the nature and substance of a law transgressed.

Because Chillingworth renders himself incapable of expressing his perceptions, however, he denies to others the possibility of codifying his role within the community; this makes him a failure with regard to his own purposes and to his potential as a productive member of his society. He has denied to this community the language necessary to be able to make sense of experience by refusing to contribute his perceptions—represented here as the first of their kind within the colony—to society's code of norms. Just as the strangeness of Hester's *A* infuses it with power, so too the secrets in Chillingworth's knowledge make his choice of nonparticipation extraordinarily damaging. He withholds the especially important knowledge accessible only in the elusive liminal areas, those places explicitly beyond the known social world that cannot be entered by choice but only by circumstance, historical necessity.[25] Thus, Chillingworth's linguistic failures and denials play a crucial role because of the abnormality that they conceal. So far from playing the prophet, Chillingworth stifles his voice until he exists within an almost prelinguistic state. As he flies into a wild dance of repressed language upon finally seeing the minister's secret pain branded on his chest, Chillingworth's manner of victory celebration is precisely what manifests his failure:

> After a brief pause, the physician turned away.
>
> But with what a wild look of wonder, joy, and horror! With what a ghastly rapture, as it were, too mighty to be expressed only by the eye and features, and therefore bursting forth through the whole ugliness of his figure, and making itself even riotously manifest by the extravagant gestures with which he threw up his arms towards the ceiling, and stamped his foot upon the floor! (138)

Consumed by "ghastly rapture," the "extravagant gestures" of the moment have no translation into language. As one who ventures beyond the norm—both in terms of personal consciousness and the fiction's own geography—only to return speechless rather than prophetic, Chillingworth's social failure is commensurate with his personal betrayals.

Hawthorne layers Chillingworth's role with additional irony by describing Chillingworth's methods of uncovering secrets with language and imagery reminiscent of the narrator's description of his own story telling process. However, the distinction is one of vision. While the reading of the Puritan past that Hawthorne does through his narrator is infused with a belief in progress and a search for foundations, Chillingworth's parallel reading is only backward looking and so must be destructive. Chillingworth is not a reader who advances through the revelation of secrets; he is a voyeur, waiting for the explosive results of a fact that he already knows. His failure is even greater than suggested in the common leech/host image often used to characterize his relationship with Dimmesdale; he is less than a leech because Dimmesdale, the nearly lifeless figurehead, lacks the substance to be a host.

This doctor's revelations about his patient's misery are not achieved through confidence but through silence. Between the poles of rhetoric and gesture and embodied in the complete lack of communication between Dimmesdale and Chillingworth is only a "nameless horror" (156), a "silence, an inarticulate breath" (124)—only this to define a world without a language sufficient to its experience. This absence of name, confession, or confrontation, which characterizes the Chillingworth/Dimmesdale relationship, is a model of the linguistic vacuum within which Hawthorne places Puritan Boston; the bipolar opposition that the two men create represents the range of experiences of language possible before the radical transformation of Hester and her symbol.

With regard to the community's evident need for self-empowerment through new vocabulary and language, Dimmesdale is both a victim and a failure as culpable as Chillingworth. He fails to take responsibility both for his own transgression and his own language; in fact, Dimmesdale actively avoids such responsibility through careful orchestrations and manipulations of circumstance. He speaks in abstractions and chooses contexts that are more theoretical than experiential; that is, he speaks in contexts where words are not expected to bring about ordinary understanding of the present tense (or to make "a bright transparency of to-day"), but rather where they are elevated immediately into symbolic thought. He speaks from the pulpit, and so his confessions are impersonal. There he takes responsibility for the general state of sin, and adultery (as action, or at least as thought) is foremost among the failures that give substance to that general state.

Although implicating himself in that generic state of fallenness, however, Dimmesdale moves no closer to confession of his own specific transgression, of its place in history. If he could leave behind his support system of the pulpit and the crowd—even if he could say the same words, but to an individual in the town, outside of the church context, he would be using language for a different—and more fundamental—purpose: to establish mutual understanding. Though like Hester, Dimmesdale plays a symbolic role largely controlled by the community, he accrues some of his own guilt and responsibility in his attempts to step outside of his own consciousness, to objectify himself as a symbol, and then to manipulate that objectified role. Like Chillingworth, Dimmesdale is given the chance to tell a "true" (that is, experiential) story. Dimmesdale's refusal to take on that role is far more complex than Chillingworth's brute repression, however: Dimmesdale's response is not silence but a careful narrative that, ironically, through the very perfection of its design, becomes as ineffective (for both his culture's needs and ironically his own designs) and as far from revelation as simple denial.

As a preacher for a group of nonseparatist Puritans whose intentions were not schism but reform, Dimmesdale naturally receives the benefits of some inherited respect for his station. The expectations that come with his social role are not easily or quickly abandoned. Even Hawthorne's audience shares some degree of this attitude, and as the *North American Review* points out, it may cause readers to be "cheated" into sympathizing with Dimmesdale if they carry with them the "habitual respect for the sacred order, and ... faith in religion."[26] However, it is quickly evident that Dimmesdale is perceived as a good speaker because he reinforces comfortable perceptions. In the description of Dimmesdale as "a young clergyman, who had come from one of the great English universities, bringing all the learning of the age into our wild forestland" (66), Hawthorne suggests that this preacher has been met by an uncritical reverence based specifically on Old World principles. Dimmesdale's accomplishments are well suited to the "shelter and concealment" (214) of England and its universities, perhaps, but ineffectual for pioneer life in the wilds of New England" (214):

> Notwithstanding his high native gifts and scholar-like attainments, there was an air about this young minister,—an apprehensive, a startled, a half-frightened look,—as of a being who felt himself quite astray and at a loss in the pathway of human existence, and could only be at ease in some seclusion of his own. Therefore, so far as his duties would permit, he trode in the shadowy by-paths, and thus kept himself simple and child-like; coming forth, when occasion was, with a freshness, and fragrance, and dewy purity of thought, which, as many people said, affected them like the speech of an angel. (66)

His "scholar-like attainments" become as empty and artificial as a modern reading of Hawthorne's language makes them sound, now that Dimmesdale is in this "forestland."[27] Similarly, feeling "quite astray and at a loss in the pathway of human existence" is certainly an unfortunate image to put forth to one's followers, particularly at a time when these followers urgently need to cut pathways into a New World. Finally, for his congregation to perceive these manners as "dewy purity of thought" "like the speech of and angel" is an extraordinary leap of faith—clearly no one knows either Dimmesdale's thought or an angel's speech but may at best intuit both; such leaps of faith entirely bypass the primary epistemological necessities of colonial living.[28]

The Dimmesdale his congregation knows is not a man but little more than a cipher (albeit one functioning as a figurehead) into which all community expectations go—at his carefully chosen times and in his manipulated circumstances. Dimmesdale does not conform, and yet his contradictory nature ironically helps perpetuate a static social order. By embodying the antisocial and contextualizing it within accepted parameters, he reinforces an unquestioning embrace of the status quo rather than forcing the expansion of the boundaries of social understanding. With the goals of ordering his perceptions, designing his world, and thus converting history and human truth into lies of social belief, Dimmesdale appears afraid to be the prophet and to lose his life in the process; he is afraid to "let the wick of his life be consumed completely by the gentle flame of his story."[29]

Dimmesdale's communication outside of the pulpit reflects this fear. Much like his community's cultural consciousness, Dimmesdale embodies an unresolved dichotomy, the tortured condition of defense, in which patently experiential knowledge—the individual experience of lived history—is contained (in two senses) within familiar and formulaic language. Clearly Dimmesdale has "lived"—and, compared to his fellow Puritans within the novel's world, perhaps, he has done so with some depth of sensitivity and passion. It may be that these same traits generate the system of rhetorical defense by which he must protect himself—by which he expresses preference for the safety of structure and stasis over the dynamics of cultural process.

Dimmesdale voices specific, true, and dangerous facts, but his mode of expression ensures that these facts are transformed before entering the ears of his congregation; this orchestration is so complete that his extraordinary fear and tremulousness—qualities that push the community to question his nature—are revered, and he is elevated further from history's carnal world into the sphere of spirit: "He had told his hearers that he was ... a thing of unimaginable iniquity.... [T]hey heard it all, and did but reverence him the more.... He had spoken the very truth, and transformed it into the veriest falsehood" (143–44). This he does by depending upon a predictable (rather than new) interplay of history and language; he depends upon his context, upon his mastery of that context, and thus, upon the effects of that context on his words.

As Dimmesdale sets up a confession scene filled with portentous distractions, his reliance on a given set of expectations to absolve him from the consequence of his words is clear: He ascends the scaffold in the night, not because he is finally "driven hither by the impulse of ... Remorse" (148) but because he is attracted by the gothic horror of the setting, sure to account for any frightening events that might occur that night.[30] There is "no peril of discovery" in this context even after a scream escapes from him, because in the town's collective belief, aided by the black of night, such a sound sooner would be thought of as "something frightful in a dream, or [taken] for the noise of witches; whose voices, at that period, were often heard to pass over the settlements or lonely cottages, as they rode with Satan through the air" (149). In this way Dimmesdale's confession has been quite brilliantly (if perhaps unconsciously) orchestrated in such a way that its message will be transformed completely before being codified by the town. Every one of Dimmesdale's actions shows that he seeks inscription within an established story; he rejects the role of truth teller in favor of setting himself within layers of inscription that will protect him from the simplest and most fundamental consequences of word and thought. His reliance on rhetoric, context, and expectation provide him safety but at the cost of any possible cultural potency.

In the aftermath of his adultery, then, it is not surprising that Dimmesdale's mistakes are many and varied yet always related to the intemperate use of language—whether as deception or as radical revelation. His period of transformation just before delivering the Election Day sermon is marked significantly by multiple temptations related to language, suggesting the wearing away of his defenses. He suffers impulses to teach profanity to small children and to speak blasphemously to the elderly and is nearly consumed by these desires. Clearly Dimmesdale's passion allows him to approach a new—even revolutionary—framework for language use.

Ironically, however, his final reversal will only prove his utter entrapment. He cannot free himself from the extremes of language use; he cannot locate the foundations of meaning to his all-too-plentiful words. This failure is clear in the narrator's inability to record those words of his final sermon—directly or symbolically—within the text; those words, it would seem, swim somewhere beyond the historical eye of the narrative. Because of his self-disabling language, Dimmesdale cannot fuse his life in history to its symbolic definition; he has both lived and spoken, but the link between these two acts has been severed.

Dimmesdale's final confession is, then, self-destructive without the potentially redemptive promise of contributing to the developing colony. He makes yet another mistake as he explodes the mystery of his experiences by attempting to define in his forever powerless words that which has much more cultural force than mere information. His efforts at reintegration fail because his personal identity has long since ceased to be his own. He cannot just change it at will any more than Hester can make herself a new life in the Old World; the two of them are in some sense communal property. There is a unique problem with Dimmesdale, however: Both in his language and his social identity he has come to embody an abstract system that demands the *universal* consent and faith of the community. He can change his language and his identity, but he cannot achieve reintegration because—in that change—the universal belief that he had embodied challenges itself from within and crumbles under its failure to maintain the status of an absolute. Multiplicity of interpretation attests to an inherent flaw in the pure ideal—and here, in the figure of Dimmesdale, purity stands as the entire basis for belief.

What Dimmesdale fails to do is to participate actively in the growth of the culture. Though his vision in the Election Day sermon is apparently one of the future, his life is locked in the past, and he has been able to construct no present ground on which to stand and unite these trajectories of time. In the mid-nineteenth century, popular heroes of the Puritan era derived their greatness in large part from their bond to the future and through the present responsibility for leadership that such a bond engendered; they were decidedly not men of the past. Sustaining the traditional model of the Christian hero's necessary submission to divine purpose, a widespread, mainstream, belief in nineteenth-century America suggested that the greatness of such Puritan figures rested in (to use Horace Bushnell's terms) "their unconsciousness"—their selfless dedication and their "secret love" for the advancement of an order, which they might establish but not bring to completion.[31] But Dimmesdale is impatient. Frustrated by years of repressing his story, he leaps beyond what might eventually be the "silent growth of centuries," and in doing so, he once again fails to contribute to his society—now not through deception, but through another mistake of an overdetermined consciousness, the inability to allow for the fulfillment of an ideal by forces beyond subjective consciousness.

Unlike "the story of the scarlet letter[, which] grew into a legend" (261)—gained cohesion, transmissibility, and meaning in Hester's absence—Dimmesdale's story has a far less profound effect on his world. Some in his audience believe him and some do not; the diversity of interpretation mirrors the fragments of the ideal system, which he had perpetuated falsely and then broken necessarily. There is the initial promise that the crowd's response to the sermon—"a strange, deep voice of awe and wonder, which could not as yet find utterance" (257)—might emerge in a "bright transparency" in later ages, but that promise expires with the same excessive speed as has attended Dimmesdale's telling of the story.

After "many days" rather than generations or centuries, "time sufficed for the people to arrange their thoughts in reference" to the meaning of Dimmesdale's sermon (258); little time is necessary when the story bears no great promise, only the fragmentation of belief. As a character who has depended on his society for his (false) identity, Dimmesdale's revelation leaves him without a role. His death is not the patriotic culmination of the truth teller "with high aspirations for the welfare of his race" (130); rather, it is the only end to a Puritan who had made himself unreal (ultimately vulnerable, fragile, and unregenerative) through his denial of his experiential life and his crippling excess of consciousness, achieved through artificial constructions of language and self-serving manipulations of ambiguity.

As opposite poles in a paralyzing trap, Dimmesdale is false rhetoric, with all of its flourishes, and Chillingworth is inarticulate gesture, with all of its passion. Their common problem is a demonstrated inability both to understand language as it emerges from history and to recognize the substantiality of the bond between the poles (and, as men, between them too; in either case, the bond is Hester—the only one who knows both of their secrets as well as her own).[32] By choosing to play the roles that they do, both

Dimmesdale and Chillingworth fail to work toward a new code for a New World, a national story in an American language.

HESTER AS STORYTELLER

The strength of this linguistic trap and its enforcement from prominent figures such as the doctor and the preacher make it no surprise that the same frame defines the language relations between Hester and her town. Previous to her transgression, Hester was a member of her society, which at its inception imagined itself as a "Utopia of human virtue." Like all such places, however, this community "invariably recognized it among their earliest practical necessities to allot a portion of the virgin soil as a cemetery, and another portion as the site of a prison" (47). From the start, even the most idealistic settlement will understand death and crime (here perhaps synonymous with sin) as part of the common lot: For idealism to thrive, there must be a simple and clear repository for whatever does not fit. The potential problem, of course, is that such aberrations need not be clear or final; the sin (or the death, in horror stories) may not fundamentally transform the subject.

Then there is a violation that cannot be sealed in a vault, and the whole order of the utopia stands threatened. Before Hester's time, Puritan Boston's static framework for knowledge and language had been tenuously sufficient. As the task of self-definition grew more complex, however, and as history unfolded in unpredictable ways, the community found the weakness in their utopian order: No longer was it clear that sin would be transformative. In fact, Hawthorne suggests that those who continue to insist upon living by the rules of the orderly utopia write themselves out of the progress of history: Of the two who believed in a future world of freer expression and love, only Hester is left.

However, because of the distance necessary to revelation in Hawthorne's model, Hester herself is prophetic by the end only in a limited sense; she is an active but speechless prophet. Just as the *A* is only the smallest step toward a linguistically potent culture, so too is Hester's own life meant only to begin and to set into motion a new and active perception of language and story. With the deaths of Chillingworth and Dimmesdale, the paralyzing bond is broken, and Hester's life itself continues to make the wilderness somehow more domestic, less mysterious: "Her sin, her ignominy, were the roots which she had struck into the soil. It was as if a new birth, with stronger assimilations than the first, had converted the forest-land, still so uncongenial to every other pilgrim and wanderer, into Hester Prynne's wild and dreary, but life-long home" (80). As the only one actively breaking down the barriers to effective language in her society, the only one fusing symbol and meaning, Hester is ironically estranged from the common symbolic frame of reference; she makes her own life as she walks through the "moral wilderness" (199). Even so, as a prophet of sorts, Hester is animated by her historical memory and a complicated, perhaps buried, drive to live her story fully and so to bring it into a future age.

A historical memory and a compelling desire to transmit: These are exactly the two qualities most essential to participation in the establishment of a national language and literature in Jacksonian and antebellum America. While Hawthorne is born into a rhetoric of nationhood, perhaps he too feels a "story" within his memory—something transmissible (paradoxically) because unexplained, something that had never been conveyed as information but that instead permeates "the life of the storyteller, in order to bring it out of him again."[33]

For the storyteller in this formulation, language presents a peculiar problem: It must encode rather than define, transmit but not expend, its story; Hester Prynne is that storyteller. Creating as she goes, Hester is a pioneer who accepts a challenge to make real words, ideas, and all fragments of language that are only empty rhetoric to the others in her society, to infuse lived meaning and historical experience into a cultural symbol. She has no one, however, not even her lover, with whom she can discuss her pioneering; the power of Hester's "magic circle" (246) of language both denies her possible consciousness of personal revelation and secures those revelations for Hawthorne's America. So much of Hester's storytelling is left to later generations.

Hester's reality is palpable. It has the dimensions of both life and symbol, "infant" and "shame." As she emerges from the prison, made a new woman, she accepts that some transformation has taken place and that her perception of the world must likewise change: "Could it be true? She clutched the child so fiercely to her breast, that it sent forth a cry; she turned her eyes downward at the scarlet letter, and even touched it with her finger, to assure herself that the infant and the shame were real. Yes!—these were her realities,—all else had vanished" (59). To say that Hester is empowered by the *A* is not to say that she enjoys this power, that it is desirable in the abstract, or even that she knows exactly what the power is. From even the little Hawthorne tells us about Hester's society, we know that she is not the only person guilty of adultery. To return to her town, however, to live out her life wearing the *A*—that is to accept a role never before taken in that wilderness utopia.

What is more, Hester, with her decorated *A*, can perform a proto-nationalistic function only because of this unique role in which symbol returns to history. According to Hawthorne's own records, not only did his chosen ending to *The Scarlet Letter* send his wife Sophia to bed with an incapacitating headache, but he too could hardly bear to see what he had left for his heroine to do: "When I read the last scene of The Scarlet Letter ... just after writing it—tried to read it, rather, for my voice swelled and heaved, as if I were tossed up and down on an ocean, as it subsided after a storm ... I was in a very nervous state, then, having gone through a great diversity and severity of emotion, for many months past. I think I have never overcome my own adamant [coolness] in any other instance."[34] He had given Hester the burden of living for another age entirely; the sacrifice entailed is overwhelming.

In his description of the American development of the English language, Noah Webster anticipates the role Hawthorne thus gives to Hester: "To cultivate and adorn [the language], is a task reserved for [those] who shall understand the connection between language and logic, and form an adequate idea of the influence which a uniformity of speech may have on national attachments."[35] To place Hester in this role is to see her enduring function as escaping—if only to a limited extent—the frame of containment that Hawthorne's plot seems to wish to force upon her, to see in her, that is, a persistent layer of the radical. Just as the magistrates imposed upon Hester a scarlet letter, which then grew to take on all manner of unexpected meanings, so too does Hawthorne's narrator impose upon her an apparently final sentence, sending her back to dark New England, and yet there her tombstone assures us—her life will continue to generate among its many meanings at least a few of residual illegibility, a few that is, that will escape expected narratives.[36]

Thus we are reminded that the reading of Hester's life—particularly as a symbol whose meanings reach downward and inward into the private world of love, as well as outward into culture, and upward into moral (and/or transcendental) meanings—makes it compulsory for audiences to return, to reread, and finally to acknowledge the irrecoverable losses of history and memory. The interpreter cannot help but sense distance, even intrusion, as we—with the romance's "curious investigator"—look upon the "dust of the two sleepers" with "one tombstone [carved] for both" (262). Hawthorne's extraordinarily meticulous historiography ensures that, again with the wandering investigator, the text's interpreter stands at a place in history distant from Hester and yet also nowhere near an age that can find itself utterly separate from her.

Hester Prynne and her *A* thus leave us in the most complicated of situations, neither trapped nor free, as we move back and forth between interpretive positions. The romance, Hawthorne makes clear, has not finished the task of imagining. Not only are we turned back to the *A* as we imagine the tombstone, but we should also recall in the end that there is another manuscript to read, another origin to the story of Hester Prynne: "Prying further into the manuscript, I found the record of other doings and sufferings of this singular woman.... The original papers, together with the scarlet letter itself,—a most curious relic,—are still in my possession, and shall be freely exhibited to whomsoever, induced by the great interest of the narrative, may desire a sight of them" (35). To return and to reread: That is ever Hawthorne's imperative to us, and in this image of a manuscript outside of the romance itself, we are compelled to acknowledge the layers of storytelling, which make that task endless. In our distance from certainty we will surely envision the ruptures of revolution, but in our insatiable appetite for imaginative interpretation, we continue to enact their repair.

NOTES

1. In terms helpful to an understanding of this change in the culture's code of self-definition, Victor Turner has distinguished between the functions of the "liminal" and the "liminoid"—the change in the relation of the transitional (or transgressing) character to the status quo. While in traditional cultures (in Turner's terminology), the liminal condition is "demanding" and "compulsory," the "liminoid" (modern cultures' version of the liminal) is a condition of will and choice in which "great public stress is laid on the individual innovator, the unique person who dares and opts to create." Furthermore, Turner argues, liminality in traditional cultures "secretes the seed of the liminoid, waiting only for major changes in the sociocultural context to set it agrowing." In this model, to the fictional Puritans of Boston, Hester is clearly and simply liminal. Her status as an outsider is an enforced punishment. In Hawthorne's representation of Hester's personal history, however—in the course of her life and in her entrance into the United States of 1850—Hester more and more resembles the "liminoid"; she is the harbinger of a modernity fusing new cultural contexts to the seeds that allow them to grow (Turner, "Liminal to Liminoid, in Play, Flow, and Ritual: An Essay in Comparative Symbology," *Rice University Studies* 60 [1974], 53–92).

2. Colacurcio, *The Province of Piety: Moral History in Hawthornes Early Tales*, 457.

3. Anne W. Abbott finds Hawthorne's "favorite metaphor of the guillotine" to be one of the undesirable and "unpoetical" aspects of the romance.

4. Hester herself envisions such a future—albeit a future from which she excludes herself—as she instructs Pearl in the celebration of Governor's Day: "[T]o-day, a new man is beginning to rule over [the colony]; and so—as has been the custom of mankind ever since a nation first gathered—they make merry and rejoice; as if a good and golden year were at length to pass over the poor old world!" (228).

5. Benjamin, "The Task of the Translator," in *Illuminations*, 74–75.

6. Hawthorne, "Endicott and the Red Cross," in *Twice-Told Tales*, 436. The "grim beadle" in *The Scarlet Letter* echoes this sentiment: "'A blessing on the righteous Colony of the Massachusetts, where iniquity is dragged out into the sunshine'" (54).

7. Benjamin, "The Task of the Translator," in *Illuminations*, 80.

8. [Anne W. Abbott], 147.

9. In terms helpful to understanding the magistrates' sincere but inadequate use of language, Mary Douglas describes the evolution of cultural roles: "All the attribution of dangers and powers is part of this effort to communicate and thus to create social forms" (*Purity and Danger*, 101).

10. For Hawthorne, of course, purely rational language would be as insufficient as the purely transcendental. For a discussion of this conflict, see Philip Gura, *The Wisdom of Words: Language, Theology, and Literature in the New England Renaissance*.

11. Here again, the imagery is specifically revolutionary: See p. 163, in "Another View of Hester":

> It was an age in which the human intellect, newly emancipated, had taken a more active and wider range than for many centuries before. Men of the sword had overthrown nobles and kings. Men bolder than these had overthrown and rearranged—not actually, but within the sphere of theory, which was their most real abode the whole system of ancient prejudice, wherewith was linked much of ancient principle. Hester Prynne imbibed this spirit. She assumed a freedom of speculation, then common enough on the other side of the Atlantic, but which our forefathers, had they known of it, would have held to be a deadlier crime than that stigmatized by the scarlet letter. In her lonesome cottage, by the sea-shore, thoughts visited her, such as dared to enter no other dwelling in New England; shadowy guests, that would have been as perilous as demons to their entertainer, could they have been seen so much as knocking at her door.

12. Charles Feidelson Jr., *Symbolism and American Literature*.

13. On the religious and educational importance of language to the New England Puritans, see Baron, *Grammar and Good Taste*, esp. 119–39.

14. Hawthorne, "Endicott," in *Twice-Told Tales*, 435.

15. For evidence of this dominant tone, we need look no further than John Winthrop's famous sermon—"A Model of Christian Charity" (1630)—on board the *Arbella*, as it sailed toward the soon-to-be-established Massachusetts Bay Colony.

16. For the implications of deviance specifically within Puritan culture, see Kai T. Erikson, *Wayward Puritans: A Study in the Sociology of Deviance*.

17. Douglas, *Purity and Danger*, 38. This is the moment at which emergent, involuntary, cultural memory has the greatest potency. Taussig argues that the appearance of involuntary memory "fuses the real with the imaginary" (*Defacement*, 142).

18. In Hawthorne's model this glittering letter might be compared to Endicott's reflective and unlettered breastplate in "Endicott and the Red Cross" because of its power to reflect the symbolic sum total of the Puritan colony—past, present, and future. See Sacvan Bercovitch's "Endicott's Breastplate: Symbolism and Typology in 'Endicott and the Red Cross,'" *Studies in Short Fiction*.

19. Here again we might contrast the contained power of the regicides within New England legend. While retaining some substantial claim to secrecy, these men do not carry with them a story that cannot be predicted or controlled. Their revolution has been defeated; they are thus images of lost possibility and the hopes that such memory can foster, rather than images of radical futurity. The social turmoil suggested by the magistrates' lack of control comes from the particular quality of "social pollution" that enables Hester to be both sinner and saint to her community. She embodies the type of deviance that Douglas calls "danger from internal contradiction, when some of the basic postulates [of a

society] are denied by other basic postulates." Douglas says that such a case is characteristic of a social "system [that] seems to be at war with itself" (*Purity and Danger*, 122).

20. Hawthorne makes the connection between Hester and the Puritan sermon as explicit as that between Dimmesdale and the sermons: "If she entered a church, trusting to share the Sabbath smile of the Universal Father, it was often her mishap to find herself the text of the discourse" (85).

21. As I have suggested throughout this chapter, I believe that Hawthorne's world of historical symbolism mirrors the ideology of northern liberalism in 1850 in that both worlds delegate the (democratic) epistemological burden to society, though by noting the reflection it is not my purpose to present Hawthorne's tone as didactic.

22. Following Taussig, we might say that because Pearl, as a child, cannot "keep" a secret in the same way that adults can, so she also cannot "be kept by it" (*Defacement*, 121).

23. As Michael Taussig notes, there is "something so strange emanating from the wound of sacrilege wrought by desecration" that the exile that comes with defilement becomes a form of magic, and that "desecration [is] the closest many of us are going to get to the sacred in this modern world" (*Defacement: Public Secrecy and the Labor of the Negative*, 1).

24. Hester is, at the start, a peculiar figure of the Virgin Mary; not only does she obscure the paternity of her child, resulting in social exile, but the tale ultimately also makes clear that she carries the child of the resident Man of God. However resonant these plot lines are, though, the parallels decidedly do not result for Hester in any of the experiences of transcendence familiar to the New Testament story.

25. Douglas defines this "double play on inarticulateness" that invests Chillingworth with a potential power and makes his refusal to tell his story all the more damaging to the social order: "First there is a venture into the disordered regions of the mind. Second there is the venture beyond the confines of society. The man who comes back from these inaccessible regions brings with him a power not available to those who have stayed in control of themselves and of society" (*Purity and Danger*, 95).

26. [Abbott], 141.

27. That is to say, the language seems to me characteristic enough of Hawthorne that it may not carry any intentional irony, but in combination with the details elaborated in this chapter, an ironic reading seems merited by the overall tone of the passage.

28. What interests me here is the double abstraction, which renders the analogy only more difficult to imagine than either of its component parts and clearly undoes the primary function of analogy, which is to render the abstract more accessible to a world resistant to such language.

29. Benjamin, "The Storyteller," in *Illuminations*, 108–9.

30. Larry Reynolds makes a fascinating point when he connects the image of the scaffold to the European revolutions of 1848. Reynolds demonstrates that to attribute the scaffold to the Puritans is a "historical inaccuracy"; instead, he argues, Hawthorne must be using the term as a synecdoche for the guillotine. See *European Revolutions and the American Literary Renaissance*, 84.

31. See Bushnell, *The Fathers of New England*, 7, 12–13, 30–31.

32. Hester's bond to Dimmesdale is clear, and so too should be her bond to Chillingworth, when we posit the powers of secrecy within the novel. As Brook Thomas argues, "Chillingworth's 'new secrets' [as learned among the Indians] might be associated with a 'primitive' realm that Hester's vision of an enlightened future hopes to overcome, but the 'promise of secrecy' that once again binds husband and wife suggests a possible connection between the two" ("Citizen Hester," 191).

33. Benjamin, "The Storyteller," in *Illuminations*, 89, 91–92.

34. Hawthorne, 1855 entry in *The English Notebooks*, 225.

35. Noah Webster, *Dissertations on the English Language*, 18; as quoted in Baron, *Grammar and Good Taste*, 45.

36. David S. Reynolds is among the critics who sees the end of *The Scarlet Letter* differently, arguing that it provides evidence that "Hawthorne explore[d] the subversive and then recoil[ed] to the pious." In this ending Reynolds sees what he argues is a frequent strategy in Hawthorne's work, the "strategy of tacking a benign moral conclusion onto a deeply disturbing tale" (*Beneath the American Renaissance*, 121–22).

Chronology

1804	Nathaniel Hawthorne (originally Hathorne) is born on July 4 in Salem, Massachusetts, the second child of Nathaniel Hathorne, a sea captain, and Elizabeth Clarke Manning Hathorne.
1808	Father dies of yellow fever in New Guinea.
1821–1825	Attends Bowdoin College, Maine.
1828	Publishes *Fanshawe* anonymously and at his own expense.
1830	Begins to publish many sketches and tales anonymously or using a pseudonym.
1837	Publishes *Twice-Told Tales*.
1839–1840	Works as measurer of salt and coal at Boston Custom House.
1841	In April, joins and invests in Brook Farm community at West Roxbury, Massachusetts, but withdraws by end of year.
1842	Marries Sophia Peabody and lives in Concord, Massachusetts. Neighbors include Emerson, Thoreau, and Margaret Fuller.
1844	Daughter Una is born.
1846	Publishes *Mosses from an Old Manse*. Son Julian is born. Works as surveyor for Salem Custom House until 1849.
1847	Rents house in Salem.

1850	Publishes *The Scarlet Letter*. Until 1851, lives in Lenox, Massachusetts.
1851	Publishes *The House of the Seven Gables* and *The Snow-Image*. Daughter Rose is born. Moves to West Newton, Massachusetts.
1852	Purchases and lives at Wayside in Concord, Massachusetts. Publishes *The Blithedale Romance*, *A Wonder-Book for Girls and Boys*, and a campaign biography of Franklin Pierce.
1853–1857	Appointed by President Pierce, serves as U.S. Consul in Liverpool, England.
1857–1859	Lives in Rome and Florence.
1860	Publishes *The Marble Faun*. Returns with family to Wayside.
1863	Publishes *Our Old Home*.
1864	Nathaniel Hawthorne dies on May 19 in Plymouth, New Hampshire, and is buried at Sleepy Hollow Cemetery, Concord, Massachusetts.

Contributors

HAROLD BLOOM is Sterling Professor of the Humanities at Yale University. He is the author of 30 books, including *Shelley's Mythmaking*, *The Visionary Company*, *Blake's Apocalypse*, *Yeats*, *A Map of Misreading*, *Kabbalah and Criticism*, *Agon: Toward a Theory of Revisionism*, *The American Religion*, *The Western Canon*, and *Omens of Millennium: The Gnosis of Angels, Dreams, and Resurrection*. *The Anxiety of Influence* sets forth Professor Bloom's provocative theory of the literary relationships between the great writers and their predecessors. His most recent books include *Shakespeare: The Invention of the Human*, a 1998 National Book Award finalist, *How to Read and Why*, *Genius: A Mosaic of One Hundred Exemplary Creative Minds*, *Hamlet: Poem Unlimited*, *Where Shall Wisdom Be Found?*, and *Jesus and Yahweh: The Names Divine*. In 1999, Professor Bloom received the prestigious American Academy of Arts and Letters Gold Medal for Criticism. He has also received the International Prize of Catalonia, the Alfonso Reyes Prize of Mexico, and the Hans Christian Andersen Bicentennial Prize of Denmark.

JOEL PFISTER teaches at Wesleyan University. He is the author of *Staging Depth: Eugene O'Neill and the Politics of Psychological Discourse* and other titles; he also coedited a title on the cultural history of emotional life in America.

SACVAN BERCOVITCH teaches at Harvard University. He authored the *Cambridge History of American Literature*, an eight-volume set, and *Reconstructing American Literary History*. He is the editor of many titles, including *Prose Writing, 1820–1865*.

CHARLES SWANN teaches at Keele University in the United Kingdom. He is the author of *Nathaniel Hawthorne: Tradition and Revolution*. He also has published on such authors as Dickens, Hardy, Melville, and Crane.

EMILY MILLER BUDICK has taught at the Hebrew University of Jerusalem. She has published numerous titles, including *American Romance Fiction: The Nineteenth Century* and *Engendering Romance: Women Writers and the Hawthorne Tradition, 1850–1990*.

JANICE B. DANIEL has taught at Morehead State University in Morehead, Kentucky. She has published on Zora Neale Hurston and has delivered papers on Hawthorne, Virginia Woolf, and Aldous Huxley as well as on Hurston.

MICHAEL T. GILMORE teaches at Brandeis University. His books include *Surface and Depth: the Quest for Legibility in American Culture*. He is a contributor to the *Cambridge History of American Literature*.

LELAND S. PERSON teaches at the University of Cincinnati. He is the editor of a book of some of Hawthorne's work, *The Scarlet Letter and Other Writings*. Also, he has published *Aesthetic Headaches: Women and Masculine Poetics in Poe, Melville, and Hawthorne* and other titles.

RICHARD KOPLEY teaches at Penn State's Commonwealth College. He has published *Prospects for the Study of American Literature: A Guide for Scholars and Students* and has been the editor for a publication of Edgar Allan Poe's work.

MARGARET REID has taught at Morgan State University in Baltimore. She is the author of *Cultural Secrets as Narrative Form: Storytelling in Nineteenth-Century America*.

Bibliography

Barlowe, Jamie. "Rereading Women: Hester Prynne-ism and the Scarlet Mob of Scribblers." *American Literary History* 9, no. 2 (Summer 1997): 197–225.

———. "Response to the Responses." *American Literary History* 9, no. 2 (Summer 1997): 238–243.

———. *The Scarlet Mob of Scribblers: Rereading Hester Prynne*. Carbondale: Southern Illinois University Press, 2000.

Bell, Millicent, ed. *Hawthorne and the Real: Bicentennial Essays*. Columbus: Ohio State University Press, 2005.

Berlant, Lauren Gail. *The Anatomy of National Fantasy: Hawthorne, Utopia, and Everyday Life*. Chicago: University of Chicago Press, 1991.

Bloom, Harold, ed. *Hester Prynne*. Philadelphia: Chelsea House Publishers, 2004.

———. *Nathaniel Hawthorne's* The Scarlet Letter. Philadelphia: Chelsea House Publishers, 2004.

Budick, Emily Miller. "Hawthorne, Pearl, and the Primal Sin of Culture." *Journal of American Studies* 39, no. 2 (August 2005): 167–185.

Colacurcio, Michael J., ed. *New Essays on* The Scarlet Letter. Cambridge: Cambridge University Press, 1985.

Daniels, Cindy Lou. "Hawthorne's Pearl: Woman-Child of the Future." *American Transcendental Quarterly* 19, no. 3 (September 2005): 221–236.

Donoghue, Denis. *The American Classics: A Personal Essay*. New Haven: Yale University Press, 2005.

Gatti Taylor, Olivia. "Cultural Confessions: Penance and Penitence in Nathaniel Hawthorne's *The Scarlet Letter* and *The Marble Faun*." *Renascence: Essays on Values in Literature* 58, no. 2 (Winter 2005): 135–152.

Gilmore, Michael T. "Hidden in Plain Sight: *The Scarlet Letter* and American Legibility." *Studies in American Fiction* 29, no. 1 (Spring 2001): 121–128.

Goddu, Teresa, and Leland S. Person, eds. "*The Scarlet Letter* after 150 Letters: A Special Issue." *Studies in American Fiction* 29, no. 1 (Spring 2001).

Gollin, Rita K., ed. *The Scarlet Letter*. Boston: Houghton Mifflin, 2002.

Herbert, T. Walter. "Response to Jamie Barlowe's, 'Reading Women....'" *American Literary History* 9, no. 2 (Summer 1997): 230–232.

Hull, Richard. "Sent Meaning vs. Attached Meaning: Two Interpretations of Interpretation in *The Scarlet Letter*." *American Transcendental Quarterly* 14, no. 2 (June 2000): 143–158.

Idol, John L., Jr., and Melinda M. Ponder, eds. *Hawthorne and Women: Engendering and Expanding the Hawthorne Tradition*. Amherst, Mass.: University of Massachusetts Press, 1999.

Jarvis, Brian. *Cruel and Unusual: Punishment and U.S. Culture*. London; Sterling, Va.: Pluto Press, 2004.

Johnson, Claudia Durst. *Understanding* The Scarlet Letter: *A Student Casebook*. Westport, Conn.: Greenwood Press, 1995.

Kennedy-Andrews, ed. *Nathaniel Hawthorne:* The Scarlet Letter. New York: Columbia University Press, 2000.

Khan, Jalal Uddin. "Patterns of Isolation and Interconnectedness in Hawthorne's *The Scarlet Letter*." *Indian Journal of American Studies* 27, no. 1 (Winter 1997): 1–11.

Kreger, Erika M. "'Depravity Dressed Up in a Fascinating Garb': Sentimental Motifs and the Seduced Hero(ine) in *The Scarlet Letter*." *Nineteenth-Century Literature* 54, no. 3 (December 1999): 308–335.

Kumiko, Mukai. "The Social and Artistic Avant-Garde in *The Scarlet Letter*: The Meaning of Embroidery." *Journal of the American Literature Society of Japan* 2 (2003): 1–18.

Last, Suzan. "Hawthorne's Feminine Voices: Reading *The Scarlet Letter* as a Woman." *Journal of Narrative Technique* 27, no. 3 (Fall 1997): 349–376.

Millington, Richard H., ed. *The Cambridge Companion to Nathaniel Hawthorne*. Cambridge, England: Cambridge University Press, 2004.

Morey, Eileen, ed. *Readings on* The Scarlet Letter. San Diego, Calif.: Greenhaven Press, 1998.

Murfin, Ross C., ed. *The Scarlet Letter*. Boston: Bedford Books of St. Martin's Press, 1991.

Pease, Donald E. "Hawthorne in the Custom-House: The Metapolitics, Postpolitics, and Politics of *The Scarlet Letter*." *Boundary 2* 32, no. 1 (Spring 2005): 53–70.

Pourteau, Leslie K. "Pearl, the Ordinary: Perceived Sin and Projected Guilt in *The Scarlet Letter*." *Proceedings of the Philological Association of Louisiana* (1992): 121–126.

Ramdya, Kavita. "Hawthorne's Resistance to and Appropriation of Sentimental Writing in *The Scarlet Letter*." *McNeese Review* 42 (2004): 41–60.

Rowe, Joyce A. *Equivocal Endings of Classic American Novels*: The Scarlet Letter, Adventures of Huckleberry Finn, The Ambassadors, The Great Gatsby. Cambridge; New York: Cambridge University Press, 1988.

Thickstun, Margaret Olofson. *Fictions of the Feminine: Puritan Doctrine and the Representation of Women*. Ithaca: Cornell University Press, 1988.

Thomas, Brook. "Citizen Hester: *The Scarlet Letter* as Civic Myth." *American Literary History* 13, no. 2 (Summer 2001): 181–211.

Tomc, Sandra. "A Change of Art: Hester, Hawthorne, and the Service of Love." *Nineteenth-Century Literature* 56, no. 4 (March 2002): 466–494.

Weinauer, Ellen. "Considering Possession in *The Scarlet Letter*." *Studies in American Fiction* 29, no. 1 (Spring 2001): 93–112.

Acknowledgments

"Sowing Dragons' Teeth: Personal Life and Revolution in *The Scarlet Letter*" by Joel Pfister. From *The Production of Personal Life: Class, Gender, and the Psychological in Hawthorne's Fiction*: 122–143. © 1991 by the board of trustees of the Leland Stanford Junior University. Reprinted by permission.

"The A-Politics of Ambiguity" by Sacvan Bercovitch. From *The Office of* The Scarlet Letter: 1–31. © 1991 by The Johns Hopkins University Press. Reprinted by permission of The Johns Hopkins University Press.

"*The Scarlet Letter* and the Language of History: Past Imperfect, Present Imperfect, Future Perfect?" by Charles Swann. From *Nathaniel Hawthorne: Tradition and Revolution*: 75–95. © 1991 by Cambridge University Press. Reprinted by permission.

"Hester's Skepticism, Hawthorne's Faith; or, What Does a Woman Doubt? Instituting the American Romance Tradition" by Emily Miller Budick. From *New Literary History* 22, no. 1 (Winter 1991): 199–211. © 1991 by *New Literary History*, The University of Virginia, Charlottesville. Reprinted by permission.

"'Apples of Thoughts and Fancies': Nature as Narrator in *The Scarlet Letter*" by Janice B. Daniel. From *American Transcendental Quarterly* 7, no. 4 (December 1993): 307–319. © 1993 by The University of Rhode Island. Reprinted by permission.

"Hawthorne and the Making of the Middle Class" by Michael T. Gilmore. From *Rethinking Class: Literary Studies and Social Formations*, edited by Wai Chee Dimock and Michael T. Gilmore: 215–238. © 1994 by Columbia University Press. Reprinted by permission.

"The Dark Labyrinth of Mind: Hawthorne, Hester, and the Ironies of Racial Mothering" by Leland S. Person. From *Studies in American Fiction* 29, no. 2 (Spring 2001): 33–48. © 2001 by Northeastern University. Reprinted by permission.

"The Matter of Form" by Richard Kopley. From *The Threads of* The Scarlet Letter: 97–109. © 2003 by Rosemont Publishing and Printing Corp. Reprinted by permission.

"From Artifact to Archetype" by Margaret Reid. From *Cultural Secrets as Narrative Form: Storytelling in Nineteenth-Century America*: 106–131. © 2004 by the Ohio State University. Reprinted by permission.

Every effort has been made to contact the owners of copyrighted material and secure copyright permission. Articles appearing in this volume generally appear much as they did in their original publication with few or no editorial changes. In some cases foreign language text has been removed from the original essay. Those interested in locating the original source will find bibliographic information in the bibliography and acknowledgments sections of this volume.

Index

Characters in literary works are indexed by first name (if any), followed by the name of the work in parentheses